# Heaven on Earth

Travel that doesn't cost the Earth

Green

# Heaven on Earth

Travel that doesn't cost the Earth

Green

SARAH SIESE

# CONTENTS

## South America

## North America

## Europe

## Central America

# Middle East

# Asia

# Africa

# Australasia

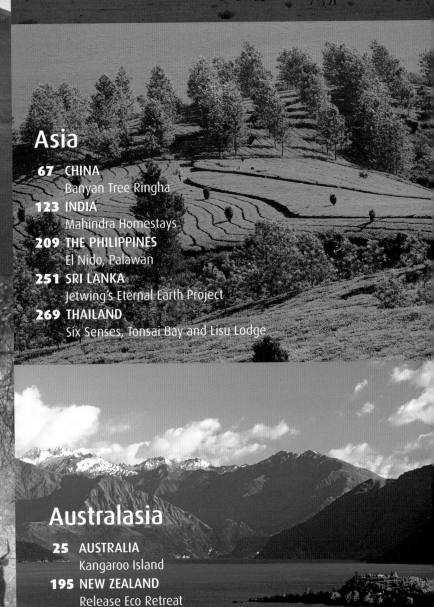

# DESTINATIONS

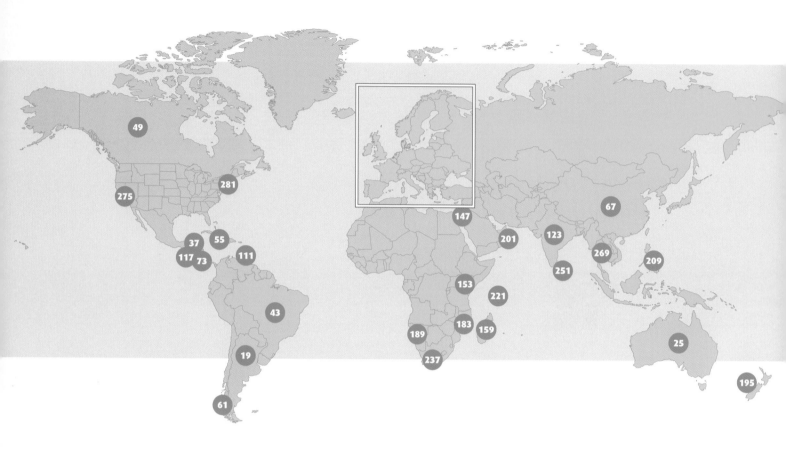

## PAGES

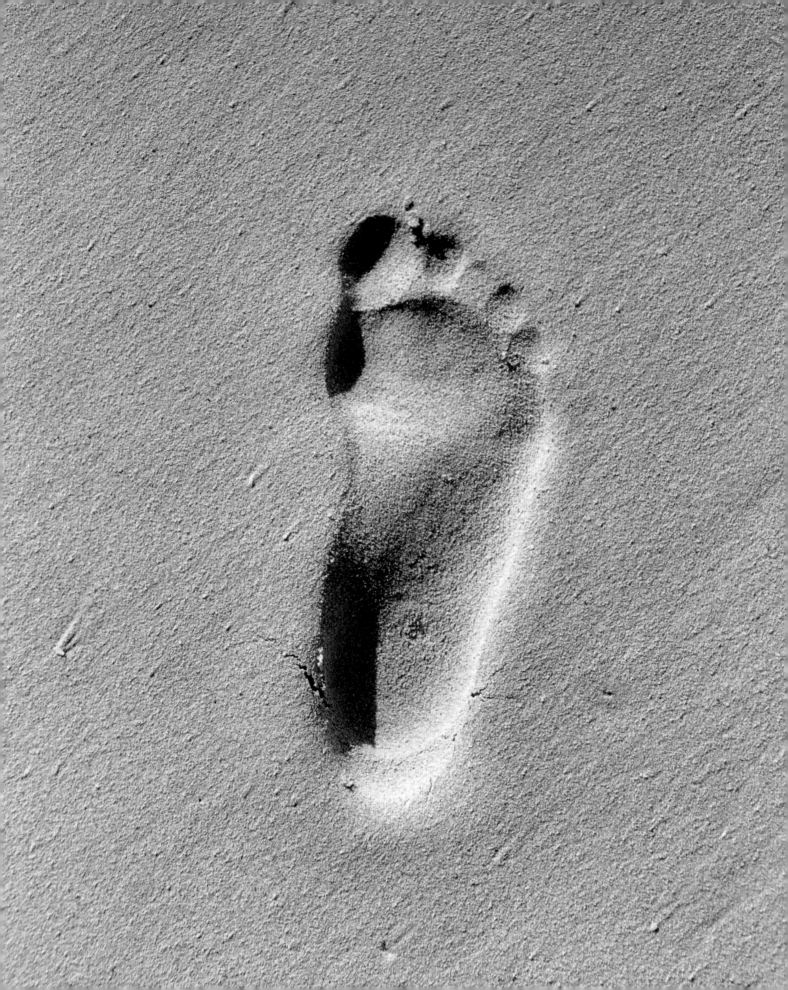

# INTRODUCTION

Before I started researching this book in 2006, I had a limited idea about what eco-friendly meant when it came to tourism. I was familiar with certain practices at home, like recycling our used plastic, glass and paper and was already using low-energy light bulbs and eco-tricity. I walked to the shops when I could and generally avoided unnecessary car journeys. Other than that, it didn't really affect my life and it certainly didn't occur to me to investigate a hotel's green policy.

Since then, the issues around global warming and, in particular, $CO_2$ emissions, have amassed and are rarely out of our daily news bulletins. We are all aware of what is happening but in many respects feel we have little control over what we can actually do.

I was shocked to find out that deforestation accounts for 24 per cent of $CO_2$ emissions and … aviation, by comparison, counts for 3 per cent. I believe that travel, and flying in particular, has been made a scapegoat in this debate and that we should be looking at other issues more critically. In a global world, flying is often the only way to reach far-flung corners of the Earth – many of which depend on tourism as their primary source of income.

It seems it's all about going back to traditional standards and good old-fashioned common sense. When I was growing up in the 70s it was common practice to finish everything on my plate ('think of those starving people'), close a door ('were you born in a barn?'), turn out a light when leaving a room and be expected to look after my belongings, which were meant to last a lifetime. The extremes of disposable living in the late 80s and 90s subliminally rankled with my conscience – I knew it wasn't right to 'chuck it out' the moment it no longer held a use but I, like everyone else, was a child of our time and soon got used to convenient plastic bags, perfect-looking fruit and vegetables, a new phone every time I renewed my mobile contract and began to take it all for granted.

But taking everything for granted is something we can no longer do with the Earth – icebergs are melting, the air is polluted and the unhealthy balance we triggered a quarter of century ago has now tipped the balance.

So should we carry on travelling? The answer in short is yes. But sensitively. Much of the tourism industry offers exemplary examples of responsible living. Being in the limelight has meant that no stone has been left unturned and hotels around the world are doing their bit to neutralise their carbon footprint and to offer sustainable tourism that benefits the community and protects the environment.

Green is about recognising that buildings should be built to last, ideally made from locally sourced materials, fitting in sympathetically with their surroundings. Wind, sun and hydro are incredible, natural sources of energy – clean, renewable and free of pollutants. The best food is always the local produce that has come fresh from field, river or sea to plate in under a day, that doesn't need wrapping in cellophane to preserve or enhance. Combine this with sharing time with indigenous people who know their country best and you are on to a winner.

So should we travel? I repeat, yes. It's innate in our psyche to find out how others live and what their landscape looks like. It helps us to grow. It gives us understanding and the desire to preserve ways of life that are centuries old.

*Heaven on Earth Green* is a book about the world's best eco tourism, ranging from conventional hotels that have taken environmental concerns on board, to inspirational outdoor adventures that leave no trace.

It includes everything from urban stalwarts of hospitality to unknown rural gems. Whether it's city, beach, mountain, skiing, safari, camping, pampering, sailing, or adventure – we have personally vetted each of our favourite eco places from all over the world.

I hope you'll be empowered by the choice of green experiences. Every chapter features a menu of environmentally friendly activities inimitable to each destination. I also hope you'll take time to find a computer and log on to stuffyourrucksack.com before you travel and see where you can make a difference.

Enjoy your travelling, but remember to give something back and to be grateful for the opportunity.

# CLIMATE CHANGE

The IPCC (Intergovernmental Panel on Climate Change) 2007 report states that, 'Warming of the climate system is unequivocal, as is now evident from observations of increases in global average air and ocean temperatures, widespread melting of snow and ice and rising global average sea level.'

Essentially, climate is driven by the sun's energy. How much energy remains in the earth system and how much is reflected back out into space depends on the composition of the atmosphere (of gases, clouds and particles) and the reflectivity of the surface. Changes in either will affect the energy balance, and so change the climate. This is a natural process and climate has always been changing – indeed, without the greenhouse effect whereby energy is trapped in the system and heats it up, the world would be too cold to inhabit. The problem is not the change itself but the speed with which it is happening, its impact on an environment already rendered fragile by human activity, and the fact that humanity is driving it.

The three main greenhouse gases are methane, nitrous oxide and, most importantly, carbon dioxide. The two main sources of $CO_2$ are emissions from fossil fuel use and deforestation – one releasing carbon by burning ancient biomass and the other by burning its modern equivalent. $CO_2$ concentrations are now far higher than at any time in the past 600,000 years and emissions continue at an accelerating rate. It is now clear

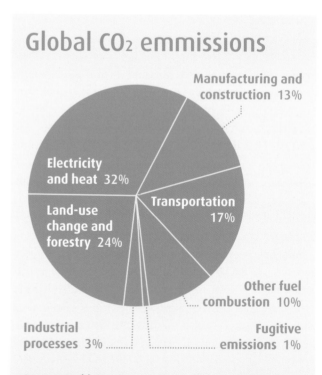

## Global CO₂ emmissions

Manufacturing and construction 13%

Electricity and heat 32%

Transportation 17%

Land-use change and forestry 24%

Other fuel combustion 10%

Industrial processes 3%

Fugitive emissions 1%

**Source:** World Resources Institute, Climate Analysis Indicators Tool (CAIT) version 3.0 (Washington DC: World Resources Institute, 2006)
**Note:** Transportation emissions include international transport emissions, referred to as 'international bunkers'

(with more than 90 per cent confidence) that they are warming the planet and so shifting the climatic regime.

It is still difficult to predict exactly what effects will occur in particular places, but the overall impacts will be profound, shifting climatic zones, altering rainfall patterns, and raising sea-levels and storm frequencies. Up to 40 per cent of all species could be threatened in the process. Furthermore, changes following the predictions are already occurring. These are most marked in the most sensitive regions – towards the poles and in alpine and semi-desert regions – but in the long run it will be the poorest countries that will bear the brunt.

www.carbonbalanced.org

### To fly or not to fly, that is the question

The debate on aviation is controversial and often very confusing. The statistics that are thrown at us seem to totally contradict each other, depending which side of the argument you're coming from.

The chasm basically boils down to one thing – whether you look at the issue from a global or a personal level.

At a global level aviation looks like a small offender, contributing a mere 3 per cent of $CO_2$ emissions. However, on an individual level, scientists have come up with a per capita annual footprint allowance that can be swallowed by just one long-haul flight to Australia.

So there lies the dilemma. Flying in itself is not the worse offender. How much you fly or, for that matter, drive, can send your personal $CO_2$ tally stratospheric. Aircraft are not uniquely bad – in fact the per-mile emissions are comparable to driving a car the same distance but flying distances are usually huge. And because flights allow us to travel thousands of miles in just a few hours their carbon costs are high.

A return flight from London to New York produces 0.8 tonnes of $CO_2$ per person, one to Australia is over 5 tonnes of $CO_2$, well over what scientists consider to be an acceptable annual footprint. You'd be forgiven for thinking that short haul is, therefore, better that long haul. Not so. A large percentage of the damage is done at take-off and landing, so a short-haul flight actually produces more $CO_2$ per mile than long haul.

It all boils down to how you look at it. If you do choose to fly there are schemes galore that can help off-set your personal footprint (see Cool Earth page 14). Offsetting offers a way to compensate for the carbon emissions you produce. It usually involves paying into a scheme that invests

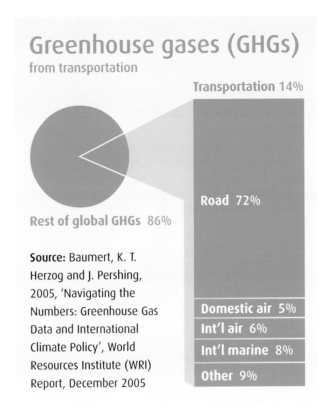

## Greenhouse gases (GHGs)
from transportation

Transportation 14%

Rest of global GHGs 86%

Road 72%

Domestic air 5%
Int'l air 6%
Int'l marine 8%
Other 9%

**Source:** Baumert, K. T. Herzog and J. Pershing, 2005, 'Navigating the Numbers: Greenhouse Gas Data and International Climate Policy', World Resources Institute (WRI) Report, December 2005

in re-forestation or renewable energy – that is, projects that will reduce carbon emissions by an equal amount to those created by activities such as air travel, driving or heating a building. Offsetting doesn't mean you don't need to worry about saving energy. The most effective way to help fight climate change is to cut down on the amount of energy you use and reduce your personal carbon footprint.

But, and it's a big but, the tourism debate is so much bigger than your personal footprint or the $CO_2$ damage of your flight. It would be a mistake to offset your flight and then rest on your laurels, thinking that's my bit done for the world.

Tourism is the number one export for over a third of developing nations who, with one in 11 jobs, rely on visitors to exist. They need our money, which is why we have listed key activities you can enjoy in each area that support the local economy, directly benefitting the communities while protecting the environment.

There are a few questions we can ask ourselves before booking a holiday, most pertinent of all, 'Am I harming or am I contributing to the environment and social community I am visiting and where is my money going?' If it's to a fat-cat businessman who puts his profit first and exploits his workforce, then think again.

# PLAN A RESPONSIBLE TRIP

Top tips

As a traveller, you will have an impact on the culture and environment of the place you are visiting. Here are some rules of thumb to make this impact positive.

### Consider your choice of transport

A flight will dwarf all other elements of your holiday in terms of carbon emissions. Use online calculations to learn about the footprint of a particular journey and see how long it would take you to make the equivalent carbon saving by cutting down on car journeys or using low-energy light bulbs.

www.climatecare.org/responsibletravel

### Avoid short-haul and indirect flights whenever possible

If you do fly, try to avoid short-haul flights where there are viable alternatives, as the fuel-hungry take-off and landing make up a greater proportion of the journey's overall emissions. Similarly, flying indirect to save a few pounds can radically bump up your emissions tally due to the extra take-off and landing.

### Consider your accommodation

Many areas popular with tourists struggle with water and energy supplies and have limited waste and recycling facilities. Before you book somewhere to stay, check its website or brochure for a statement on sustainability or responsible tourism. Anywhere doing its fair share will be shouting about it and may have an eco label.

### Find out about local issues

Find out if there are energy or water shortages or particular development or conservation issues in the destination you are planning to visit and make sure you don't contribute to them by your behaviour while away by your choice of accommodation or tour operator.

See the Travel Foundation and Tourism Concern for more information. www.tourismconcern.org.uk, www.the travelfoundation.org.uk

### Report bad practice

If you spot hotel staff ignoring environmental policies, for example by washing towels daily, report it to the management. Similarly, if you encounter exploitive practices in destinations or among tour operators, complain to the company you booked through and write an on-line review.

You can report animal exploitation via the Born Free Foundation's Travellers' Alert campaign at www.bornfree.org.uk

### Be culturally aware

Learning a few words of the local language can help you interact with locals in a far more respectful and rewarding way than stumbling through with English plus hand gestures. Learn about local customs and religious beliefs and modify your wardrobe and behaviour accordingly.

### Think local

Travellers pay fleeting, and often seasonal visits, to their destinations. Choose tour operators and hotels that employ local people, ideally year round, and source as much food and other supplies as possible from local producers. Make sure you get out of your hotel or resort to visit local restaurants, shops and markets and always tip with cash. In markets, don't let the love of bartering get in the way of paying a fair price.

### Give something back

Our love of exotic, off-the-beaten-track holidays has brought us into greater contact with societies struggling with poverty, conservation, development and sometimes exploitation. Although it can be very difficult, try not to give money to child beggars as this encourages the practice when they should be in school. A donation to a local project, charity, health centre or school is more likely to end up in safe hands.

You can also find out about local projects and items in short supply by using the www.stuffyourrucksack.com website.

### Minimise your environmental impact

Taking your litter with you is obvious. But refraining from buying corals, shells or other precious products made from endangered plants and animals and helping to preserve local wildlife is equally important.

### Take your habits with you

If you recycle, avoid unnecessary car journeys and avoid wasting water at home, don't binge on holiday. Use public transport in your destination, keep heating, lighting and air conditioning to a minimum and shower rather than use a bath. As many island and mountain destinations have limited waste and recycling facilities, it pays to leave unnecessary packaging on holiday purchases at home.

### Don't play golf in a dry zone

More and more developing world countries believe that they must provide golf courses for Western tourists, even in water-poor areas. These either drain water reserves or depend on desalination plants that use vast amounts of energy.

# COOL EARTH

**Supercharge your carbon emissions with Cool Earth.**

### Offsetting

Each year an area of rainforest the size of Britain disappears. This rapid destruction is one of the biggest causes of global warming on the planet, emitting more than six billion tonnes of carbon dioxide into the atmosphere every year; that's more than the entire US economy.

Every acre of endangered rainforest locks up over 260 tonnes of carbon – compare this with the average UK household, which is responsible for 10–15 tonnes of carbon emissions every year. By protecting one acre of rainforest you can literally supercharge your carbon responsibility.

While we can all recycle, use clean energy and generally be green, a new way to make a big contribution to being carbon positive and to offsetting your holidays is to join Cool Earth.

Cool Earth protects huge swathes of endangered rainforest that, without protection, will disappear, drastically reducing the world's ability to absorb carbon emissions to devastating effect.

### How does it work?

Contact Cool Earth and sponsor an acre of the Amazonian rainforest. Once you have selected which of the projects you want to support and made your donation, you will

Gervais – all passionate about preventing climate change by avoiding deforestation and supporting the communities that live there.

### Key points

- Cool Earth is a charity that protects endangered rainforest that may disappear if left unprotected
- Once sponsored, the land is protected for a minimum of 10 years
- Educational work with local communities ensures that forest land is worth more left standing

automatically be allocated your own acre, protected for at least 10 years. You will then receive a sponsorship certificate and be able see it on Google Maps through the Cool Earth website. Cool Earth will then keep you up to date on what is happening on the project and how your money is helping to protect this vital resource.

### What do they do with your money?

Part of your donation is spent on acquiring or protecting land on behalf of the local community. All land is vested back to the local population; Cool Earth then helps them to help themselves by ensuring that the forest is worth more by leaving it standing, than it is logged. They also employ locals as rangers, build schools and supply drying facilities for crops in order to increase their value. The list goes on. Donations ensure that land is protected for a minimum of 10 years, and in many cases in perpetuity.

### Who is Cool Earth?

Cool Earth was founded in 2007 by Frank Field, MP, and Johan Eliasch, the UK government's Special Representative on Deforestation and Clean Energy. The advisory Board includes Sir Nicholas Stern, former Head of the UK Government Economic Service, and Mark Ellingham, the founder of Rough Guides. Supporters include Sir David Attenborough, Bill Bryson, Philip Pullman and Ricky

## Contact

**Tel:** 0800 0930624
**Web:** www.coolearth.org

# STUFF YOUR RUCKSACK

Help the world

'It's so easy to make a difference. How many times have you been travelling and visited a school or community or local charity that you would love to help? The school needs books, or a map or pencils; an orphanage needs children's clothes or toys. All things that, if only you'd known, you could've stuffed in your rucksack. But once you get home you forget, or you've lost the address, or worry that whatever you send will be stolen before it even gets there...'

Kate Humble

## What does Stuff Your Rucksack do?

If you mean the founding members of Stuff Your Rucksack (SYR), then very little. The members of SYR are either very busy with their day jobs, or in the case of BBC's Kate Humble, never in the UK.

SYR is driven by travellers who take the time to give a little feedback about charities and organisations they've found while travelling or on holiday, or in some cases, by the organisations themselves. It's a user-driven site where simple, but very real needs can reach a wider audience.

The idea has two facets: the first – a person who has found an organisation that needs stuff can leave the details of that organisation on the SYR website; the second – potential visitors can visit the site to find out what simple things are needed that will make a big difference.

There is some degree of vetting that goes into deciding whether to list organisations, however SYR is clearly not able to have people 'on the ground' in all these countries so advises travellers to use discretion and care when visiting an organisation found through their website. The site also offers a facility to allow any users to leave feedback and a picture of their visit to encourage other people.

## Stuff Your Rucksack's ethos

SYR was very much Kate Humble's idea. Inspired by years of travelling, particularly in poorer parts of the world, she

found it frustrating to visit a school that desperately needed something as simple and easy to pack, as A4 lined paper. If only she had known a few days previously, she could have slipped some in her luggage.

As such, it's always been about one-to-one help. SYR offers no fulfilment service of its own and doesn't pretend to have all the answers or to be experts in the issues surrounding global poverty. It simply wants to connect people's needs with other people's thoughtfulness and generosity.

## Where do they reach?

SYR's database of organisations currently covers 64 countries spread across the world. As you'd expect, most organisations are to be found in developing countries. There are a few in places you may not expect though, so wherever you're travelling it's worth a quick look on the site before you leave. I was able to drop some toys in at a children's home in Sri Lanka last Christmas, literally five minutes' walk from the city centre. Ultimately, they are hoping to have listings in every country.

Wherever people travel, there is an opportunity to help the communities.

## What can people do?

Anyone travelling in the near future can help by looking at the website to see what they can take. If not, then SYR asks you to keep your eyes peeled while you're away to see if there are any organisations that future visitors can help. Sign up at SYR on your return and list the details.

## Contact

**Web:** www.stuffyourrucksack.com

# ARGENTINA
## Estancia Los Potreros

Way off the beaten track, on the top of the Sierras Chicas, nestled between the pampas and the Andes in the heart of the beautiful region of Córdoba, lies a paradise for people who love horses. Surrounded by nearly 15,000 acres of secluded grassy wilderness, Estancia Los Potreros is an idyllic retreat for hikers and nature lovers.

Primarily a working ranch breeding Aberdeen Angus cattle and Paso Peruano pacing horses, the estancia has remained in the same Anglo-Argentine family for four generations. Its origins go back to the establishment of Córdoba city in 1575 with the estancia house dating from 1679, when the principal occupation was breeding mules for the silver mines in Peru – and it was from this activity that the name Los Potreros, meaning 'enclosures for equines', is derived.

Today, English-educated brothers, Robin and Kevin Begg, and their wives, Teleri and Louisa, run Los Potreros with the help of their children, offering a unique combination of colonial-style estancia life with long-distance riding in exquisite landscapes.

The estancia breeds horses and the farm is the key source of employment for a number of local people. Kevin and Robin are keen supporters of pure organic farming, avoiding all growth hormones, pesticides, insecticides or chemical fertilizers. They are careful not to overgraze and keep the stocking rate to a minimum level that allows the natural grasses to regenerate. Cattle and horses are free range and graze particular paddocks to create natural fire-breaks during the winter.

Shooting is banned on the farm and wild animals are 'protected', including puma, which on average, kill one foal a year and an unknown number of calves. Dead cattle or horses are left to enter the food chain, a policy that encourages condors, vultures, foxes and other wild life.

Although recycling is just beginning in Argentina, bottles are returned to the winery to be filled up with Los Potreros' own delicious wine. Water is sourced direct from the land's natural springs, and 90 per cent of electricity is generated from renewable sources from on-site wind turbines and solar power cells.

On the community front, Estancia Los Potreros has given important support to the local rural school for many years. Augmented by guest donations and the sale of gift items, the farm has provided a number of services, including solar power, a well, an orchard and a bread oven.

The riding terrain is vast and varied, ranging from steep rocky paths down tree-studded gullies to open, grassy hilltops and earthen roads. From the top of the oldest mountain range in South America, you can see the city of Córdoba, 50 kilometres away, sitting in the pampas below; from the other side of the range you can see the Punilla Valley and the Sierras Grandes beyond. Underfoot – or

above **Guests and gauchos**    opposite (from top) **Vintage fun, the sitting room and honeymoon suite**

crushed by a hoof – the intoxicating scents of peperina, wild mint, thyme and palo amarillo rise in the breeze.

The estancia comprises a traditional adobe Córdoba farmhouse surrounded by acacia, coco and molle trees and a burst of wild flowers, including red, white and purple verbena fronting a large grass patio where Argentine *bochas*, or bowls, is often played. All seven bedrooms have wood-burning stoves, giving the place a very special atmosphere, with comfortable antique beds and original Argentine coffers lending an authentic air. Each room has a private bathroom with both a bath and a shower, and fresh meadow flowers adorn the side tables. In attending to visitors nothing is too much trouble for the family hosts or long-established staff, and the overall atmosphere is that of a house party.

Guests eat in the formal dining room seated on Chippendale furniture. A relaxed breakfast (if you haven't departed on an early ride) is usually taken on the stone patio under the bamboo pergola. All food is sourced locally and tastes so much the better for it. Meals are varied and delicious with plenty of opportunity to try regional dishes. *Locro* is an eclectic dish, *empanadas* must be tried and there are

above **Running wild and free**

regular impromptu tastings of local wines for interested guests. Lunches can be sumptuous *asados*, Argentine barbecues when endless cuts of meat are offered until the taker can accept no more, or, on a ride, picnics with well-deserved drinks in the shade of weeping willows beside fast-flowing, crystal-clear streams.

Around the ranch you'll frequently happen upon friendly encounters with local people. Gaucho culture and reverence of the horse are never stronger than here, and bring with them the oldest traditions of Argentina. To 'ride like an Argentine' probably refers to stylish polo players, but the gaucho is at the root of this tradition and everywhere people appear stuck to their saddles at work or at play.

Most people come to ride with the gauchos – a sure way to get a true insight into rural life in Argentina. The horses, all bred on the estate, are handsome, well kept and docile, and the thick sheepskins over British army saddles make for a very comfortable ride. There are plenty of opportunities to canter, although most of the riding is done at a fast walk if riders are using the ranch's superb string of Paso horses. The unique Peruano, pure descendants of the horses of the Conquistadors, can take you at canter speed while still walking – an unbelievable experience! There are also large, smooth-gaited Criollos, crossbreeds and Peruano-Criollo crosses. It is no surprise that the estancia is celebrated for its exceptional horses.

# Green menu

**Play polo** No visit to Argentina would be complete without the chance to try your hand at a game of polo. The estancia specialises in introducing this extremely fun and highly addictive sport to guests who have not had the chance to try it before. A short lesson on the ground and some practice 'stick and ball' is followed by a game, set at a pace to suit riding abilities. Warning – this could be the start of an extremely expensive habit.

**Experience the smoothest ride you'll ever have** With a riding herd of over 80, there is something for everyone. The horses are responsive, sure-footed and willing. The varied work that they take part in, including rounding up cattle and playing polo, combined with the natural lifestyle they lead in an un-stabled environment, means that they are always fresh, interested and keen to do their jobs.

**Go trekking** With thousands of acres of private land to explore, the estancia offers plenty for even the most dedicated trekking enthusiast. A range of self-guided walks take visitors to high spots on the farm, or to hidden rock pools for a refreshing dip. Take a walk down to the cattle farm to see the gauchos in action, or make your way to 'The Top of the World' to see the tremendous views over the Punilla valley.

**Spend hours birding** The bird life is interesting year-round. Ornithologist Paul MacDermot noted, 'A couple of condors were briefly seen, and roosting in the bushes near the house were a pair of absurdly tame horned owls about six inches long. Other wildlife spotted were some Cuis (guinea pig) and a wild pig with a baby, which is a rare sight.'

**Ride in the moonlight** For four days on either side of the full moon, 'full moon rides' take place – it's an opportunity not to be missed.

**Enjoy wine tasting** Argentina is the fifth largest producer of wine in the world and Córdoba has records showing that 10,000 vines were planted the year after its foundation in 1574. Today riders, walkers and birdwatchers alike all enjoy the Córdoba wine produced by the Bodega Caroyense, who produce and bottle the only private wine in their cellars on behalf of the estancia.

## When to go

Córdoba is known for its good weather and healthy climate – *siempre de temporada* ('always in season') is the old slogan. October to March is warm and the vegetation turns a lush fresh green as the fruit literally drops from the trees.

## Contacts

**Estancia Los Potreros** Casilla de Correo 4, La Cumbre X5178 WAA, Córdoba, Argentina
**Tel:** +54 11 6091 2692
**Web:** www.estancialospotreros.com
**Rates:** From US$360 daily all-inclusive charge per person.

# AUSTRALIA

## Kangaroo Island

Teeming with kangaroos, koalas, wallabies, seals, sea lions, penguins and goannas, KI – as it is affectionately known – is the best place in Australia to see a menagerie of free-roaming, native animals in their natural habitat, including species that are rare, even extinct, on the mainland.

Although still little known, KI is the third largest island off Australia with 450 kilometres of shoreline and almost 33 per cent of its area covered in pristine wilderness and conservation parks (21 in total). Such protection has enabled the island to retain its rich diversity of flora and fauna. Since the island was separated from the mainland over 10,000 years ago, animals and plants have evolved along different biological lines, free of feral pests and predators, such as foxes, creating species found nowhere else in the world.

Even on a day trip from Adelaide you are likely to spot koalas and wallabies (5,000 of the latter for every human inhabitant), emus and kangaroos (KI even has its own sub-species), possums and penguins, seals and sea lions and abundant birdlife.

*National Geographic Traveller* magazine recently ranked Kangaroo Island the best island in the Asia Pacific region and equal fifth in a survey of 111 islands around the world. A judging panel of 522 experts ranked the islands by comparing their commitment to sustainable tourism and preserving the environment for future generations of tourists. The entire island has barely changed since explorer Matthew Flinders first stepped ashore in 1802, to the extent that any road that's covered in bitumen is known locally as a 'highway'.

Arguably the highlight of its several natural history highlights is Flinders Chase National Park, set in 74,000 hectares and home to both the iconic Remarkable Rocks, the huge, weather-shaped granite boulders perched on a dome standing 75 metres out of the sea (think Henry Moore meets Salvador Dali), and Admiral's Arch, an impressive landmark that some 6,000 native New Zealand fur seals call home. Another contender would be Seal Bay, one of only two places in the world that visitors can walk, with a National Park Ranger, amongst a breeding colony of rare Australian sea lions.

The island's natural calendar reveals an incredible diversity of wildlife activities. Between December and February, for example, at the peak of summer 'down under', fur seals give birth to chocolate-brown pups while koalas, wallabies and kangaroos produce tiny young, which are born naked and blind.

In autumn, glossy black cockatoos and little penguins begin nesting and black swans begin their courtships with wing-raising, neck-stretching and loud trumpeting.

Come spring, September to November, wildflowers are in abundance, including around 40 endemic floral species, Cape Barren geese nest on top of the native iris grasses to

incubate their eggs and platypuses lay two eggs in a burrow up to 20 metres long.

## Southern Ocean Lodge

As a break from enjoying the island's wild pleasures, visitors can enjoy some of the finest accommodation in Australia. Options include Southern Ocean Lodge on the south-west coast at Hanson Bay, which borders two national parks and offers stunning ocean views from its 21 luxurious suites. In keeping with the natural attractions of the locations, guests are offered a full range of activities, including coastal trekking expeditions, kayaking, mountain biking, wildlife-viewing and star-gazing.

Key to the island's green credentials, Southern Ocean Lodge's developer has set up a fund to support environmental projects on the Island over the next 10 years. Projects likely to benefit include the ongoing restoration and management

above **Koala at Hanson Bay**   right **View at Southern Ocean Lodge**

above **Southern Ocean Lodge**

of the glossy black cockatoos' habitat and the further research into the 15 threatened plant species on Kangaroo Island. Other elements in the Lodge's approach to sustainable tourism include converting waste water and sewage into clean irrigation water (which is used on the gardens), extensive recycling and composting, water harvested from all roof surfaces and stored in tanks, and the latest heat pump technology for an energy-efficient, hot water system.

In terms of conservation only one hectare was cleared for the Lodge or approximately one per cent of the total 102 hectares purchased as private land. The remaining 99 per cent has been placed under a Heritage Agreement to protect against future development. The Lodge is situated on an important wildlife corridor between two national parks and the management has plans in place to protect the corridor. A 250-metre-long boardwalk has also been erected between the Lodge and the beach to minimise the impact of guests.

# Green menu

Spy on sea lions Watch sea lions in their natural habitat of coastal vegetation, dunes, beach and ocean at the fabulous Seal Bay Conservation Park.
www.parks.sa.gov.au

Wildlife-watch Visit Flinders Chase National Park for bird life, plants and a wide variety of animals such as echidnas, Cape Barren geese, koalas, kangaroos, wallabies and brush-tail possums.
www.environment.sa.gov.au

Be exceptional Experience the wildlife, natural history, hospitality and heritage of the island with a local expert.
www.exceptionalkangarooisland.com

Take a dive Swim with dolphins, visit a seal colony and observe a variety of seabirds and marine creatures in their natural environment.
www.kangaroomarinecentre.com.au

Go wild Join a minimum-impact wilderness trip.
www.wildernesstours.com.au

Hit the food and wine trail Kangaroo Island boasts 30 vineyards, pure honey, exceptional seafood, cheese and olive oil. The trail highlights food producers and the growing wine industry.
www.goodfoodkangarooisland.com

## When to go

June to August may not be the best in terms of the weather but it's the time when the land mammals, who feed predominantly at night, dawn and dusk, frequently come out by day, and koalas, and kangaroo and wallaby joeys start to emerge from the mothers' pouches to feed. In the skies above, visitors can watch the arrival of waders on their migration from Siberia and ospreys indulging in spectacular courtship fights. At sea, Southern right whales pass from Antarctic waters to the Great Australian Bight to calve.

## Contacts

**Southern Ocean Lodge** Hanson Bay, Kangaroo Island
**Tel:** +61 02 9918 4355
**Web:** www.southernoceanlodge.com.au
**Rates:** From £1,778 per person for three nights based on two sharing, including return flights from Adelaide, three days 4WD car hire and three nights in a Flinders Suite, including all meals selected drinks and some guided adventures and experiences.

**Bridge & Wickers**
**Tel:** +44 (0) 20 7483 6555
**Web:** www.bridgeandwickers.co.uk
**Rates:** All deals are available to anyone booking their trip through Bridge & Wickers, a travel agency committed to working solely with locally owned Maori or Aboriginal travel companies wherever possible. It donates £10 for every person booked to a charity dedicated to supporting a local eco initiative or community, according to the destination you choose.

# AUSTRIA
Scenic Vorarlberg and Rogner Bad Blumau, Styria

If there were such a thing, Austria would probably win the award for the World's Greenest Country – 70 per cent of its power comes from renewable sources and 60 per cent of waste is recycled. The southern city of Graz is the first in the world to have converted its entire municipal bus fleet to run on bio-diesel, and Salzburg and Vienna are close behind.

### Grosses Walsertal, Vorarlberg
The fact is that environmentalism is a way of life in Austria. Sustainability is in the blood. Nowhere is this more evident than in Grosses Walsertal in the province of Vorarlberg. A dramatic, V-shaped valley cloaked in thick forests of ash, beech and fir and lush meadows of herbs and wildflowers, it was designated a UNESCO Biosphere Reserve in 2000 on account of the role its inhabitants play in maintaining this stunning Alpine landscape.

'It takes a lot of work to keep the high-altitude meadows in a good condition', explains Kurt Stark, manager of an artisan dairy in the pretty village of Sontagg. 'In some of the high pastures there are more than 80 different species to every square metre. As a result, the cheese made here develops a wonderful richness and depth of flavour that is like no other you will ever taste.'

But sustainability in Austria isn't just about tradition. Vorarlberg is home to a group of architects who have developed a progressive approach to building and in doing so have helped to make their region probably the most energy-efficient in the world.

'Our passive buildings,' explains architect Hermann Kaufman, 'are built from local wood wherever possible. Sustainably sourced wood uses very little energy to produce and actually helps with climate change because it is a natural store of carbon.' And with up to 30 centimetres of insulation, triple glazing and ingenious heat recovery and ventilation systems, they use 10 per cent of the energy it takes to heat the average European home.

Incredibly, Vorarlberg is home to three of the seven villages with the EEA's five-star rating, reflecting the province's strong environmental conscience. Kaufmann puts this down to community spirit. 'Vorarlberg is a small region where everybody knows everybody. If you do something good, everybody will know about it, so you have a really good opportunity to make a positive contribution to the community.'

When it comes to sustainability, there's no shortage of places to stay, with many of the region's hotels and guesthouses signed up to the government's Umweltzeichen sustainability scheme, including the Gasthof Krone, an old coaching inn overlooking the square in the picturesque village of Hittisau, which has recently been sensitively renovated giving it a smart, contemporary twist. Even if

above **The Gaudì-esque exterior of Rogner Bad Blumau**

you don't stay, its award-winning restaurant is well worth a visit. Alternatively, stay high in the mountains of the Grosses Walsertal in a hut or farmhouse, looking out over the mountain pastures, knowing that your stay is having very little impact on your beautiful surroundings.

### Rogner Bad Blumau, Styria

Rogner Bad Blumau in the province of Styria attracts thousands of international visitors every year looking to get in touch with nature's healing properties in this remote corner of south-eastern Austria. This strikingly unique hotel and spa is built over a hot spring discovered in the late 1970s, which has the highest mineral content of any spa in Europe.

The facilities are fantastic. Not only can guests bathe in one of eight thermal pools – both indoor and outdoor – they can also indulge in more than 200 relaxing and therapeutic treatments.

What really sets Bad Blumau apart, however, is its holistic approach to sustainability. 'The aim of the spa when it was conceived by Robert Rogner in 1993 was to integrate it

harmoniously with nature and within the local communities,' says general manager Hannes Czeitschner. And it is this philosophy that has inspired the hotel's strikingly unusual and unique appearance.

Its designer, Austrian artist and environmental champion Friedrichsreich Hundertwasser, wanted to create a synergy between man, nature and architecture at Bad Blumau. 'Hundertwasser said that if we take away from Mother Nature, then we have to give back in some way,' says Czeitschner, 'so he gave all the buildings grass roofs, making them invisible from above.'

To complement the fluidity of the surrounding landscape, Hundertwasser decided the hotel should have as few straight edges as possible. So he devised an enchanting Hansel and Gretel exterior, and a wonderfully irregular interior, where the meandering walkways feel like you've wandered into a rabbit warren. There are also more than 2,400 uniquely shaped windows and 330 distinctive columns to reflect nature's diversity.

When it comes to the nuts and bolts of sustainability, Rogner Bad Blumau is second to none. The water from

above and below **Scenic Vorarlberg in Winter**

the spa, which bubbles up at a temperature of 110°C, is used to heat the entire complex and to generate up to half of its electricity. The hotel champions recycling and demands that all its suppliers meet stringent environmental criteria set by the Austrian Institute for Sustainability.

Its commitment to the environment is matched by its support of the local economy. 'Blumau used to be one of the poorest villages in the country,' says Czeitschner. 'People used to move away from the area to find jobs because they didn't see any future in the village. So working with local people has always been an important part of what we do.'

As a result, 80 per cent of the food served – including milk, cheese and yoghurt, as well as fruit and vegetables, beef, honey and pumpkin-seed oil – comes from local farmers, all of whom now work to organic standards and 90 per cent of the staff come from within a 50-kilometre radius. 'It's all part of the same idea really,' continues Czeitschner, 'to integrate what we are doing here harmoniously, whether we're talking about the architecture and the local landscape, energy consumption and climate change or the business and the local economy.'

# Green menu

Listen to music Take in one of Europe's best music festivals, Schubertiade, which specialises in Franz Schubert's Lieder and takes place in the pretty village of Schwarzenberg every year during the last two weeks of June and the first two weeks of September.

Follow the energy trail There is an eight-kilometre path that starts in the village of Langenegg and connects a series of natural energy points. With a human sundial, a lookout with a 360° revolving bench, water features and herb gardens along the way, it's great for young children.

Imbibe herbal teas, lotions and potions Sample the best herbal tea you'll ever drink, brewed with wild mountain herbs and flowers, then learn to make your own drinks, soaps and cosmetics with the Alchemilla Project's director Susanne Türtscher.

Go mountain trekking For the ultimate Alpine experience, spend a week trekking between mountain huts, hiking through lush meadows and picnicking among the wildflowers.

Work on a farm Stay on a traditional, working farm, where you can help with milking, cheese- and hay-making and learn about the farmers' relationship with nature.

Enjoy relaxing therapies Choose from hundreds of natural therapies available at Bad Blumau. The simplest is to float in the deliciously warm waters of the Vulkania spring, best under a moonlit sky on a winter's night with the steam wafting past in the breeze. Not only is it sheer bliss but the water does wonders for your skin, muscles and joints.

## Contacts

### BREGENZERWALD

**Gasthof Krone** Am Platz 185, 6952 Hittisau, Austria
**Tel:** +43 5513 6201
**Web:** www.krone-hittisau.at
**Rates:** From €98 for a double room bed and breakfast, €138 half board.

### GREAT WALSER VALLEY BIOSPHERE RESERVE

**Mountain Hut** Garmilhütte auf der Alpe Oberpartnom, Oberhaus 65, A-6741, Raggal, Austria
**Tel:** +43 5553 263
**Web:** www.tiscover.at/garmilhuette
**Rates:** From €50 for the entire hut (sleeps 11).

**Farmhouse** Haus Häsischa, A-6741 Marul 20, Austria
**Tel:** +43 5553 378
**Web:** www.raggal.net/haushaesischa
**Rates:** From €17 bed and breakfast.

### BAD BLUMAU

**Rogner Bad Blumau** A-8283 Bad Blumau 100, Austria
**Tel:** +43 3383 5100
**Web:** www.blumau.com
**Rates:** From €125 per person per night half board.

## When to go

There is skiing in both Bregenzerwald and the Great Walser Valley during winter; November and December tend to be best for snow, although January is quieter. For the wildflowers, May to July is best, but you won't get up to the highest meadows until June. Rogner Bad Blumau is great all year round, although *al-fresco* bathing in the winter is a real treat. You'll avoid the crowds in January.

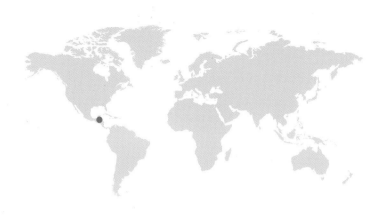

# BELIZE
## Jungle lodges

Shouldered between the Peten forests of Guatemala, and Mexico's Yucatan Peninsula, Belize is a spectacular-looking destination. In fact, many tourists in the know regard this relatively tiny, wedge-shaped Central American country as the Caribbean's best-preserved alter ego.

With its large ratio of sea to land, Belize offers massive opportunities for both serious divers and snorkellers. In particular, the shallow, offshore chain of islands know as 'cayes' are a diver's dream. They front dazzlingly vivid turquoise waters and straddle a coral reef second only in size to Australia's Great Barrier Reef.

### Turtle Inn, Ambergris Caye
Ambergris Caye, named in colonial whaling days after the substance used to make perfume, is the largest of the 200-odd tiny islands that dot and dash Belize's coastline, and was the country's first tourist destination. Then, as now, it was a popular diving location.

Despite the trinket shops, small bars, and tiny sand-strewn airstrip that have appeared since, the place still seems geared for the locals. San Pedro is its compact capital, possibly where Madonna set her hit song, 'La Isla Bonita', and, much like the rest of Belize, the low-key atmosphere has helped establish it as a hot destination for publicity-shy celebrities.

So too, Francis Ford Coppola – who established the second of his luxury eco lodges, Turtle Inn, right on the

powder-white sands of noodle-thin Placencia Peninsula. Despite its rustic touches, the inn strikes an oddly sophisticated note within the context of this southern Belizean sleepy community. But Coppola knows how to set a scene. The 18 bedrooms are thatch-roofed, roomy, Balinese-inspired cabanas, created using the skills of local stone-masons and craftsmen, and decorated with well-chosen artisan furniture.

Outdoor showers, and screen doors enable you to feel at one with the beach environment. Even the airy 'desert island' dining room is tasteful, with artefacts placed just-so, and lighting pitched to evoke the beauty of a film still.

'Mr Francis' as the people who work here affectionately refer to him, is a frequent visitor – and a firm believer in realising his eco dream. OK, you may get Sicilian pizza on the menu but the arugula and wild garlic come straight from the inn's gardens, and guests have every chance to interact with local people, through contact with the staff and on hikes and excursions arranged by the inn.

If you stay here, you will also have the opportunity of enjoying Belize's three coral atolls – out of a total of just four in the Caribbean. Quite the most stunning of these is Lighthouse Reef, the outermost atoll, in the centre of which is the country's unique Blue Hole.

This is technically a 300-metre-wide sink hole that drops to the bottom of the lagoon and opens out into a web of

caves and crevices. Its 130-metre depth is what lends the hole its startlingly blue intensity of colour – and it was Jacques Cousteau who popularised the phenomenon, making it the most famous dive site in Belize.

While you are there, don't miss enchanting Half Moon Caye, located in the south-eastern corner of the atoll. Belize's first marine conservation area, it was declared a National Park in 1981, moving on to become one of the country's World Heritage Sites in 1996.

Half Moon is a veritable Eden, home to 98 species of birds, including red-footed boobies, ospreys and warblers. Land and sea animals include the charmingly named Wishy Willy, and both Loggerhead and Hawksbill turtles, which come ashore annually to lay their eggs.

## Jungle lodges

But the islands and seaboard are not Belize's only big draw. While Belize remains relatively low key, eco lodges are the tourist accommodation currently in favour. Hopefully, and providing cruise visitor numbers are kept in check, this trend will continue. In the countryside, their rustic look and self-sufficient ethos blend well with the unspoilt jungle surroundings.

Ecotourism is big news for this former British colony. Its rich visual interior includes hiking trails through virgin rainforests that cover 65 per cent of the country. The ancient Mayan sites are pretty much crowd-free, and comfortable jungle lodges offer paradise surroundings that you share

previous page (main) **Turtle Inn**
previous page (thumbnail) **Blancaneaux**
left **Bedroom at Blancaneaux**    above **Beach heaven at Turtle Inn**

above **Pool villa at Chaa Creek**     opposite **Turtle Inn**

with the local wildlife, including possums, scarlet macaws, toucans and hoarse-voiced howler monkeys.

### Blancaneaux Lodge

Up in the west, among the fertile foothills of Belize's largest national park, Mountain Pine Ridge, is Blancaneaux Lodge. Another of Coppola's properties, the area initially reminded him of the 'jungle paradise' he had enjoyed while shooting *Apocalypse Now* in the Philippines. And familiar objects from that film – the slow-whirring fan that Martin Sheen lay under – as well as black-and-white photos of Marlon Brando looking mean and moody, decorate Blancaneaux's clubby bar.

Thatched cabanas scale rocky slopes that rise above the fast-flowing Privassion river – each features an open-air living room with a hammock, off which are the bedrooms decorated simply with brightly patterned Guatelmalan rugs and teak furniture. A riverside spa offers traditional Thai massage and a massive open-air hot pool.

Blancaneaux's eco credentials span creating their own hydro-electric power, using their own filtered water and tending a huge organic garden that provides 75 per cent of the lodge's vegetables, fruits and nuts – everything from aubergine and cabbage to eggs and herbs.

### Chaa Creek

Some five miles to the west of Blancaneaux, and also in the Cayo district – arguably Belize's most beautiful – is the Lodge at Chaa Creek. An immaculate 365-acre private nature reserve and eco resort set in the foothills of the Maya Mountains, it boasts 23 steeply thatched rondavels, all of which enjoy great views from extensive balconies over the grounds – the best being the romantic tree-top Jacuzzi suites.

The hammering of woodpeckers, and the whooping cry of macaws are a constant background noise – huge fat caterpillars with stripy Dennis-the-Menace bodies rest on fragrant frangipani trees, and the lodge boasts its own on-site rare Blue Morpho butterfly breeding centre.

Eco credentials are high at Chaa Creek. Waste glass is ground down into building material – so too, cans. Originally though, the lodge was a small farm, and owner Mick Fleming would paddle half a day downstream to sell his radishes and tomatoes at the local market. Twenty-five years later, that same farm has grown into a sizeable organic business, employing 100 local people, and utilising traditional Mayan techniques. All manner of goodies are produced here – banana, cacao, sorrel, pineapple and sugar, even cotton.

# Green menu

### TURTLE INN

**Visit the Cockscomb Basin Wildlife Sanctuary** The world's first Jaguar reserve in Belize's unfathomably vivid jungle is home not just to the country's indigenous cat, but also armadillos, ant-eaters, tapirs and birds.

**Canoe down monkey river** Pootle through mangrove estuaries rich in wildlife. Keep a sharp eye out for manatee, howler monkeys, crocodiles and enormous, rare butterflies.

**Cast your line** Go sports fishing in the most productive of Caribbean waters. Cast your line for barracuda, king mackerel or bone fish – or simply enjoy a laid-back guided kayak tour of Placencia's lagoon, where dolphins are frequently spotted.

### BLANCANEAUX

**Discover Mayan sites** Belize's colourful Mayan heritage is within easy reach of the lodge, particularly Caracol, the country's most extensive site, and the largest in the Mayan world.

**Canoe through Barton Creek Cave** Go canoeing in this hugely important millennium-old sacred Mayan site, where you can trace a velvety-dark route through its somewhat creepy depths. Look out for shards of pottery and skulls on rock shelves, remnants of sacrificial victims 'fed' to the gods. The Maya called this subterranean sacred world 'Ixbalba', or place of fear, and it is easy to see why.

### CHAA CREEK

**Take a leisurely ride** Enjoy sunset canoeing along the Macal river or horseback riding through the rainforests.

**Discover the world of the medicine man** The Rainforest Medicine trail, set up to commemorate the region's last Mayan bush medicine expert, Dom Elijio Panti, is a fascinatingly steamy walk through tangled trees and sappy leaves where you learn which plant is good for insomnia, why wild custard apple is brilliant for head lice, and how the Tapaculo tree helps cure diarrhoea. Samples of these plants are currently being sent to Kew Gardens in London.

## Contacts

**Turtle Inn** Placencia Village, Placencia, Belize
**Tel:** +501 523 3244
**Web:** www.turtleinn.com
**Rates:** From US$385 for two per night in a seafront cottage, including breakfast.

**Blancaneaux Lodge** Mountain Pine Ridge Reserve, Central Farm, San Ignacio, Belize
**Tel:** +501 824 3878
**Web:** www.blancaneaux.com
**Rates:** From US$270 for two per night in a riverfront cabana, including breakfast.

**Chaa Creek** P.O. Box 53, San Ignacio, Cayo District, Belize
**Tel:** +501 824 2037
**Web:** www.chaacreek.com
**Rates:** From US$160 for two per night in a Garden Jacuzzi Suite, including breakfast.

**Reef and Rainforest**
See page 77.

## When to go

Subtropical Belize is warm and humid, especially along the coast. The mountains have pleasant cool breezes, and the lowland jungles are usually steamy and humid at any time of year. The best time to visit is outside the rainy season (May to November) and between December and March.

# BRAZIL
Refúgio Ecólogico Caiman

The Pantanal region is a vast (and I mean vast – it's the size of France), land-trapped waterlogged basin, directly below the Amazon, covering 210,000 square kilometres of Brazil, Bolivia and Paraguay.

Its flat, low-lying plains are flooded annually by the hundreds of rivers and ponds that stem from the giant Paraguay river, which crosses the biome from north to south, connecting the Pantanal to the Paraná river basin. Reminiscent of Africa's Okavango, it is equally dramatic and photogenic. At times it's wild and rugged, at others the marshlands look like golf courses with natural bunkers and hidden roughs, groomed to perfection by the white Indian cattle that roam.

Each year hundreds of cubic kilometres of water are lost through direct evaporation, turning the Pantanal into the largest window of fresh water evaporation in the world. Most of the year it is hot and rather humid and provides a perfect habitat for over 20 per cent of the world's species, including the endangered jaguar, the capybara (the world's largest rodent, which looks like a dog-sized guinea pig), the giant anteater, alligator-related caiman and stunning royal-blue hyacinth macaw. It's a birder's paradise with 385 species calling this patchwork of giant puddles their home. You'll see more birds in 10 minutes in the Pantanal than in 10 days in the Amazon.

The area's most precious commodity is, undoubtedly, water, which defines the nature of the seasonal wetlands and the habits of the region's wildlife. When the floods recede, the water accumulated during the summer slowly starts to evaporate. The vegetation becomes drier and the landscape fills with yellowish tones while animals seek out water and food. In the winter months the lack of water on the plains is a defining factor – the rains are rare, the air is dry and there are very few drinking holes. Most of the water is in the larger lakes and rivers and is sought by mammals, birds and reptiles alike. The fish population is also concentrated in these waters, fighting for food and keeping an eye out for predators. When the rains come at the end of September, spring reappears and the landscape becomes greener as the trees slowly flourish once more.

### The camain refuge – an ecological vision
Caiman's story, like so many eco successes, is the result of one man's passion for his country and vision for the planet. This particular estancia, located in the Mato Grosso do Sul in the southern Pantanal, was formed in 1910 by British investors wishing to create a large cattle farm. They sold out in the 1950s to Brazilian investors who kept it going until 1985 when they divided it into separate farms. Among these was the Estancia Miranda, reformed and renamed by the current owner, Dr Roberto Klabin, as the Caiman Ecological Refuge.

opposite, above and below **Riding and canooing through the marshlands between the caiman**

Today it covers an area of 53,000 hectares bringing together three complementary activities: the Estancia Caiman, an extensive cattle farm with over 50,000 Brahman cattle; Caiman Lodge, a pioneering eco tourism operation with three separate lodges; and a nature conservation programme, which hosts scientific projects such as the hyacinth macaw project (whose population has grown from 1,500 to 5,000), and the jaguar conservation project (which monitors 42 resident cats using tagging and hidden cameras), while maintaining a private reserve encompassing 5,600 hectares.

The knowledgeable naturalist Fernanda Melo has trained all six 'caimaners', local bilingual guides who accompany daily walking and riding tours, sharing their vast knowledge of local fauna and flora. Within hours you'll learn the distinctive soundscapes – the early-morning yell of the chachalacas act like the Pantanal's alarm clock. 'Gradual interdependence' sounds like one of those psychobabble phrases but, Klabin has proved that it is possible to reach a sustainable and harmonious level of human presence in the Pantanal. Man and nature are living hand in hand.

Following the Gold Rush in the 17th century, cattle raising has been the region's most important economic activity for over 200 years and it continues to define the local culture of the Pantaneiros. For a 'campeiro' (cowboy) a typical day starts with an early-morning 'Quebra-torto' (a high-energy breakfast of coffee and rice cooked with dried beef). Working the cattle is a challenging and unpredictable task and the campeiros leave home not knowing what time they will return. Before preparing the horses they discuss the day ahead over a ritual drink of *Terere*, a type of iced tea made with the leaves of yerba mate, a tree common in western Brazil. Pantaneiros are straight-forward people who value the beauty of the land where they live and work. The caiman community consists of over 120 employees and their families. They all collaborate to maintain the social and environmental equilibrium of the Refuge and receive comfortable housing, medical and dental care and schooling for their children. Interestingly, each family

receives 5lbs of beef each week to deter poaching. It's a great success story but nothing is taken for granted.

There are three accomodation options: the 10-bedroomed Sede Lodge; the more rugged Cordilheira Lodge and, most spectacular of all, the newly renovated Baiazinha Lodge.

Sede Lodge is the original home of the Klabin family offering comfortable estancia-type rooms around an enclosed courtyard. It's close to the unmissable environmental interpretation centre, a huge lagoon ideal for bird watching and the small community of the Pantaneiros who work on the Refuge. It represents the social and cultural heart of the estancia.

Cordilheira Lodge, situated to the north with eight simple guestrooms is more remote. Peace reigns supreme under the flame trees and the hammocks beckon for a daily siesta.

The splendid Baiazinha Lodge, meaning 'Little Bay', has just eight double guestrooms (complete with pool, hammocks and a private nature library) overlooking the tranquil waters of the flooded basin. The prolific wildlife provides endless entertainment – colourful parrots fly through the air, shy marsh deer bounce through the water alongside herds of capybara, while caiman bask in the sun.

The Refuge's electricity is sourced from the national grid but solar power heats all the water, which comes from a local well. Food is sourced from Roberto's other nearby ranch, whenever possible, and also from the nearby town of Miranda.

Fare is both regional and delicious. Apart from mouth-watering beef dishes, fresh-water fish are a great option. The flavours are always strong and spicy. Try the succulent but strange-looking pacu, a fruit-eating fish with a quirky face. Other typical dishes include the *arroz carreteiro*, made of rice and sun-dried beef, accompanied by *farofa* (yucca flour toasted in butter or oil with banana).

Caiman lives up to its namesake. It has been estimated that over 30 million caiman live in the Pantanal. Up to six metres in length they roam the grasslands and waters, feeding on fish and small mammals. They look dangerous but, fortunately, prefer to keep out of humans' way and only attack if provoked.

To visit the Pantanal is to take a different type of safari – for the 'Big Five' you'll have to go to Africa but for jaguars, giant anteaters, tapirs, capybaras and magnificent birdlife it doesn't get better than the Pantanal.

below **Scenic trails criss-cross the estate**    opposite **A capybara and Baiazinha Lodge**

# Green menu

Watch animals at night Stars, torches, action. One of the highlights could be the giant anteater, endangered jaguar, shy tapir or the shining red eyes of the caimans at night.

Go biking Take a bike and cycle along the 80 kilometres of roads and trails built by Roberto over the last 20 years – it's flat and easy to ride.

Take a canoe trip Row in a three-seat Canadian canoe around the bays of the Sede and Baiazinha Lodges. Listen to the waterbirds cry, the capybaras bark and the caiman grunt.

Saddle-up Hop on a horse and you'll experience and see so much more than if you use any other form of transport.

Be a cowboy for a day (*Dia de Peão*) Live the life with an authentic campeiro for a day. Begin with the ritual of choosing and 'settling' of the horses, then get herding and even try lassoing practice. After a busy morning, eat typical *matula* at lunch followed by more work in the afternoon ending with a refreshing *Roda de Terere*.

Go bird watching Take a walk with some binoculars to observe some of the spectacular local species, including the some of the area's most symbolic birds, the jabiru stork, buff-necked ibis, the amazing hyacinth macaw, nanday and monk parakeets and the toco toucan.

## When to go

Although birdwatching is great all year round, there are two seasons with quite distinct characteristics: the wet season (November to March) is the favourite time for wading birds such as storks, herons, egrets, spoonbills, ducks and other species that feed on fish, crustaceans and plants in the flooded plains. Rain usually falls in the afternoon and temperatures range from 20–40°C. The dry season (April to October) is better for spotting mammals and sees the colourful plumage displays and breeding of macaws, oropendolas, woodpeckers and flycatchers. The whole area turns dry and temperatures range from 10–30°C.

## Contacts

**Refúgio Ecólogico Caiman** Av Brigadeiro Faria Lima, 3.015 Cj. 161 Itaim Bibi, São Paulo, SP Brazil CEP 01452-000
**Tel:** +55 (11) 3706 1800
**Web:** www.caiman.com.br

**Journey Latin America (see p.65)**
**Tel:** +44 (0) 20 8747 8315, +44 (0) 161 832 1441
**Web:** www.journeylatinamerica.com
**Rates:** From US$314 per person per day, including all meals and activities.

# CANADA
## World Wide Opportunities on Organic Farms

Canada is big. As the second largest country in the world, spanning six time zones and stretching from the Atlantic to the Pacific and north to the Arctic oceans, it covers almost 10 million square kilometres and is made up of 10 provinces and three territories.

Escaping into nature is easy. You can be strolling along a city pavement and within minutes wind up in the middle of a rainforest. Forests stretch from the Atlantic to the Pacific coasts, and up to the Arctic tree-line limit in the north. They occupy 45 per cent of the landmass and are home to roughly two-thirds of the estimated 140,000 species of plants, animals and micro-organisms that thrive in Canada. Quebec alone has over 123.5 million acres of forested land.

The primary goal at the 2008 GMIST (Gros Morne International Summit on Sustainable Tourism) was 'to promote Canada as a world leader in the burgeoning field of sustainable tourism'. And it doesn't come greener than volunteering to work on a farm.

The concept is simple – join the Canadian chapter of Wwoofers (World Wide Opportunities on Organic Farms) and hook up with over 800 hosts from coast to coast. You can live on a farm for a week or more, volunteer your time and sweat, and receive lodgings and meals in return.

If your idea of a holiday is to lounge by the pool with a margarita, stop reading here. But if you've always dreamed of farming the land, this trend sweeping Canada is for you. Hoe, plant, pick and weed away your holiday on a *bona fide* working farm – it's a trend that has sprouted like corn on the prairies.

I rose to the sound of the roosters (my new alarm bell), grabbed a hoe and hit the veggie patch on 130-hectare, certified-organic Keewatin Farm under the wide-open prairie skies near Regina in Saskatchewan. The farm is centred around a lovely old Edwardian red-brick house featuring two porches – front and back – so visitors can enjoy sun or shade depending on the weather. Not far from the house – just below the barn – is a small prairie valley whose spring-fed water flows enthusiastically to join the river in the famous Qu'Appelle Valley. The area is home to dozens of indigenous species, including hawks, foxes, rabbits, gophers and, of course, coyotes.

Helping Elaine McNeil and husband Will Oddie with their breeding herd of Canadien horses was an unexpected joy. There was always grooming to be done and plenty of stable chores. After that it was time to saddle up for an energising trot or take off on a hay ride with Canada's sturdy national horse at the end of the reins. I felt like Laura Ingalls in *Little House on the Prairie*. Others spent the afternoon picking Saskatoon berries. We all finished each day cooling off with a cold drink on the farmhouse porch while gophers and foxes stole by, ignoring us

opposite **The joys of farming in British Columbia**

completely. A good night's sleep was practically guaranteed after all our exertions, bedding down at the B&B – Bed and Bale – in the Edwardian red-brick farmhouse. If you're lucky you'll hear coyotes howling as the Northern Lights flicker across the sky.

A workin' holiday? That's right, the down-and-dirty kind. As more people realise that the average food item in North America has travelled some 2,500 miles from farm to table, they want to see what's cooking just down the road and fresh from the field.

Desk jockeys are increasingly getting in on the buzz, going low-tech on their days off, signing up for agri-tourism holidays, playing farmer for a week. The work might be

making maple syrup, winding mohair wool on a bobbin, collecting cranberries or picking pumpkins, then learning how to cook them into something gourmet from a chef. The physical work, steady pace and connection with the earth soothes the soul, especially if you are an urban bunny, more used to tapping on a keyboard than tapping into the rhythms of nature. Some farms exchange room and board for volunteering. And there are hundreds of farms to choose from coast to coast. So don your dungarees, grab your garden gloves, hit the dirt and start living the good life.

above **Lassoing is quite a skill**   right **Rural comfort**

# Green menu

Cycle through Pemberton Meadows Pedal yourself along a 50-kilometre natural buffet in Pemberton Meadows farmland, British Columbia, just north of Whistler. Every August, 1,300 farm and food enthusiasts cycle along a rural street party on Slow Food Cycle Sunday. Meet local growers and work up an appetite for tasty pit stops along the way.
www.slowfoodcyclesunday.com

Get to know the local food scene Take a guided gourmet safari of Salt Spring Island, British Columbia, visiting the Gulf Island's boutique wineries, vineyards and cheesemakers that supply the nation's best chefs. Dine on fresh, local cuisine at Hastings House Country Estate Hotel; on Saturdays, add a visit to the town's funky market.
www.islandgourmetsafaris.com

Enjoy rustic comfort Stay in Le Gîte de l'Ardora, a 150-year-old historic farmhouse on New Brunswick's Acadian Peninsula. This place is near the sea at a farm that raises cows, geese, pheasants, blueberries and... oysters.
www.ardora.ca

Visit Capricorn View Farm Tour the facilities and get to know Capricorn View Farm, a family-run goat-meat and milk farm at Bloomfield, Ontario. Learn about their handmade goat-milk soap and help out with barn work before sitting down to a lunch of goat meat and cheeses.
www.capricornview.com

Pick grapes, drink wine Love wine? Head to The Grange of Prince Edward Estate winery in Ontario at autumn harvest to help pick grapes on 25 hectares of vineyards. Then sit back and sip the results.
www.grangeofprinceedward.com

Stay on a farm Sleep in a cabin at Pioneer Farm, O'Leary, an off-the-grid organic farm in coastal PEI, then pull on your grubbies. The morning's chores? Helping owners Judy and Jim Bertling gather eggs for your breakfast and feed 'Wiggles' the pig. Learn about sustainable practices and preserving heritage breeds. Groom and saddle the llamas to carry your picnic lunch on a trek.
www.pioneerfarm.ca

Enjoy rural luxury Take a shortcut to Provence by touring Rabouillère, a Quebec farm (an hour's drive south of Montreal) where you can overnight in rural luxury and dine on *haute cuisine* fresh from the garden. Rabouillère raises llamas, two types of sheep and 25 kinds of racing, meat and ornamental pigeons. The property's gardens bloom in season with fine herbs and edible flowers.
www.rabouillere.com

# Contacts

**Keewatin Farm** Box 2, Site 101, RR#1 Regina, Saskatchewan, S4P 2Z1 Canada
**Tel:** +1 (0) 306 779 1012
**Web:** www.canadienhorse.com
**Rates:** Available on request.

**WWOOF Canada** 4429 Carlson Road, Nelson, British Columbia, Canada, VIL 6X3
**Tel:** +1 (0) 250 354 4417
**Web:** www.wwoof.ca
**Rates:** Available on request.

Volunteering on Organic Farms is a great way to travel inexpensively, while broadening your education and practical experience. Over 800 farm hosts will introduce you to the many interesting aspects of Canadian farms and gardens.

# When to go

The best time to WWOOF is between early spring (April on the eastern side of Canada; February to April in British Columbia on the western side of Canada) to late autumn. There are numerous hosts who accept volunteers all year round.

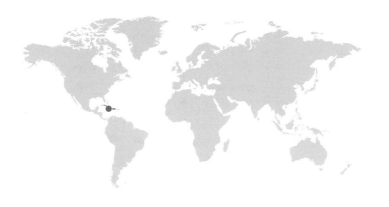

# CARIBBEAN
### Star Clippers

'We have been under sail all night,' the captain told me as I wandered onto the bridge at breakfast time, somewhere off the coast of Grenada. 'We saw whales at dawn. It was truly incredible.'

I vowed to spend the following night sleeping on deck, something passengers on the three square riggers of Star Clippers are quite welcome to do if they wish.

A Star Clippers voyage around the Caribbean is everything a cruise is not. No crowds, no over-commercialised ports, no casinos, no formality. Just a group of 228 like-minded people in search of peace, the quiet, tiny, unspoiled anchorages of the 'real' Caribbean and a chance to connect with the ocean.

Star Clippers operates genuine sailing ships, *Royal Clipper*, *Star Clipper* and *Star Flyer* – mega-yachts in the truest sense of the word. They sail in the Adriatic, the Aegean, French Polynesia, Southeast Asia and the Caribbean, the winter home of *Royal Clipper*, the largest of the three. Yes, they follow an itinerary but distances are short and the aim is to spend the maximum possible time under sail, the engines turned off.

Not only does this save fuel, but it recreates the glorious days of the ocean-going clippers of the 19th century, known as the 'greyhounds of the sea' for their speed and grace. It's a chance for passengers to experience real sailing without having to join in – unless they want to.

Star Clippers is more than the greenest type of cruise, if you must call it a cruise. It's a piece of living history, lovingly recreated by the company's Swedish owner Mikael Krafft to preserve the art of building and sailing square riggers. Krafft has been fascinated by clipper ships since he was a boy, when he would make scale models of these sleek, elegant vessels. A few decades and considerable business success later, he has turned his love of maritime history into a viable business. 'Now it's fun to build the models in a scale of 1:1,' he says.

The company currently owns three ships, with plans for a fourth, which, when it launches in the next couple of years, will be the world's biggest five-masted sailing ship. But while the vessels look traditional, as exact replicas of famous ships in history, what's going on below decks is a different story.

'The new ship is going to be extremely environmentally clean, allowing for the absolute highest standards of purifying waste water,' explains Krafft. 'At the same time, we will be installing the same technology on the three existing ships, which is an enormous investment.'

Unlike big cruise ships that disgorge up to 3,700 people onto small island communities, Star Clippers minimises its impact on the ports it visits. In the Caribbean, *Royal Clipper* calls at some of the smallest islands, often ferrying passengers ashore by tender. Shore excursions are offered, but on a small scale; passengers tend to be independent travellers who prefer to do their own thing.

For watersports, a special platform is lowered at the aft of the vessel. Diving, snorkelling, kayaking and dinghy sailing are encouraged; powered sports much less so. Instead of a lavish spa, Thai massage is offered in a pavilion on deck on all three ships (although Royal Clipper does have a beauty parlour below the waterline).

Some of the islands visited are inaccessible to large vessels and, as such, are completely unspoilt. We dropped anchor off Iles des Saintes, a tiny slice of France off the coast of Guadeloupe, with a miniature town hall, a patisserie and a couple of bars. The inhabitants here are descended from Breton fishermen.

In the Tobago Cays National Park, we stopped for a beach lunch, snorkelling in turquoise water so clear you can see right across the bay to Royal Clipper's anchor chain. Absolutely everything is removed from the beach after a call like this, where visiting vessels are not allowed to leave any debris.

Similarly, the Grenadines were sheer bliss, catching a morning breeze and slicing between dark green hummocks of islands fringed with brilliant white, no noise apart from the rustle of wind in the sails. I lay in the bowsprit nets either side of the ship's figurehead and dolphins rode the bow wave beneath me, zipping along at speed, racing the ship.

Even in the bigger ports, Royal Clipper stays away from the crowds. In Dominica, we dropped anchor at Prince Rupert Bay and I joined a fairly tough hike through the rainforest up to Trafalgar Falls, my guide pointing out the local flora and fauna along the way.

When we visited Antigua, the ship sailed majestically into Falmouth, the 18th-century naval base, instead of going

left **Under sail**   above **The bar**

above **Birds ete view of the deck**

alongside in St Johns with all the big cruise ships, whose passengers prefer shopping malls to the crumbling glory of Nelson's Dockyard. It's a much more authentic experience, mingling with the genial yachting community rather than shuffling around the duty-free shops with thousands of bargain-hunters.

In St Lucia, the ship sits in Marigot Bay, one of the loveliest anchorages in the Caribbean, while passengers snorkel or go ashore to shop in the markets and visit the famous twin peaks of Gros and Petit Piton.

I never did manage a whole night on deck as my cabin was too comfortable, albeit compact, but during the course of the week, I learned a bit about navigation from the Captain's daily talk and hauled on a few lines, somewhat feebly compared to the rugged deckhands.

There isn't much in the way of evening entertainment but one night, a crackly old black-and-white movie, *Around Cape Horn*, was projected onto a sail stretched across the aft deck, telling the tale of a terrifying voyage by clipper through the world's toughest ocean in a fearsome storm.

After it had finished, I lay on a sun-lounger, gazing up at the dazzling night sky, reflecting that not only was this cruising with a clear conscience, but actually the best imaginable way to travel by sea.

# Green menu

Travel under sail The Royal Clipper sails two itineraries in the Caribbean, Grenadines and Windwards. The Grenadines itinerary includes Barbados, St Lucia, Dominica, Antigua (Falmouth Harbour), St Kitts, Iles des Saintes and Martinique. The Windwards voyage, which can be bolted on to make two weeks, calls at Barbados, the Grenadines, Grenada, Tobago Cays, St Vincent, Bequia, Martinique and St Lucia. The season runs from November to April. It is also possible to extend your stay at either end of the cruise and spend a few days in one of the numerous boutique hotels on Barbados, many of which have excellent green credentials.

## When to go

Star Clippers has one ship, *Royal Clipper*, which sails in the Caribbean from November to April when the weather remains warm (a very pleasant tropical climate) and relatively dry.

*Star Clipper* is in the Far East during the Winter months, doing both a northern and southern itinerary, which embarks and disembarks in Phuket as well as a Phuket – Singapore sailing. All of the itineraries are 7 nights.

During the summer months *Star Clipper* is in the Eastern Mediterranean, sailing around the Greek Islands, operating 7-night itineraries, which include the northern and southern Cyclades. There is also a 10/11-night itinerary between Venice and Athens.

The *Star Flyer* is in Tahiti all year round offering 7, 10 and 11 night itineraries, which all embark and disembark in Papeete.

## Contacts

**Star Clippers** Crown House, Crown Street, Ipswich, Suffolk IP1 3HS
**Tel:** +44 (0) 1473 292029

**Web:** www.starclippers.co.uk, www.starclippers.com for the international site
**Rates:** From £1,065 for a week, plus £110 port taxes, including meals and watersports (except diving). Flights and transfers are not included.

# CHILE

EcoCamp, Patagonia

Now here is a good quiz question: Where in the world is closer to Sydney than London and yet only three hours behind GMT? The answer is the Torres del Paine National Park in the Patagonian region of southern Chile.

Patagonia is a geologically diverse region with striking mountain formations, smoking volcanoes, flat, barren pampas and expansive ice fields. It is crowded with glaciers, lakes, fjords, ancient forests and wildlife such as guanacos (a relative of the llama), pink flamingos, giant condors and shy huemuls deer. It may be at the end of civilisation – next stop is Antarctica – but it offers some South America's most magnificent and challenging trekking and riding.

It's also home to Torres del Paine National Park, a World Heritage Site of the first order, which can offer a colossal choice of adventures, ranging from a soft stroll to hardcore rock climbing, among myriad peaks and lakes, with expeditions to glaciers and opportunities to visit the remote Tierra del Fuego.

The name EcoCamp had me envisioning discomfort, cold, wet and misery. What I found was warmth, of both the physical and social nature, top-rate hospitality and guiding, delightful international company and a view that defines Patagonia itself – the great granite Torres – popping out above my pillow each morning. It was communal living at its best, camaraderie when you wanted it, space and privacy when you didn't and at the end of four days I felt

like I'd lived the great outdoors 100 per cent and without a single sacrifice. Each night trekkers share their tales sitting on comfy sofas around the log burner and then sleep like logs in the snuggest fleece sheets and mega-tog duvets you've ever felt.

Over recent years the growth in visitor numbers has placed huge stress on the infrastructure of hotels and services inside the park, creating some serious environmental problems and throwing the existence and quality of tourist services into disrepute. But in January 2000 EcoCamp welcomed in the new millennium by choosing this remote World Biosphere Reserve – without doubt one of the most beautiful and enthralling spots on the planet – as the perfect spot to open the first true eco hotel in Patagonia. It makes quite a statement.

The story started when the Chilean adventure company Cascada Expediciones embarked on a study of alternatives to hotels. The goal was simple, to 'find a prototype solution that could reconcile the care of a fragile environment with the provision of a suitable low-impact infrastructure with a decent level of comfort for visitors'. They asked, 'would it not be reasonable to ask people visiting these remote places, so pristine and delicate, to focus their energies on preserving what they saw for the future?'

Their answer came in the form of the EcoCamp: modern accommodation, which is comfortable, transportable, and

above **Patagonian ponies**    opposite **Panorama at the gateway to the Torres del Paine National Park**

suitable for the rigours of the Patagonian climate equipped with environmentally friendly systems for the disposal of sewage and rubbish and an efficient use of renewable energy. The result is arguably aesthetically stylish, definitely safe and eco-friendly and is situated in a quiet private corner of the park, marked out by a vast shaded area on the map 'terreno privado'.

EcoCamp maintains the nomadic spirit of the ancient Kawesqar inhabitants who once travelled along the fragmented coast from Golfo de Penas to the Strait of Magellan looking for food and shelter. They were a people who lived in harmony with Mother Nature and built their huts out of wood, furs and leather, using only organic materials found at each site. The 21st-century EcoCamp design was inspired by their traditional hut, implementing

an easy form of engineering. A number of isosceles triangles form the semi-hemispherical structure of the domes, providing important uniform distribution of the stress of severe wind loads, which often exceed 160–180 kilometres per hour – a traditional, lightweight, flat-sided tent would be utterly vulnerable. The rounded sides minimise external surface contact with the cold winds thus lowering the impact on the warm interiors. Hey presto! It's snug, strong and very airtight.

The camp itself comprises 15 dormitory domes. At its heart are two giant domes (9 metres in diameter and 4.5 metres tall) that fulfil the purpose of resting area, dining room and kitchen. Meals are a communal affair with breakfast laid out like a fine buffet setting you up for the day: bacon and eggs, ham, cheeses, fruits, nuts and

yoghurts. You make and pack your own lunch in re-usable sealed bags from a selection of fresh meats and salads, muesli bars and chocolate brownies. Dinner is a hearty three-course meal with warming soup, various local lamb dishes followed by a traditional pudding. One thing's for sure – you won't go hungry.

An additional bathroom dome, the same size as the dining dome, has showers with constant hot water, compost lavatories, three washbasins and mirrors decorated with fresh berries, lichen and bark from the woods. In a nutshell, it's all you need – warmth, hot water and great food.

A more sensible template for eco tourism is impossible to find. Guests find themselves exposed to nature, as in camping, but with the comfort of a hotel. The transient settlement interferes as little as possible with the

environment – even building wooden boardwalks to keep the grassland pristine. In fact, it's barely visible from afar and reflects the nomadic ethos of portability, leaving very few tracks of any existence when relocated every winter, allowing the terrain to recover fully.

EcoCamp wants travellers to embrace the blustery weather as an integral part of Patagonia and squalls of wind persistently flap the outer canvas reminding you that nature is knocking at your door. Having slept snuggly between those snuggly fleece sheets, you generally wake up any time after 6 a.m. – by which time the dome is already flooded with daylight – to the sound of horses' hooves or a woodpecker somewhere nearby… and that view. Few can resist the urge to grab a camera and catch the first light striking the mountains.

above **Guanaco**    opposite **Eco tent and its interior comforts**

With only 15 tents there's a strong feeling of intimacy. One of the most impressive aspects of the EcoCamp is that its energy comes from 100 per cent natural and renewal sources, including hydro, solar and turbine. Solar energy has been widely used in Patagonia especially during summer when the days can have 17 hours of daylight but wind energy is still at an experimental stage as the wind blows very irregularly with strong currents at certain hours and then not a breeze for days.

In this world of eroding wilderness, an eco trip to the remote region of Patagonia looks too good to be true but it's every bit as wonderful as the photos. You can trek the giant 'W' through virgin beech forests; gaze in wonder as colossal glacial icebergs carve into the freezing slate-blue waters of Lago Grey; feel healthily insignificant at the foot of the towering granite peaks of the Torres del Paine; and when the stars come out, forget it all and just lie in total silence underneath the Southern Cross.

# Green menu

**Go walking** Most visitors come here to trek and the most famous walk of all is the aptly named 'W' that winds its way around the park's best-known peaks. It can take anything from three days to a week to complete the trek depending on your level of fitness and the pace you choose.

**Shear a sheep** If you have never visited a sheep farm, you are in for quite a treat. While most of South America is cattle country, Patagonia is definitely sheep territory. Cerro Guido, half an hour from EcoCamp and just outside the national park, is a 100,000-hectare farm with 45,000 sheep. The old communities reflect times gone by with 100-year-old carts and machinery still in operation.

**Enjoy a day in the saddle** A horseback ride is a great option for walk-weary legs and a fantastic way to cover huge stretches of the park. Crossing wide streams, ascending vertiginous paths, cantering along the lakeside or just ambling past a group of guanacos is easy in the saddle. Hacks of various lengths can be arranged from EcoCamp.

## When to go

The camp runs from October to April each year. Summer (mid-December to mid-March), with its mild temperatures and long days, is the most favorable season to visit Patagonia. Expect changeable weather and strong winds whenever you visit.

## Contacts

**Cascada Expediciones** Don Carlos 3219, Las Condes 755-0139, Santiago, Chile
**Tel:** +56 2232 9878
**Web:** www.ecocamp.travel

**Journey Latin America**
**Tel:** +44 (0) 20 8747 8315, +44 (0) 161 832 1441
**Web:** www.journeylatinamerica.com
**Rates:** From £663 per person based on two sharing, including three full days trekking in Torres del Paine National park for 5 days, 4 nights (excluding flights).

Since 1980, Journey Latin America has been dedicated to running responsible holidays to Latin America. Their credentials have been recognised by AITO with the highest achievable three-star Responsible Tourism status. They support four small charities in Latin America, all of which focus on long-term development; through education, healthcare and conservation. They have achieved a 70 per cent take up on $CO_2$ off-setting – funds are used by TICOS to develop projects that have both carbon savings and wider sustainable development benefits for local communities.

# CHINA

## Banyan Tree Ringha

With just over 1.3 billion people, China is the world's largest and most populous country. This hugely fast-growing economy has fuelled a demand for energy, with China producing 6.1 billion tonnes of $CO_2$ every year, overtaking the US as the world's biggest polluter. On average, two new power stations are built every year to cope with this demand, but in 2005 this rose to an even greater five 300-megawatt power plants a week. Chinese cities seem wrapped in a grey cloud, with respiratory and heart diseases related to air pollution the leading causes of death; China is literally choking.

On the face of it, China would appear to be the least 'green' and environmentally friendly country on Earth but I discovered a place where the air is so clear it's like breathing champagne. Banyan Tree Ringha is in China's Yunnan province, a mountainous area 3,200 metres above sea level. Getting there involves taking a plane to Kunming International Airport, followed by an internal 50-minute flight to Diqing Airport and a scenic 40-minute car ride. You'd be hard pressed to find a more secluded hideaway. The spectacular location inspired author James Hilton to name it Shangri-La, the setting for his classic 1933 novel *Lost Horizon* and today the area has been designated the official Shangri-La by the Chinese government. Historically and culturally it forms part of Greater Tibet.

Banyan Tree Ringha opened in September 2005, the first of the brand located in China. But what are its eco credentials? When the parent firm Banyan Tree Holdings was set up, the company faced a choice: to pick a location, bulldoze its way through, disrupt the surrounding communities and end up with a purpose-built resort, or to develop an eco-sensitive approach that complemented the location and offered opportunities to the local community. Banyan Tree Ringha opted for the latter and its ideals are encapsulated in its approach to the accommodation itself. The resort consists of authentic Tibetan farmhouses. These were bought from nearby locals, then carefully removed from their original locations and reconstructed at the new site. This involved a meticulous process where individual logs were numbered like a giant model kit. This ensured that no newly cut timber was required and that the original character of the buildings was preserved. Each villa has a Tibetan name – that of the original owner of the house. There are 32 spacious suites and lodges featuring fireplaces, wooden balconies that offer awe-inspiring valley or river views and handcrafted wooden bathtubs in what were once yak stables. The rooms are all on two floors and there's just one way to describe them – huge. The smallest, a Tibetan Suite, encompasses 204.5 square metres.

Banyan Tree Hotels and Resorts are known for their sensitivity to the environment. Reclaimed water for irrigation, ceramic dispensers and biodegradable soap and shampoo are subtle indicators of their commitment to

above and opposite **Secret valleys and lost horizons around Ringha**

sustainability and environmental responsibility. Like many hotels and resorts, the Banyan Tree Ringha helps to reduce water consumption and detergent pollution by asking guests when they want their bed linen and towels changed.

Water for the resort comes from a spring in the mountains while the main energy supply is provided by the Chinese government with the necessary backup generator. When it comes to recycling, plastic and glass go to a rubbish house near the property where villagers take it and sell it to a recycling factory for their own benefit.

The villas are so impressive and comfortable that you're in danger of spending more time in your room than you should. It's the location that lifts this resort into the sublime, and it's a location that should be explored.

There's a range of adventurous tours on offer using the resort's 4x4s or there are trekking programmes on foot or on horseback. Sixty-five per cent of the staff are locals, employed in all departments while additional locals are contracted to provide trekking and guiding assistance. The treks enable guests to visit farmhouses for an authentic meal of hot-pot dishes and homemade yak-butter tea and cheese. There are six villages in the nearby valley and Banyan Tree rotates these visits to each home in each village so that everyone in the area benefits.

They pursue the same policy when it comes to horse rentals. The treks are a great way of engaging with the local community and finding out about the Tibetan way of life, as well as soaking up the stunning scenery. The hotel is also involved in a string of community initiatives that includes supporting the school and its 34 pupils, providing locals in the Ringha Valley with tools and utensils every six months, and stocking the local clinic with medicine and materials.

Famous for its award-winning spa, guests at Ringha are able to indulge in a wide range of pampering body treatments and massages. The signature Ringha massage is a two-hour session involving Eastern techniques that induce a sense of total well-being. The spa has also developed several treatments to help guests ease their muscles after a day's strenuous trekking.

There are two restaurants at Ringha; Llamo Restaurant with an all-day dining menu of Tibetan and Western food, and Chang-Sa serving traditional hot-pots, steamboats and snacks. The two must-haves at the latter are the Tibetan hot-pot and Tibetan barbecue, which are delicious. Local products are used as much as possible, so expect yak meat, Tibetan farm chicken and all manner of vegetables, including seasonal Tibetan wild mushrooms and local cabbage.

The wine, an interesting combination of grapefruit and barley, is also local.

Banyan Tree Ringha imparts a unique sense of place to its guests and through its cultural and environmental initiatives has, in turn, contributed to the local community. The group has plans to open eight more properties in China over the next five years, including Sanya, Hangshou and Beijing. While China's eco tourism is very much in its infancy, hopefully it will catch on fast with places like this starting a trend for eco-friendly choices.

above **Songzanlin Monastery**　　right **Local grandmother and infant**

# Green menu

**Take the Shangri-La culture tour** A fascinating insight into Tibetan life, visiting farmhouses, sampling homemade yak-butter tea and visiting the 800-year-old Ringha Da Bao Si Monastery. There is also a craft tour where you can see carpenters at work.

**Go trekking** There are several treks on offer including a gentle acclimatisation trek, a village trek (and lunch), river or lake excursion, pony treks or more strenuous walks up into mountains to a height of 3,700 metres.

**Visit Songzanlin lamasery** Visit the largest Tibetan Buddhist lamasery in Yunnan Province.

**Indulge in spa treatments** Don't miss one of the signature treatments, including a rice-wine bath or a heated soft river-stone massage

**Buy local handicrafts** The Banyan Tree Gallery is the place to buy intricate and ethnic souvenirs, including Tibetan handicrafts.

**Enjoy Tibetan song and dance** Every full-moon night, the local Tibetan staff and their families perform a short song and dance item at the Plaza.

**Learn about Tibetan cooking** Every Sunday, the resort's Executive Chef prepares two authentic Tibetan dishes and shares his knowledge of cooking, Tibetan culture and the Tibetan way of life.

**Support the Green Imperative Fund** This provides critical financial support to worthy environmental action and community-based projects. For every night a guest spends in a Banyan Tree property, a small contribution under an 'opt out' arrangement is requested. Banyan Tree will match their contribution dollar for dollar, to develop The Green Imperative Fund.

## When to go

There are four distinctive seasons in Ringha. Spring (March to May), Summer (June to August), Autumn (September to November) and Winter (December to February). May and June are the best time for flowers, July and August are the peak season and also the most popular for mushroom hunting. In September and October, you get the great autumn colours and blue skies and in the winter expect freezing temperatures and snow. In mid-June, Shangri-La plays host to a horseracing festival that sees several days of dancing, singing, eating and horseracing.

## Contacts

**Banyan Tree Ringha** Hong Po Village, Jian Tang Town, Shangri-La County, Diqing Tibetan Autonomous Prefecture Yunnan Province, PR China 674400
**Tel:** +86 887 828 8822, +65 6849 5800 (reservations)
**Web:** www.banyantree.com
**Rates:** From US$400 for the Tibetan Suites and US$700 for Tibetan Lodges.

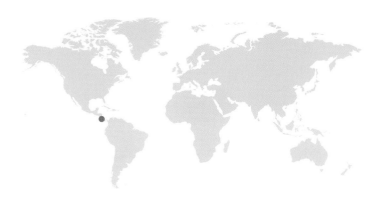

# COSTA RICA
## Lapos Rios

Costa Rica is the teacher's pet of the eco tourism class, and this small Central American nation regularly gets straight As on issues green. It's not just Lapa Rios, the subject of this review, that flies the green flag – a cast of thousands of eco lodges and projects would also be mentioned in dispatches, and a staggering 25 per cent of the country is set aside in National Parks – the highest percentage of any nation on the planet. Call me cynical, but while some destinations pedal repackaged product as eco-friendly in order to move with the times, Costa Rica has been walking the walk for years. Responsible tourism is embedded as the fundamental principle in the country's tourism mantra – even the Tourist Board's strapline is 'No Artificial Ingredients'.

Impressive, I see you nod, but only to be expected from a country that abolished its own armed forces in 1948 preferring (in the aftermath of a bloody civil war) to spend millions on improving the day-to-day lot of its citizens rather than rearming to the teeth in the face of an improbable invasion by their pacifist Panamanian neighbours.

In fact, the only cross-border incursions in recent years have been those by hordes of Hawaiian-shirt-wearing American tourists, but don't let that put you off. It may mean that the cuisine on offer in Costa Rica rarely soars to heights much beyond super-sized burgers and shakes (although Lapa Rios is an exception), but gringos from the States demand and receive a level of service of which

Europeans holidaying on their own continent can often only dream. That Ticos (as Costa Ricans refer to themselves) make such naturally warm hosts only makes the experience of travelling here all the more pleasurable.

Costa Rica is a picture-perfect and pocket-sized country with two beautiful coastlines separated by a spine of extremely active volcanoes. For all but the most backpacker-budgeted travellers, access to the furthest-flung corners is by light aircraft, which offers a wonderful perspective on the varying and distinct eco systems that make this such a fascinating destination. The wetlands of the Caribbean Coast give way to jungle, interspersed with the massive banana plantations that provide so much of the country's income; next come the cloud forests of the mountainous interior and then it's down to the tropical rainforests of the Pacific coastline, all within an hour's flight.

### Lapa Rios

Visitors bound for Lapa Rios land on a dusty landing strip in the no-horse town of Puerto Jimenez on the south-western Osa Peninsula, with a handily located graveyard at the end of the runway for those who misjudge the crosswinds. The Lapa Rios office is the only building, emblazoned with a warning – 'This is the last time you will have phone or email contact'. While this is enough to induce heart palpitations in most Eururbanites, the

feeling of genuine release from the manacles of 24-hour contact is immensely liberating and very much in keeping with the whole experience.

It's then into a dependable Land Rover Defender for the hour's bottom-bouncing drive to the resort, through a strange landscape of white-sand beaches and arable pastures, not unlike a scene from the west coast of Scotland, but with Brahmin cattle chowing down in the foreground and rainforest-clad hills as a backdrop. The driver of every passing vehicle offers the surfer's salute of fist with thumb and little finger spread, which embodies the Ticos' philosophy of *Pura Vida* – a commitment to celebrating a peaceful way of life.

On arrival at Lapa Rios, and after the obligatorily warm welcome, guests are talked through the wide-ranging eco credentials of what is Costa Rica's flagship green initiative, before taking one of the most memorable walks imaginable to their bungalow. This neck of the rainforest is crawling, slithering, scuttling and hopping with more wildlife than you can shake a stick at (not advised). From the dawn chorus of howler monkeys hailing the rising sun to the cane toad the size of a pound of sugar with which we had a Costa-Rican stand-off on our doorstep, this entire place is animate. As for the flora, not an inch of soil is bereft of plant life, and it is little wonder that *National Geographic* declared the Osa Peninsula 'the most biologically intense place on earth'. Quite some claim.

left **Pool villa**    above **Swimming pool**

above **Brahmin cattle**

The 16 thatched and extremely comfortable bungalows all have terraces with hammocks, and the focal point of the main lodge is a hardwood stairwell soaring three storeys from the restaurant floor so guests can see out over the dense rainforest canopy down to the ocean. All the man-made structures blend into the surroundings, and the fact that Lapa Rios enhances this special location rather than detracting from it is entirely down to the vision and dedication of the American owners John and Karen Lewis. Back in 1990 when Al Gore had eyes only for the White House, they bought 1,000 acres of mostly primary rainforest bordering the world-famous Corcovardo National Park. The creation of Lapa Rios lodge helped fund the ongoing project and the entire area is now protected in perpetuity.

Ecologically, Lapa Rios is the benchmark for eco lodges the world over. No trees were felled for its construction

and solar panels are used to heat water. Use of pesticides and herbicides is restricted to the thatched roofs and 25,000 palms have been planted to replace old thatch. Guests pre-order their meals to avoid food waste, minimal use is made of non-recyclable containers and the lodge has introduced the local regions' first recycling. It provides protection for over 1,000 acres of pristine rainforest and reports all illegal logging and cutting activities to the local authorities and the press and, in order to cultivate 'monkey bridges', it also refuses to comply with local laws that require the rainforest canopy to be cut back above roads around the reserve.

Its educational remit towards its guests, staff and the locals survives close scrutiny and the local children can now enjoy a formal education in the school built by the lodge, something their parents never had the opportunity to do.

When it comes to the eco test Costa Rica, like the dazzling macaw that symbolises it, passes with flying colours.

# Green menu

**Visit coastal primary rainforest** A visit to the National Park of Corcovardo, where you can follow tapir tracks along the beach is an absolute must.

**Enjoy a perfect point break** Surf dudes of any standard will enjoy the perfect point break beneath the resort. Surfers are a notoriously territorial bunch, but at Lapa Rios, you'll be welcomed out to the waves by even the gnarliest boarders – it's just that sort of place.

**Visit the reserve** Access to the private reserve is only allowed with professional guides, which makes for a magical, uncrowded experience.

**Plant a tree** Guests can volunteer for a reforestation programme to plant native trees.

## When to go

The dry season is from December to April and while the temperature remains fairly constant throughout the year (think 20–25°C) the rest of the year sees increased rainfall.

## Contacts

**Lapa Rios** Puerto Jimenez, Osa Peninsula, Costa Rica
**Tel:** +11 506 2735 5130
**Web:** www.laparios.com
**Rates:** From US$245 per person per day for full board, non-alcoholic beverages, the round trip Puerto Jimenez/Lapa Rios and one guided tour into the Lapa Rios Nature Reserve per person per stay.

**Reef and Rainforest**
**Tel:** +44 (0) 1803 866965
**Email:** mail@reefandrainforest.co.uk
**Web:** www.reefandrainforest.co.uk, www.familytours.co.uk

Since 1989, Reef and Rainforest has pioneered the principle that the best way to help preserve endangered tropical forests is through sensitive, small-scale tourism, which provides a viable alternative to logging and agriculture – a premise that is now established thinking. They choose lodges, resorts and hotels that conserve wilderness and put funds back into local communities, and seek out the best locations to see wildlife truly in the wild. Reef and Rainforest supports a number of conservation charities, including the Belize Audubon Society, Durrell Wildlife Conservation Trust and the Shark Trust, and also offers a dedicated Family Wildlife Adventures programme.

# CYPRUS
## Rural Cyprus

Cyprus, the southernmost island in the Mediterranean, basks in year-round sunshine. Even in the winter months, the island enjoys mild temperatures (around 15°C) with an average of six hours sunshine a day.

What I love so much, though, is that a stone's throw from the bustling coastal resorts is a different world of mountain villages, cool, pine-scented forests, rural crafts and solid, stone-built houses, that have been there for centuries.

### Rural tourism
The landscape comprises a long spine of mountains, the Troodos, falling away into broad coastal plains to the north, south and east. The hilly interior is almost entirely rural, peppered with hundreds of tiny villages, with life centering around the Greek Orthodox church and the local *kafenion*, where old men pass the time of day, flick their worry beads, drink strong Cypriot coffee and play backgammon.

Orange, lemon and banana plantations line the less developed areas of coastline, and silvery olive groves grow inland, while vineyards cling to the southern flanks of the mountains. Farmers herd goats and sheep, bred for their meat and the exquisite halloumi cheese, while donkeys are still used to carry heavy loads, bearing the traditional wicker panniers that are made in some of the mountain villages.

It appears idyllic, although life is tough for these villagers, with young people migrating to the coast and traditional skills and crafts dying out. Rural tourism, though, has injected new life into some of the island's poorest areas as holidaymakers are discovering the joy of waking up to the sound of cockerels crowing and donkeys braying.

### Sustainable rural tourism
In 2006 the Cyprus Sustainable Tourism Initiative (CSTI) was formed by various members of the tourism industry in Cyprus who are taking an active part in promoting rural tourism. Their activities include the introduction of a series of six village routes (three have been completed to date) to encourage visitors to 'discover the real Cyprus' by exploring the less well known regions of the island.

The Cyprus Tourism Organisation has developed six wine routes where one can visit some of the smaller wineries and sample the wines. These are located in charming villages with traditional architecture and truly hospitable people.

The Akamas National Park, in the north-west of the island, is home to one of the last breeding sites in the Mediterranean for the green and loggerhead turtle. There are a number of interesting hiking trails to follow and jeep safaris that enable you to explore the rugged landscape and its fascinating gorges.

In villages scattered around the island, a number of beautiful renovated stone houses and studios with traditional interiors – high ceilings, galleried living areas, cool stone

above **Stavrovouni Monastery in the Larnaka District**     below **Seascape walking**

floors and wooden fittings – are available. Some have outdoor ovens, for preparing slow-baked *kleftiko*, and might even have a lemon tree in the garden for juice to squeeze over the *souvlakia*.

By staying in these villages, guests are encouraged to experience rural life at first hand, joining the locals picking fruit and olives, learning to cook traditional dishes, make halloumi and accompanying local fishermen out to sea.

## Special-interest activities

Cyprus has always been a superb walking destination and has several well-marked trails, but in 2005, a new challenge for serious hikers arrived in the form of the E4 European Long Distance Path, a network of footpaths extending all the way from Gibraltar across mainland Europe, supported by the CTO and the Forestry Department.

The marked trail covers hundreds of kilometres from south of Paphos to the western point of Akamas, the entire length of the Troodos mountains and out to Cape Greco, the beautiful, rugged south-eastern point of the island beyond Ayia Napa.

A number of expatriates who have fallen in love with the island are taking an active part in eco tourism, offering various activity holidays, including mountain-bike holidays in the north-west of the island, around the sleepy village of Polis and the Akamas Peninsula. Guests stay in a traditional stone house and take daily rides in groups of up to eight, over donkey trails, forest paths and unmade roads, visiting some of the island's most beautiful and remote spots and leaving no footprint whatsoever.

Other special-interest activities are horse-riding holidays in the Troodos mountains and foothills, particularly along

above **Vines around Lofou and Vasa**

the Kamilostrata, or Camel Road. This trail was created in medieval times to transport copper by camel from the Pera Pedi mines to the coast for export. Today, the path meanders through beautiful pine and deciduous forest and crosses several magnificent stone bridges, built by the Venetians who once occupied the island.

### Vakhis Project

The expats may be leading the way in activity holidays but nobody does Cypriot food like the Cypriots, and nowhere is there such an impressive revival of the 'slow food' movement. In 2006, the CTO launched the Vakhis Project, named after a famous chef who lived in Kition (now buried underneath modern-day Larnaca) in AD 300.

Restaurants with a Vakhis certificate meet certain criteria of using local ingredients – olives, almonds, figs, pulses, herbs, citrus fruits, lean meat and fresh seafood – and prepare their food according to traditional recipes. These can be found in villages such as Kakopetria, in the Troodos mountains and Lofou and Vasa, in the wine region. Cypriot cuisine is varied, satisfying every taste from meat-eaters to vegetarians. Local herbs and spices, such as oregano, basil and cinnamon, add both aroma and flavour. One of the best ways to sample Cypriot cuisine is to try meze, which can consist of 21 dishes, including dips, salads, local cheeses, seafood and the delicious barbecued meats – a popular export to leave you with fond memories of a beautiful island and its hospitable people.

# Green menu

**Go into the woods** Take a picnic to one of the CTO's forest picnic sites – my favourite is Smigies, near Akamas, with the wind whispering in the pines, barbecue pits and an all-wood children's playground.

**Take a bike or hike** Put on your boots or hire a bike to explore the Akamas peninsula (don't drive). Stop at Lara Bay to talk to the turtle conservationists who camp here all summer, guarding the turtle nests. (You can skinny dip (unofficially) at one end of the beach).

www.rural-cyprus.com

**Watch the birds** Take a birdwatching trip around the island's marshes, salt flats, reservoirs and forests with the local NGO Birdlife Cyprus.

www.birdlifecyprus.org

**Join a local festival** Enjoy Carnival in February, Orthodox Easter, the Flower Festival in May or the unique Kataklysmos (Flood Festival, at Pentecost) in June, with boat races, swimming competitions, folk dancing and food stalls.

**Support the Cyprus Handicraft Service** This helps to train traditional craftsmen and women and to preserve rural arts and crafts. It was set up in 1975 to provide work for refugees and those displaced by the 1974 Turkish invasion but has grown into a thriving cottage industry with showrooms in Nicosia, Larnaca, Limassol and Paphos.

**Discover Cyprus's culture** Follow the CTO's recommended sightseeing routes for archaeology, wine, mountain villages and monasteries.

www.specialcyprus.org

**Eat organic olives** Visit the award-winning olive park, which has the island's first truly ecological olive mill as well a museum, shop, artists' corner, organic restaurant, playground and pony rides.

## Contacts

**Cyprus Tourism Organisation**
Useful guides on cycling, riding, walking, food, festivals and archaeology
**Tel:** +44 (0) 207 569 8800
**Web:** www.visitcyprus.com

**Cyprus Agrotourism Company**
Umbrella organisation for marketing village houses
**Tel:** +357 22 34 00 71
**Web:** www.agrotourism.com.cy

## When to go

Cyprus is a year-round destination with more than 300 days of sunshine. January and February are mild and sometimes wet, with snow (and skiing) in the Troodos. Come in February for the almond blossom. From March to May, the countryside is soft, green and abundant with wildflowers and perfect for hiking and biking. July and August are hot and dry – for activities, spring and autumn are better. Visit in September for the grape harvest and Limassol Wine Festival. Even in November, you can still swim in the sea on sunny days.

# DENMARK
## Copenhagen

Copenhagen is a capital city with the charm and fresh food of the seaside, a history of 1,000 years ranging from the wild and woolly to the elegance of Renaissance and Baroque splendour and an enviable welfare system that carries you (at a price if you are earning) from the cradle to the grave. The fact that, at the World Summit in Copenhagen in 1995, Denmark was one of the only countries to forgive a sizeable amount of Third-World debt, is surely indicative of its responsible attitude to the world around it.

The ethos of healthy living strikes you from the first – bike-power rules, with a third of the population using pedal-power to travel around the city, saving 100,000 tonnes of $CO_2$ emissions every year. There are wide bike lanes everywhere and it's not just young men in cycle shorts and helmets filling them; you'll see plenty of people ferrying about their small children, animals or shopping in carts on the front of their bikes. Traffic is minimal – I walked from Vester Søgade to central station and beyond at 9.30 a.m. and barely had to look right or left to cross the roads, although obviously, it's busier at certain times than others. Rush hour generally means that you are more likely to be run over by a bike than a car.

Politically, economically, ecologically and health-consciously astute, the Danes do not close their eyes to the dangers that may lie ahead and have taken the threat of global warming and its sister issues of chemical toxicity and

environmental damage to heart. However, oddly enough, they find recycling a bit complicated – it is mandatory to sort glass, batteries and paper (and this is paid for through taxes) but the municipalities incinerate everything else so recycling other materials is still a problem.

## Guldsmeden hotels

The delightful boutique Guldsmeden hotels, of which there are three, all lie along, or just off, Vesterbrogade, the ancient road once lined with green fields that led to the western gate before the city walls came down in the 1850s, the pent-up poor moved out and the red-light district set in. Vesterbro (Westgate), is now an up-and-coming, slightly edgy area, where plenty of young creative businesses start their lives in design and craft studios and there is a vibrant nightlife in and around the old meatpacking district.

The brainchild of Sandra and Mark Weinert, the chain comprises three hotels in Copenhagen, another in Arhus. All offer a sophisticated, white-washed, ethnic charm coupled with a warm welcome, friendly staff, and the mod-cons (and flat-screen TVs) that you would find in a more urban-cool designer hotel. Walk through the doors and forget the city; the Guldsmeden oozes the relaxation and charm of a Mediterranean hideaway with crisp cotton Egyptian sheets, dark-wood or Balinese furniture, romantic four-poster beds decorated with cowrie shells, thoughtful feminine touches,

above and opposite **Spa and bedroom at the Guldsmeden Axel Hotel**    below **17th-century houses in the Old Town**

including a range of organic spa products developed in cooperation with local suppliers, and fresh and copious organic breakfasts, served up on lovely blue-and-yellow Mexican china. At the Axel flagship hotel (closest to Rådhuspladsen), you will also be able to enjoy the soft-towel charm and organic products of their new spa (including the restaurant's rescued free-trade coffee grounds in a body scrub prepared daily; and although the seal-skin throws gave me pause, on further investigation I learnt that they were bought from Royal Greenland, which trades directly with the remaining seal-hunting Inuit communities on Greenland, for whom this is a means of survival and who would have used every part of the animal and not just the skin).

Everything that is viable is being done or investigated: kitchen and cleaning products are fully eco-friendly (better for the staff as well as the environment); all suppliers are organic and all building material is long lasting and wood is sourced from plantations; it has just been confirmed that solar roof panels are suitable for the roof of the Axel Hotel

and after much research, a green energy supplier who fulfils all the Weinert's criteria for intelligent energy production has been found in Norway (green energy can often have a powerfully negative impact on the surrounding landscape if the company does not have a policy for regrowth). Recycling grey water is on the cards but still in the future, awaiting the technology that will filter out an adequate amount of harmful bacteria. In addition, the Weinerts take corporate social responsibility very seriously and ask their guests to donate €2 (15DKK) for every day of their stay to the Children's Heart Foundation, a sum that the hotel happily matches.

## Hotel Alexandra

Hotel Alexandra is another boutique hotel, quite unlike anything else you will have experienced. Two minutes' walk from Rådhuspladsen but away from the bustle of the square, this is not only an eco-friendly hotel that has been the proud holder of the Danish Green Key sustainability award for the last 11 years, it is also a living art experience, in which every piece of furniture has been bought at auction, with an emphasis on Danish art from the 1930s to the late 1950s. Nothing is bought new and nothing is thrown away – if it has served its purpose in the hotel, it is sold on again and the money reinvested in 'new' furniture. Each elegant room is decorated and named after a designer – it's not every day you can lounge in iconic Arne Jacobsen 'Swan' or 'Egg' chairs without fear of a museum curator leaping upon you spluttering with rage.

No eco detail is too small to implement, even to 'stopping the housekeeper from reflushing the loos, when checking after the rooms have been cleaned,' says Jeppe Mulhausen the hotel manager. 'In fact, the average hotel uses 250 litres of water per guest, we manage to average 140. And, of course, we are keen for the guests to be involved. They can choose how often we wash their linen and if they stay for more than one night and forgo having their room cleaned, we give them 100DKK of vouchers to spend in the (organic) restaurant.' On top of that, rubbish is separated into seven different types for recycling, there's no packaging at breakfast, all left-over food is recycled for animals and buying green energy is on the cards.

above right **Kongens Have with a view of the turrets of Rosenborg Slot**
right **The conservatory at Geranium Restaurant**
oppposite **The Winter Garden at the Ny Carlsberg Glyptotek art gallery**

# Green menu

Walk the city Copenhagen is very manageable on foot but if you get weary, jump onto a bike. If you can't quite summon the energy, let someone else do it for you and take a bicycle taxi.

Bike for free Every summer the city council provides 2,000 free bikes to ride around the central area. It's rather like finding a trolley at the supermarket – locate a rack, put in your 20DKK, and off you go.

Paddle the waves Take to the waterways under your own power and kayak your way past the ancient island of Slotsholmen and through the canals of colourful Christianshavn.
**www.kajakole.dk**

Snack organic Copenhagen is home to over 2,000 eateries, many of which are organic. For a snack, visit one of the Emmerys chain of bakeries for delicious pastries and bread or the new Organic supermarket Egefeld in Vesterbro.

Eat organic For a sit-down lunch or evening meal try out BioM near Nyboder for an all-out, delicious organic experience (even the paint on the walls is organic) and if you have several more krøner to spend, book ahead for Geranium, Copenhagen's new organic-biodynamic Michelin-starred restaurant in Kongens Have, the lovely palace grounds of the 16th-century, turreted and moated Rosenborg Slot. If you go for supper, you get the chance to wander the regal pathways after the gates close at dusk.
**www.biom.dk, www.restaurantgeranium.dk**

## When to go

With the exception of January to March, when it is cold, dark and windy, any time in Copenhagen has its plusses. Spring and summer have 16 to 18-hour-long days with average temperatures of 16°C and plenty of opportunity for being outside under high blue skies; winter averages just five hour's daylight and temperatures as low as 0°C but Copenhagen does 'cosy' extremely well and the run up to Christmas, with its lights, markets and Tivoli extravaganzas, has an atmosphere not to be missed.

## Contacts

**Hotel Guldsmeden Axel** Helgolandsgade 11
**Tel:** +45 3331 3266
**Web:** www.hotelguldsmeden.com
**Rates:** From £170 for a double room, including breakfast and taxes.

**Hotel Alexandra** HC Andersens Blvd 8
**Tel:** +45 3374 4444
**Web:** www.hotel-alexandra.dk
**Rates:** From £152 for a double room, including breakfast and taxes.

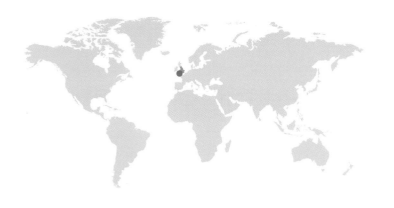

# ENGLAND
## Trevenna, Cornwall

The UK might be considered a late starter on the eco front when compared to the likes of Austria. However, owing to increased awareness and a tangible demand for guilt-free breaks, eco tourism offerings are steadily gaining momentum. One of the best is situated in one of England's most historic counties.

### Trevenna, Cornwall

In the heart of Cornwall's Bodmin Moor is an inspiring example of how green can also be hip. Thirty-something owner-manager Jonathan Rowe is a former city lawyer, who has rediscovered his rural roots (he's a fifth-generation farmer) and is now getting his hands dirty in the eco hotel business. Over the last two years, he has overseen the conversion of five barns at the centre of his family's 142-acre farm into luxury holiday homes, sleeping between two and eight people. All mod cons but it's all green too. WiFi, digital TV and efficient under-floor heating all come as standard as do power showers, the heated swimming pool and guilt-free outdoor Jacuzzi (all heated from waste from the local timber yard), not to mention panoramic views from most windows.

Yesterday's turnip tip is today's chrome-and-limestone bathroom and what was once the Shippon (the barn for rearing young calves) now comfortably accommodates a family of five. Then there are the farmhouse meals cooked by Karen Rowe full of local ingredients and delivered to your door on request.

Jonathan seems to enjoy everything from flower arranging, 'from years of duty at St Neot's church' (which is, incidentally, worth a visit for the stained-glass windows and intriguing graveyard) to understanding the ins and outs of 21st-century eco-friendly plumbing and electrics.

Trevenna is a working programme for sustainable tourism with a triple bottom line, from its support of local people (who can work where they love to live) to using the expertise of the emergent eco-economy business prototypes, which all aim to protect the environment.

'Local' definitely means 'best' here. Bathrooms are filled with products from the nearby lavender farm and a welcome pack choc-a-bloc with regional farm products, including delicious smoked bacon, Cornish cheese and apple juice from a local press. To top it all, the local winery at Camel Valley even produces award-winning bottles of fizz.

What makes Trevenna particularly special, however, are the hearts of the people who live and work there. The log-burner in each barn, lit to welcome guests, is a good indicator of the great attention to detail and special Cornish welcome.

The property is highly recommended by COAST and the GBTS (Green Business Tourist Scheme), which gives local guidance on everything from where to get stationery

above **The Eden Project**

to fixing leaky taps. If you think green has to be mud huts or jungle treehouses then check this place out.

The area's biggest pull, attracting over a million visitors a year, is undoubtedly the Eden Project. A wondrous 21st-century 'global garden' that explores humankind's dependence on natural resources.

Ten years ago the place was a barren, exhausted china clay pit. Today, the gigantic domes house crops, landscapes and wild plants reflecting the amazing diversity of our planet. There's also internationally acclaimed architecture and art, which draw inspiration from nature; and a stage on which people working to make our world a better place tell their stories.

Massive Biomes (one of which is the biggest greenhouse in the world) and millions of plants bear witness to what can be achieved by a can-do attitude and the tenacity of the human spirit. Eden is as potent a symbol of hope for the future as you could find anywhere on earth.

It's an organisation that believes in 'learning by doing' and tries to run its operations in ways that help address some big questions. Questions like: How do we ensure the economic benefits of our work go back into the local economy? How do we manage food supply and waste? Or how do we construct buildings in a way that reflect the needs of the 21st century? Inspirational indeed.

# Green menu

Step back in time Visit Lanhydrock house and gardens – it looks as though the Victorian Robartes family have just stepped out into the room next door. A perfectly preserved time capsule of 19th-century upstairs-downstairs living, with all the visual trappings of everyday life.

Go down under Walk through Carnglaze Caverns, underground caverns of cathedral proportions, including a subterranean lake, which have been hand-created by previous generations of local slate miners.

Bike or surf For a high-adrenalin rush learn to kite-surf across the sea or take a scenic guided bike trail along the cliff paths.
**www.mobiusonline.co.uk**

Go green The Lost Gardens of Helygon and the internationally acclaimed Eden Project are also nearby as are dozens of other amusements and National Trust attractions.

Watch the waves Climb Brown Willy (419 metres) from where you can watch the Atlantic to the north and the Channel to the south.

## When to go

Go at Easter and you'll miss the summer crowds and get all the colour of Cornwall's magnificent rhododendron, camellia and magnolia gardens.

## Contacts

**Trevenna** St Neot, Liskeard, Cornwall, PL14 6NR
**Tel:** +44 (0) 1579 320013
**Web:** www.trevenna.com
**Rates:** From £240 for two nights in the Wagon House barn, including a welcome hamper for two.

# ENGLAND
## Natural Retreats, North Yorkshire

Richmond in North Yorkshire, is one of 57 towns going by that name but alone, the one considered to be the mother of them all. It is also the historic gateway town to the Yorkshire Dales. A pretty community that grew up around an 11th-century stronghold built on the *riche-mont* or strong hill, it has a bustling cobbled market place leading to the two remaining medieval gateways to the Friary gardens and a fine selection of 18th-century, Georgian facades.

Its ruined citadel begun in 1071 by Alan Rufus – a kinsman of William the Conqueror – is the oldest stone-built Norman castle in England and the exhibition in the tower manages to re-create the town's history with some charm. Those climbing the 100-foot keep are rewarded with panoramic views. Down at ground level, there's a scenic riverside path to the tranquil ruins of Easby Abbey, only a mile away.

No surprise then that this spot was chosen as the first site for a new concept in eco tourism. Natural Retreats' intention is to create 'an awareness that sustainable holiday accommodation can be built and operated with a minimal effect on the natural landscape as well as providing valuable support to the local community'. Indeed, our welcome hamper was packed with local goodies from Richmond's top grocer and delicatessen-owner Ken Warne, who, a font of local knowledge, went on to recommend Yorkshire's best flavours during our stay.

The site's eco principles include sustainably sourced timber-framed residences with minimal foundations, living roofs of sedum, solar water heating and solar glazing. Rainwater collection is used in washing machines and toilets, enabling 50 per cent of the mains water supply to be substituted by stored rainwater. Guests can compost their organic vegetable waste in the on-site wormery and, last but not least, many indigenous trees are being re-introduced to the area, which has been approved as a Tree Appeal planting area.

There are 18 three-bedroom residences situated just below the brow of the hill, hidden from the road and sensitively spaced to give enough privacy, while retaining the sense of a community-if-you-want-it ambience. The site even has its own spring – used for drinking and showers – you can see the evidence of it as you walk around the hill, tiptoeing between ponds and marshland. Your bath will fill with water tinged with characteristic brown peat, which stains so many of the Dale's rivers belying its unpolluted state.

It's a special place. Mornings greet you with the sound of a trickling stream outside your patio door, greater spotted woodpeckers in the nearby woodland and a vista over Wainright's celebrated Coast-to-Coast footpath.

Children will adore spotting the shy Roe deer at breakfast, the teeming pond life, wandering resident moorhens and the freedom to roam. Adults will appreciate the guilt-free

designer space, no-worries pine floors, white-washed walls and requisite luxuries, including 21st-century wood burner, digital television, stereo and music system and a washroom to sluice all those muddy I've-had-fun-today clothes.

Tourism creates around 40 per cent of employment in this area, so your spending contribution goes a long way to support the local community. The path from your residence, lined with wild garlic and English sandwort, leads gently into town. A popular choice is to take a one-

hour, free, guided walk around Richmond, offered by local volunteers who'll provide the 'who's who' of the town as well as invaluable tips on current events and eateries. It's bookable at the tourist information centre each Sunday and Wednesday from June to September.

This eco tourism concept has proved so successful that over a dozen are now planned to open in national parks around the country, but like it's namesake, Richmond will always be remembered as the first.

# Green menu

**Visit local sights** Other than the castle and town walk, which are musts, visit Richmond's old railway terminus, which now boasts a craft bakery, artisan cheese-maker, micro-brewer, on-site ice-cream parlour, gallery restaurant and two cinemas.

**Be cheesy** Hunt out some locally made Wensleydale cheese – Wallace and Grommet's favourite.

**Trek the hills** There are walks galore, whatever your pace. Richmond is the gateway to Swaledale's hiking countryside – follow the footsteps of artist JMW Turner. The information centre gives great advice on all the local walks along with maps and tips.

**Discover the Forbidden Corner** Just north of 12th-century Middleham Castle (home of Richard III), the Forbidden Corner – originally built as a private folly in the Tupgill Park Estate – is a unique labyrinth of paths and passageways, chambers, tunnels, follies and surprises in a four-acre garden that feels more like 40 acres by the time you've found the exit. It delights children of all ages.
www.theforbiddencorner.co.uk

## When to go

Anytime is good given the unpredictability of our lovely English weather. That said, traditionally, August should be the best time to visit and it is also the month for the local music festival and country fairs.

## Contacts

**Natural Retreats** Aislabeck Plantation, Hurgill Road, Richmond North Yorkshire, DL10 4SG
**Tel:** +44 (0) 161 242 2970
**Web:** www.naturalretreats.com
**Rates:** From £325 for two nights for a three-bedroom residence sleeping up to six people.

# FRANCE
## Brittany

With 1,700 miles of windswept, rugged coastline, Brittany is one of France's most popular tourist regions – and it's not difficult to see why. Its small fishing villages, genteel spa resorts, acres of forests, two national parks, well-preserved medieval towns, Celtic culture and buzzing regional capital, Rennes, have long attracted holidaymakers. The excellent road, rail and ferry links make it quick and easy to get to. The Ille-et-Vilaine department, known as 'the gateway' to Brittany, is France's principal agricultural region and the country's second-largest vegetable-growing area. Add to this the influx of visitors in July and August, as well as its ancient fishing industry, and it comes as no surprise that durability and sustainability are high on the region's agenda – especially in the domain of tourism. What's more, eco accommodation comes in all shapes and sizes…

### Tree houses

You're wandering through the forest, navigating a path through the tall trees when you look upwards for a moment and something catches your eye. A wooden path links two trees, there's a wooden bridge and, hang on a minute, that looks like a thatched roof – why, it's a tree house. In a 200-hectare park near the coast, Le Domaine des Ormes has a range of accommodation, including several tree houses made from natural materials. No damage is done to the tree in attaching them either – so no screws or nails,

everything is achieved by using clamps and ropes and the trees are inspected every year to ensure their continuing health. The treehouses come at three different heights from the ground, have no electricity or water (there is, however, an eco toilet), which makes it an interesting place to get cosy with a partner and a fairytale-come-true for kids. Access is by ladder (if you are over the age of two) or by zip-line into the highest accommodation for the truly intrepid over the age of 12. Breakfast arrives in a basket and is hauled up, Swiss-family-Robinson-style, on an ingenious pulley – though they probably didn't get croissants and hot coffee on their menu. For those with no head for heights, there's also a charming, Hansel-and-Gretel land-based version called the Nature Lodge, which gets breakfast delivered on the doorstep.

### Yves Rocher

In stark contrast and hot off the press is the Yves Rocher, Brittany's first eco hotel, in the attractive village of La Gacilly – the skincare company's headquarters. Built from wood and thermal bricks, and conforming to the HQE (*Haute Qualité Environnementale*) standard, the 30-room hotel and organic restaurant is also a bird conservation area thanks to an agreement with France's Bird Protection League. The company, which provides most of the surrounding area's employment, has just launched its first organic range of

above and opposite **Treehouses at Le Domaine des Ormes**

products, which will, no doubt, be used in the spa. So as not to be a blot on the landscape, the lower buildings will be covered in grass – Teletubby fans will need to get their bookings in early.

### Hotel Lecoq-Gadby

For good food and pampering, the Hotel Lecoq-Gadby, a new four-star spa hotel in Rennes is the perfect place to go. The luxury spa uses organic, apple-based beauty products from the IsB range and its gourmet restaurant, La Coquerie, features dishes made from organic and regional seasonal produce. As well as 11 stylish rooms in the main house, there are 14 suites in the renovated outer buildings – beams, stone walls and antique furniture enhance the 'urban retreat' concept. The building work carried out conforms to France's HQE standard and solar panels provide 60 per cent of the hotel's energy needs, including heating the swimming pool. They even offer 'green' weddings.

### La Maison Neuve

Deep in the Breton countryside, La Maison Neuve is a working farm offering rustic bed and breakfast, as well

as a campsite, for individuals and groups. A herd of deer and some cattle graze in the fields as you drive into the yard, where you're greeted by the oinking of a pot-bellied pig, the clucking of hens and pet rabbits twitching their noses – kids will be enthralled. A renovated stable block houses six basic-but-comfortable rooms sleeping two to five people – just remember to bring your own toiletries. If you don't want to cook for yourself, the stone dining room is the place to go for home-made, straight-from-the-field produce – nettle soup, chicken in cider, pork with apple sauce, venison paté…. Don't forget to buy

above **One of Brittany's famous picturesque bays and villages**     below **Medieval half-timbered houses in the Breton capital of Rennes**

some to take home from the on-site shop along with some goats' cheese or local honey. This is a good place to stay for mountain biking, hiking and visiting the Bay of Mont St Michel or the Couesnon activity centre. But, above all, it is ideal for enjoying a little peace and quiet – there are no TVs.

# Green menu

**Join the voies vertes** These 'green routes' are purpose-built paths for walkers, cyclists and horse-riders, following old railway lines, tow paths and farm tracks. Route 2 follows the Ille-et-Rance canal from Rennes to St Malo.
www.voiesvertes.com

**Get active** The Couesnon Activity Centre offers outdoor pursuits for all ages and has won awards for its environmental awareness programmes and management.
www.basecouesnon.com

**Explore the Bay of St Michel** Laying claim to the highest tides in Europe, this UNESCO World Heritage Site is best explored on foot with a guide from the Maison de la Baie. Alternatively, walk the GR34 along the edge of the bay from Vivier-sur-Mer to the iconic Mont St Michel. Make sure you eat some mussels – they are the only seafood in France to have the AOC seal of approval.
www.maison-baie.com

**Visit Rennes** As well as admiring the medieval half-timbered houses in the Breton capital's old town, its Saturday-morning market is one of the largest in France and well worth a visit. While the city is easy to navigate on foot, many of the local Illenoo buses run on eco-friendly fuel derived from vegetable oil.
www.tourisme-rennes.com

## Contacts

**Le Domaine des Ormes** Epiniac, 35120 Dol-de-Bretagne
**Tel:** +33 2 9973 5357
**Web:** www.lesormes.com
**Rates:** From €104 per night for a tree house, including breakfast.

**Yves Rocher** La Grée des Landes, Rue de la Grée St Jean, 56200 La Gacilly/Cournon
**Tel:** +33 299 085 050
**Web:** www.yves-rocher.com, www.paysdelagacilly.com
**Rates:** Rates from €85.

**The Hotel Lecoq-Gadby** 156 rue d'Antrain, 35700 Rennes
**Tel:** +33 2 9938 0555
**Web:** www.lecoq-gadby.com
**Rates:** From €150 per double room per night, two sharing; from €130 for single occupancy.

**La Maison Neuve Rte de Rennes** Mont St Michel, 35490 Chauvigné
**Tel:** +33 2 9995 0564
**Web:** www.ferme-auberge-35.fr
**Rates:** From €40 per night for bed and breakfast. Half board €49 (1 person) to €120 (4 people).

**Brittany Tourist Board**
**Web:** www.brittanytourism.com (information), www.brittany-best-breaks.com (booking)

## When to go

Brittany has slightly better summers than Britain but if you want to avoid the crowds, May, June and September are probably the best time to visit.

# GREECE
## Grecotel

Grecotel is living proof that big doesn't have to mean eco-unaware. To the contrary, this luxury hotel group – the largest one in Greece, owning 34 properties around the country – has been repeatedly hailed for its environmental efforts since its inauguration in 1981. In the early 1990s, it was the first hotel company in the world to undertake eco-audits in its hotels according to EU standards and to install a dedicated environmental and cultural department, working continuously to preserve the Greek idyll.

Grecotel is very much a family affair – the brainchild of Nikos Daskalantonakis. His daughter Mari is responsible for Grecotel Hotels and Resorts, while her sister Tina and brother Yannis head up the city division, Classical Hotels. The commitment and passion of each family member is evident on the first encounter, spearheaded by Mari's fervently pro-active approach, which made her instrumental in re-introducing glass Coca Cola bottles instead of plastic and aluminium containers in the early 1990s. The family are particularly proud of their organic farms, which supply the restaurants across their resorts with ingredients produced using traditional farming techniques that date back hundreds of years. The group also assists in turtle protection, sand dune maintenance, the implementation of mass recycling, waste management, energy-saving techniques and pollution control, working hard to ensure that the impact of all its hotels is kept to a minimum.

### Cape Sounio

Leaving Athens with the imposing print of the Parthenon on my mind, we travelled for an hour along the coast to Sounion and another of the world's greatest monuments, The Temple of Poseidon. Marking the start of the Aegean Sea, where Aegeus plummeted dramatically into the water aeons ago, I can't help but feel that an air of godly power still exists as I stand on my balcony, overlooking the site. When Grecotel took over Cape Sounio to open in time for the 2004 Olympics, they underwent the arduous task of transforming it into a heavenly beachside retreat, working around the tight restrictions imposed by its position on a World Heritage Site. They succeeded. The neutral and understated bungalows dotted around this natural amphitheatre are interspersed with lush vegetation, and a small-scale organic farm garden provides produce for one of the restaurants, Cavo Calones.

But there's another reason why Cape Sounio is a flagship property in Grecotel's eco quest. Last year, the Ambassadors of the Environment programme was launched in association with marine biologist Jean Michel Cousteau, son of *the* diving aficionado, Jacques. In a bid to teach youngsters various ways to preserve all things 'green', the programme's enthusiastic team lead children from 4 to 12 years old on a host of eco-jaunts throughout the summer season. We watched little ones eagerly turning rubbish into art, baking cookies in solar-

previous page (main) **The main lagoon at Amirandes**    previous page (thumbnail) **Cape Sounio**    above **The main pool at Cape Sounio**

powered ovens then disappearing, snorkels and masks in hand, to photograph life under the sea. As they hike through the hills of Attica, along olive groves and the organic gardens at Cape Sounio, the children also take many steps towards learning to live in a more sustainable manner.

### Amirandes and Agreco

Heading south to Crete, we experienced another of Grecotel's gems. On the northern coast of Crete, east of Heraklion, lies Amirandes, the latest addition to the group. The resort takes on a special meaning for the Daskalantonakis family, who originate from this southern Mediterranean island, famed for having one of the healthiest diets in the world.

Amirandes sources much of its produce from the family's main farm, Agreco, which is located in Rethymnon – a one-hour drive away from the resort, allowing diners to indulge in a wide range of specialities without racking up a large carbon footprint.

On the farm, time appears to have stood still. Methods adopted here are entirely traditional, from the donkey-driven olive press to the water-powered flour mill. On entering the four-hectare estate, guests are greeted by a picture-postcard scene – a vine-covered taverna in a courtyard fringed by olive trees, Cretan farm buildings and an idyllic chapel where small weddings still take place. The views stretch out across the vineyards to the sea beyond and, as the sun beats down, it is hard to imagine a more scenic spot. Forget processed food, there is no middleman here. We milked goats (which is a lot trickier than you might think), then watched it be turned into delicious cheese before our very eyes. Raki-making, grape- and olive-pressing and wheat-grinding using methods dating back hundreds of years are also a great education in plant-to-plate processes and a far cry from the polythene-packed aisles of UK supermarkets. Sitting down for dinner, we were presented with course after course of freshly prepared farm-produce-inspired delicious dishes. I lost count

after 13… Cretan *paximadia* (biscotti), roasted quail, stuffed fresh vegetables with golden olive oil and Feta cheese, Sfakian pancakes filled with mouth-melting cheese and pine kernels, and wild artichokes, all washed down with Agreco wines, produced, of course, on site.

With bellies full and heads a little hazy, it was time for a siesta and so we headed back to Amirandes. Here, the design is a modern take on the palaces of Minoan times – oversized urns and torch-lit pathways surrounding a large lagoon give the feel of erstwhile grandeur, while the use of fibre-optics and clean lines bring the resort very much into the 21st century. After a healthy dose of sun, sea, sand and luxury, I returned home, happy in the knowledge that I hadn't been an entirely irresponsible traveller.

above **The beach at Cape Sounio**    below **Cape Sounio pool**

# Green menu

**Help out on the farm** Guests can experience traditional Cretan life by participating in farm activities, from baking bread and making cheese to pressing grapes or olives and crushing wheat at the antique, stone flour mill. Farm tours on weekday evenings guide guests around the estate followed by dinner.

**Watch the sun set like the ancients** Opposite Cape Sounio, just three kilometres across the bay, stands the ancient Temple of Poseidon, one of the most celebrated archeological sites in Europe. A visit at sunset is an especially memorable experience.

**Visit Athens** An hour away, Athens is a bustling modern city that owes much of its appeal to its heavy historical heritage dating back 3,000 years. It is not to be missed. Highlights include the Acropolis, theatre of Dionysos and Odeon of Herod Atticus and the ancient Agora. To relax and enjoy some greenery, head to the National Gardens, the city's 'green lung' located behind the Parliament building, where you will find Athenians escaping the heat of the summer. The park has dozens of walkways through all kinds of trees.

**Climb Lycabettus Hill** The highest hill inside Athens, Lycabettus, offers a panoramic view of the city from all sides. At the summit is a tiny 19th-century chapel of St. George. Not far is a restaurant and coffee shop. The most pleasurable ways to reach the summit are on foot or by funicular, although you can also drive up.

## When to go

The Grecotels are open from April to November. If you want to avoid the summer heat, May, June, September and October are the ideal times to visit.

## Contacts

**Grecotel**
**Web:** www.grecotel.com

**Cape Sounio**
**Tel:** +30 21 0728 0417
**Rates:** From €170 per double room, per night on a bed-and-breakfast basis, including taxes and services.

**Amirandes**
**Tel:** +30 21 0728 0417
**Rates:** From €450 for a Mountain View Bungalow per night on a bed-and-breakfast basis, including taxes and services.

# GRENADA
Spice Island eco

If Christopher Columbus had actually decided to come ashore when he passed the island he named Concepcion in 1498, he would probably have never left. Grenada, as it is called today, certainly seems to have been blessed with more than its fair share of beautiful beaches, fragrant fruits and an abundance of spices that have monikered it the Spice Isle with a people so happy and friendly that you're left in no doubt – life is good here.

Just north of South America and only 21 miles long and 12 miles wide, this speck of an island has had more influence on the world's olfactics than its size would suggest.

Plants thrive in its mountainous tropical rainforests, covered in more spices than your local deli, most notably nutmeg, Grenada's culinary superstar – none of which is left to waste. Every single part finds a use in jams and syrups, flavouring for everything from punch to eggy bread, scent and oil in soaps, perfumes and the local cure-for-all, Nut-Med.

Since 2004, a flock of experienced entrepreneurs have flown into Grenada, Four Seasons among them. Serial hotelier Peter de Savary has invested big time, with an ongoing programme to regenerate the tired harbour at Port Louis and is also building the Caribbean's first eco spa at Tufton Hall. It all looks like good news for locals who are experiencing a burst of life in their tourism industry. With only 1,500 visitor beds in Grenada, the impact should certainly be manageable; going for quality over quantity.

The capital of St George is one of the prettiest towns in the Caribbean, arranged around a horseshoe-shaped harbour dotted with outdoor restaurants, which is still used to dispatch precious spices and to land the daily catch.

To the north east of Grenada, the islands of Carriacou and Petite Martinique offer visitors a glimpse of a quieter, more leisurely pace of life. With a mix of Scottish and African ancestry, local traditions reflect the mixed ancestry of the peoples.

The largest of Grenada's sister islands, Carriacou covers 13 square miles and offers world-class snorkelling and diving on some of the Caribbean's most pristine reefs. Rich in tradition, it has many unique customs. In the village of Windward, sailing boats are still built using the traditional methods passed down by the Scottish settlers. Recent initiatives are encouraging younger people to learn the art of boat building and to produce model boats. The annual Carriacou Regatta held in July and August seeks to rekindle this art.

Petite Martinique, which is even more peaceful, is another small offshore island with a very strong culture. It is really one large hill with fine beaches on the calmer, western leeward side. About 900 people live there, enjoying one of the highest per capita incomes in the eastern Caribbean. Like Carriacou, Petite Martinique was first settled by the French and many islanders have names of French origin. Fishing and boat building are still the main occupations.

Solar rooftop heaters meet all hot water needs and pools use salt as opposed to chlorine, which actually holds positive health effects such as eliminating problems with dry skin, damaged hair and red eyes. Gas-guzzling rotary lawnmowers have been replaced with push-reel, both better for the grass and quieter for guests. Employees are encouraged to think as 'environmental agents', trained to put the resort's eco policies into practice with a 'green team' of supervisors overseeing the environmental programme. 'We are proud of our environmental efforts and how they make a difference in our operation without sacrificing the resort's luxury experience,' noted Sir Royston, adding, 'I consider our resort a true trendsetter in the growing green marketplace.'

Elsewhere, the green theme generally takes the form of villa hotels. Small clusters of privately owned residences attached to swanky hotels or restaurants like the Hummingbird villa at the pretty Calabash resort or Pineapple villa at Maca Bana where you can be as independent or pampered as you like. Maca Bana owners Rebecca and Uli Thompson have gone to great ends to 'ecotise' their little corner of the island using solar power, recycling all waste and sticking to a discreet residence of just seven villas. Either way you're looked after by locals who are passionate about their offerings, can eat a mouth-watering selection of island

Both islands can be visited in a day by ferry from Grenada, or you can spend a few nights on Carriacou in one of the small local hotels and really discover what getting away from it is all about.

### Eco accommodation

On the eco front there are big movements going on under the surface in Grenada. The swanky Spice Island Beach Resort has installed a desalinization plant, energy-efficient products and a strong 'reduce, reuse, renew' mindset. Although one of the most luxurious hotels in Grenada, it is also one of the most environmentally conscious. 'Conservation and preserving the environment are key factors in how we manage our entire hotel operation,' says owner Sir Royston Hopkin, acting chairman of the Caribbean Alliance for Sustainable Tourism (CAST).

previous page **Mount Hartman Bay Estate**
above **Maca Bana Villa**    right **Treading cocoa beans**

above **Maca Bana beach**

food – you won't be forced to try *Lambee* (conch) – and can't fail to be captured by the rhythm of Caribbean life. Grenadian hospitality is to the Caribbean what Ireland is to Europe; while you're on their turf you're considered personal guests and the friendlinessof the locals seems to know no bounds.

The local architect who designed the cave house at Maca Bana also designed the property at Mount Hartman Bay and if total peace and seclusion is what you require then there's nowhere else on the island or, indeed, the planet, quite like it. With 180-degree views overlooking tranquil Secret Harbour (on a plot once owned by the governor general), the marbled sea lulls you in a state of involuntary meditation. Its Hobbit-like architecture feels like a contradictory fusion of Teletubbies meets Bond with a dollop of Gaudi. From the drawing room, which is half-terrace, half-cave, a central stairway bordered by a trickling indoor stream (very Feng Shui) leads down to 12 comfortable suites spread between the main house, tower room and beach house.

Property manager Peter Robinson has overseen the evolution of Mount Hartman since its concept in 1994. Eco initiatives have been second nature, including solar power, reuse of grey water for the gardens (which grow plentiful amounts of cantaloupe, tomatoes, indigenous rock fig bananas, herbs, salads and pawpaw) and the use of local building materials and labour throughout. Native plants are incorporated into the landscaping, replanting endangered tree species and all kitchen waste is composted.

## Island exploration

For island exploration, you couldn't do better than the award-winning local Mandoo Seales (or his guide Alistair), widely recognised for his dedication to environmental-protection issues. His photographic memory and encyclopedic knowledge encompass everything from local and natural history to entertaining gossip and ghost stories.

He'll escort you from Grand Etang, a freshwater lake hidden in the crater of an extinct volcano, to refreshing waterfalls, aromatic nutmeg and cocoa plantations, historic rum distilleries and picturesque fishing villages, ending with a tropical cocktail as colourful as the island itself.

If I had to be stranded on a desert island I'd have but one request – please let it be Grenada.

below **St George**

# Green menu

While most will be visiting Grenada for the sun, sea and sand, not to budge from your lounger would be sinful. Tread organic cocoa beans Visit the organic cocoa production at the Belmont Estate farm, nestled in the heart of lush rainforest where you can 'tread' organic cocoa beans and learn about the process from tree to bar. Carefully selected beans are picked, fermented, dried and roasted, resulting in velvety, textured chocolate with which you'll want to fill your suitcase. Learn new skills Discover local tricks during a cookery lesson with chef Randy or Lorry in your own kitchen at Maca Bana or spend a day learning to paint with the owner Rebecca Thompson, one of the island's most renowned artists.

Sail the Caribbean Charter a yacht and sail to Grenada's northern outpost, Carriacou and up to the Grenadines, said by many to be the best sailing in the Caribbean. Follow a spice route Hike up to Concord waterfalls along pathways awaft with spices, including nutmeg, cinnamon, cocoa, mangos, avocados and pineapples. Then visit the Dougaldston Estate showcasing a yesteryear nutmeg plantation. www.mandoo@grenadatours.com

Join the local street party Support local fisherman during Fish Friday – a cacophony of colour and delicious smells that solicit the senses every week in the seaside town of Gouyave, where locals come to buy, eat and dance to the steel band in one giant street party. Explore underwater Snorkel or dive with the Scubatech team at Calabash. Owner Carsten Andres will take you to all the best sites, including the underwater sculptures at the marine park, wrecks and some of the most colourful corals in the world. www.scubatech-grenada.com

Support endangered turtles Measuring up to nine feet in length and a ton in weight the endangered leatherback turtle, born in Grenada's Levera National Park, travels the world 10 times over the course of 25 years, returning to the same beach to lay her own eggs. Nightly tours from April to August donate 100 per cent of your fee to Ocean Spirits environmental projects in Grenada.

## When to go

The north-east trade winds keep the island refreshingly cool most of the year with an average annual shade temperature of 30°C, rising as high as 35°C during the day from August to November. There are two seasons: the dry season from January to May sees the hills singed brown and rivers reduced to a mere trickle; and the wet (and green) season from June to December with heavier showers that seldom last more than an hour or two and leave the land refreshed and smelling of green.

## Contacts

**Grenada Board of Tourism**
Web: www.grenadagrenadines.com

**Spice Island Beach Resort** Grand Anse Beach, P.O. Box 6, St. George's, Grenada, West Indies
Tel: +1 473 444 4258
Web: www.spiceislandbeachresort.com
Rates: From US$700 per room per night plus taxes and service.

**Maca Bana** P.O. Box 496, St. George's, Grenada, West Indies
Tel: +1 473 444 4504
Web: www.macabana.com
Rates: From US$373 per night in a deluxe villa, sharing, plus taxes and service.

**Mount Hartman Bay Estate** Reef View Drive, Lance-aux-Epines, St. George's, Grenada, West Indies
Tel: +44 1628 829222 (bookings)
Web: www.mounthartmanbay.com
Rates: The Beach House from US$2,200 plus taxes and service per person per week.

**Hummingbird Villa at Calabash** P.O. Box 382, St. George's, Grenada, West Indies
Tel: +1 473 444 4334
Web: www.calabashotel.com
Rates: From US$295 per person per night, plus taxes and service. Children aged 12–16 sharing with their parents are free.

# GUATEMALA
## La Lancha and Chiminos Island Lodge

There is a sense of hope pervading richly verdant Guatemala that belies the destructive aftermath of its coups and decades-long civil war. And travellers here will find the somewhat formal Guatemalans to be extremely courteous, willing to help out with directions, and generally welcoming.

Sandwiched between Mexico and Belize in the north, and Honduras and El Salvador to the south, Guatemala is a stunningly wild and mountainous chunk of Central America, comprising fertile highlands, jungle-thick lowlands, dazzling green lakes, ancient Mayan cities veiled in forest overgrowth, and active volcanoes.

Ecologically speaking, the country has a fair way to go. Waves of settlers, originally lured by promises of free land, cleared enormous tracts of jungle in the north – World Wildlife Fund figures reveal that a large sector of the Maya Biosphere Reserve, which incorporates the ancient city of El Mirador, has lost 70 per cent of its forests over the last 10 years – though there are local government and US-funded conservation initiatives currently at work to stave off further destruction.

Hopefully, the growing trend for grass-roots eco tourism will go some way to undoing the ancient Mayans' prediction of global elimination for 2012. What an eco-minded lot they were, with their soothsaying: 'if humanity wishes to save itself from biospheric destruction', they warned, 'it must return to living in natural time'…

However touristy the small town of Antigua may seem, it makes a pleasant alternative to a night in Guatemala City. Just 45 minutes from the airport, Antigua was the old capital and has now been painstakingly restored as a UNESCO World Heritage site. It lies beneath three volcanoes and comprises a chequer-board of straight, narrow cobbled streets, flanked by colourful Spanish colonial houses.

Antigua is a delightful muddle of sensory assaults: students piling out of language schools for their coffee break, old men snoozing under the trees of graceful plazas and the lively chatter and pungent smells of its unmissable market. Here, silk- and jade-sellers work alongside stalls piled high with pyramids of brilliant chillies, fragrant tortillas and toppling towers of pineapples. Outside, snout-nosed, canary-yellow buses belch black fumes into the humid air and locals take to the shade for a snack café lunch. Antigua is also a great prelude to the country's wilder aspect. Head north for Flores, the capital of Guatemala's jungle-rich Peten district – famous for its gloriously overgrown Mayan ruins – and you can base yourself at a couple of charming eco resorts.

### La Lancha
First off, is Francis Ford Coppola's luxury jungle retreat, La Lancha. This eco lodge overlooks serene and vast Lake Peten-Itza, and is conveniently close to the jewel in Guatemala's Mayan crown – Tikal.

The road to La Lancha gives wonderful glimpses of rural Guatemala: pigs and horses share road space with cars, a hen pecks around an outdoor kitchen table in front of a simple one-storey, tin-roofed house – bougainvillea and banana palms provide shade for a group of women walking back from the mill, where they have ground their daily portion of corn for the evening meal. And cutting through this, are lovely glimpses of Lake Peten-Itza, where fishermen sit on small wooden pontoons ever-hopeful for a catch, and hammocks slung between trees provide sleepy comfort for others.

Eventually you take the turning for La Lancha, its steep grounds cut by narrow, gravelled walkways along which are 10 simply furnished, thatched casitas. You quickly get the impression that this lodge is truly hidden within a pristine rainforest setting.

Splash out on a Lakeview casita, since these have the advantage of big decks, great views onto Peten-Itza and, at night, you're less likely to be disturbed by the heart-thumpingly scary whoops of the howler monkeys. When you see these tiny creatures, it is hard to believe they are capable of such a peace-shattering racket.

La Lancha has some impressive eco credentials. Hand-made organic toiletries, locally sourced food and building materials, waste recycling and, despite the mini-bars, a low carbon footprint, thanks to no air con or TVs. The lodge's Guatemalteca restaurant and bar, a palm-fronded palapa, overlooks the lake and is where guests gather to enjoy

previous page **Chiminos Island Lodge**
above and right **La Lancha pool villa**

candle-lit, open-air dinners of fresh local fish, parilla-grilled meat and tortillas.

## Chiminos Island Lodge

Southeast of Lake Peten-Itza, is an another impressive eco-friendly retreat, Chiminos Island Lodge – situated on a Mayan-built 'island' erected during the last phase of their civilisation as a fortification and located in Punta de Chimino, on beautiful Lake Petexbatun.

There are just five reclaimed-mahogany, thatched bungalows-on-stilts here, all several hundred feet from each other so that you can enjoy the serenity of your own patch of jungle. Only naturally fallen logs were used to build them so the sense that you belong in your jungle setting is vivid and unforgettable. Each bungalow is decorated in a simple, warmly rustic way, with colourful, Guatemalan, woven wall hangings and tree stumps as tables. Each one also has its own water treatment plant.

Open-sided (though mozzie-protected), you will be constantly aware of the jungle sounds around you, the rich cacophony of toucan and parrot song and, of course, those howler monkeys.

Solar-lit pathways criss-cross the property, weaving a route across the jungle floor, leading you to the lobby and lodge, where drinks, dinner, hammocks and a new floating dock, just perfect for sun-bathing and fishing await you.

The cuisine at Chiminos Island Lodge relies on local traditional recipes, cooked by charming locals: cucumber soup, 'blanco' lake fish baked with herbs, local fruits, vegetables and tortillas.

above **Thatched accommodation at La Lancha**    opposite **Bedroom at La Lancha**

# Green menu

### LA LANCHA

Enjoy a lakeside picnic Take a picnic down to the edge of Lake Peten-Itza and enjoy an afternoon paddling in the cooling waters and the calming close-to-nature jungle surroundings.

Go birdwatching La Lancha is prime twitching territory. Borrow some binoculars and a mountain bike and trail one of the resort's jungle paths to catch sight of toucans, falcons and parrots.

Visit Tikal A short drive away, Tikal's enormous 2,500-year-old stony ruins rise from a rainforest that covers what was once the base for Mayan civilisation. There are thousands of structures, many of which have not yet been excavated. You can seek out root-strangled ruins and climb the six vast, steep-sided pyramids with guano-clad temples at their summits – a vertigo-inducing ascent of up to 70 metres that leaves your heart thumping and your body sweating. But what a reward you get at the top – miles of thick green forest, occasionally punctured by the peak of a nearby pyramid, and the air rich with the sound of jungle wildlife. Local guides often provide you with information that your guidebook probably will not even begin to cover.

### CHIMINOS ISLAND LODGE

Go fishing and canoeing Fish from the floating dock for robalo and blanco, the delicious white fish indigenous to the region or paddle a canoe through all the creeks and crevices of this magical lagoon – it is not unusual to spot Moreletti crocs sunbathing on the banks.

Birdwatch and hike The lodge's beautifully maintained trails lead you to the Mayan citadel – the remnants of the fortification built by the Mayans during their time here. Its jungle setting ensures plenty of opportunities to observe the rich birdlife. Lake Petexbatun is a winter stop-off for some rare North American species.

Visit nearby Mayan sites The fortified city of Aguateca is near-at-hand and it is just minutes away by boat to Dos Pilas and Ceibal.

## When to go

Guatemala has a year-round hot and humid climate, though it can get cold in the highlands at night. The dry season runs from December to April.

## Contacts

**La Lancha** Lake Peten Itza, Tikal, Guatemala
**Tel:** +502 7928 8331
**Web:** www.lalancha.com
**Rates:** From US$175 double, per night in a lakeview casita, including breakfast.

**Chiminos Island Lodge** Punta de Chimino, Laguna Petexbatún, Sayaxché, Petén, Guatemala
**Web:** www.chiminosisland.com
**Rates:** From US$95 per person, per day full board, and to include visit to the Punta de Chiminos site, use of canoes and fishing rods.

# INDIA
Mahindra Homestays

In most cases, India conforms to its cliché of being a country of incredible extremes. The last decade has witnessed rapid economic growth but her great wealth continues to mix with poverty. Due to increasing demand, the fabulous luxuries of the maharajas are recreated in some of the world's most spectacular hotels and resorts, providing a bubble for tourists to get a taster of 'Incredible India'.

It's all very well to spurn the deluxe hotels in favour of 'the real India' and sanctimoniously decrease your carbon footprint, but what's the other option? Backpacker hostels or Ashrams? Again, the problem of extremes.

But what about staying in an Indian home? This was the idea of Mahindra Homestays, a new creation by one of India's biggest and most reputable companies, which strives to minimise its environmental impact and promote sustainable tourism. For some, the idea might sound daunting; it certainly was to me as I set off to travel around the country to meet the hosts.

Staying in one of Mahindra's homestays is a surprisingly 'normal' experience. As normal as an experience can be, while staying in a home perched on the banks of the holy Pampa river in Kerala or in the midst of the dramatic high range landscape of Wayanad. The homestays might not have infinity pools and private gyms, but they are all extremely comfortable, immaculately clean and all chosen for their originality. Whether you stay in a heritage home, a modern

city apartment or a house in the middle of plantation country or rural farmland, it is the best way to get an insight into the intricacies and contradictions of India's culture without sacrificing the comforts necessary for a good holiday. What's more, the homestays programme is very much based on 'responsible tourism' – solar and other renewable energy sources are used whenever feasible, while many of the homestays grow vegetables and fruits in their own gardens and plantations. With none of the aloof detachment of big hotels, homestay tourism is particularly beneficial to the local community.

One of Mahindra's homestays, Devra (meaning 'tribal temple'), is found a few miles away from the lake city of Udaipur in Rajasthan, one of the most magical cities in the world: white palaces, including the Lake Palace Hotel, seem to float in the centre of the lake and the network of narrow streets in the old town is riddled with colourful bazaars. So near and yet so far – Devra seems wonderfully detached from all this. Looking down towards the city from the Aravalli Hills, it lies peacefully in the midst of farmland. The hosts, Major Durga Das and his wife Jyoti, designed the house to a traditional 'vaastu' style, which includes a temple where the local villagers come to worship. Meals at Devra have large amounts of home-grown organic food – milk, wheat and vegetables all come from the family's farm. Guests also enjoy going on local village walks and there could be no

better guides than the family, who speak the local language and attend the weddings and festivals of the villagers.

Over 1,000 kilometres south from Devra, in the Wayanad hilltop region of Kerala, you couldn't be further away from the bustle and grime typically attributed to India. Wayanad's high-range landscape of the Western Ghats is mostly covered by wild forest and jungle, while some of it has been tamed into plantation land producing coffee, pepper, vanilla and all sorts of spices. Hillview Homestay is a plantation home that looks onto acres of cultivated land and forest all the way to the distant mountains, a particularly beautiful sight if you wake up early in the morning to see it covered in a low mist. The Chandran family offer their guests feasts largely made up of produce from the plantation – rice, vegetables and exotic curries served on freshly cut banana leaves, followed by delicious home-grown coffee. The house, situated in a conservation area near to the Wayanad Wildlife Sanctuary, is walking distance from the Meenmuthy waterfall and the breathtaking views of Sunrise Valley.

this page and opposite **Vismayagiri Homestay and the owners Mr and Mrs Gigi**

Interlocking rivers and canals surrounded by paddy fields and lush greenery make up the Keralan Kuttanad backwaters. This is where Kaits Home is found, a short walk from the sleepy riverside village of Champakulam and 14 kilometres from the old trading town of Alleppey, or 'the Venice of the East'. The main house of Mr Jossey Thomas and his family is a farmhouse of typically Keralan architecture and guests stay in cottages on the banks of the river. The house is central to local village life: Mr Jossey employs local

farmhands and all fish is bought from the village fisherman.
There is a bird sanctuary nearby and staying at Kaits Home
gives one of the best opportunities for an eco-friendly
backwater tour – not ploughing through the river on a
houseboat, but exploring the narrow canals and ancient
villages by canoe.

It's not just that Mahindra Homestays is a method of
sustainable tourism. In a country like India, it's easy for
foreigners just to scratch the surface, to dabble in the culture
a bit without getting further than the glossy tourist brochure.
Staying in an Indian home gives you a real insight; I ended
up having some amazing conversations with my hosts and
visiting places totally off the tourist track, from ancient
village temples to hidden landscape viewpoints. Then again,
though staying in someone else's home, you're not stepping
on each other's toes. There's a perfect medium of familiarity,
independence, activity and relaxation.

this page and opposite **Bhainsrogarh Fort owned by Mr and Mrs Singh**

# Green menu

Take a backwater tour Punting in a rice-barge or canoe is the most eco-friendly way to explore the beautiful region of paddy fields and palm trees.

Visit palaces and temples Hindu palaces and temples are found throughout India and show Indian culture at its most magnificent. Many homestay hosts are Hindus and are happy to guide and give their guests a better understanding of their culture and religion. Some of the best palaces are in Rajasthan – highlights include Jodhpur's Meherangargh fort and Udaipur's City Palace.

Enjoy wildlife safaris and birdwatching In the high-range plantation areas of Kerala there are some excellent wildlife parks, including the Wayanad Wildlife Sanctuary, the Periyar Wildlife Sanctuary in Thekkady and Munnar's Eravikulam National Park and Chinnar Wildlife Sanctuary. Eco tourism initiatives operate in the parks, such as the Periyar Wildlife Sanctuary's employment of local tribespeople as park wardens and tour guides.

Go trekking In the Keralan plantation areas and in the Himalayan region of Spiti in Himachal Pradesh there are excellent opportunities for trekking from short walks through plantations and hilltop areas to tough treks for the more experienced.

Discover the local way life Trips to Bishnoi tribal villages in the Rajasthani desert, isolated townships in the Keralan plantation districts and farming communities in Spiti and the Keralan backwaters are a unique way to dip into the local ancient culture. Many homestay hosts are key community figures and so there is a degree of trust in these village visits that you would be unlikely to get in a tourist group.

Join a plantation tour In the plantation areas of Kerala (Wayanad, Thekkady and Munnar), a plantation tour is a fascinating insight into the local way of life.

Get cooking Many Homestay hosts offer cooking classes. These are informal and a friendly way to get to know your host and the Indian culture of food. Classes range from short lessons in how to cook dishes like daal and chapattis to the full-on cooking masterclass taught by Jyoti in Devra homestay.

Partake in family life Although staying in a homestay offers you as much independence as you like, it is well worth getting involved in a bit of family life. If there is a family event or wedding, many hosts are happy to invite their guests – weddings, in particular, are one of the best ways to experience elaborate Indian family custom.

## Contacts

**Mahindra Holidays & Resorts India Limited**
Mahindra Towers, 2nd Floor, 17/18 Patullos Road,
Chennai – 600 002
**Tel:** +91 44 39881000,
+44 (0) 20 3140 8422 (UK local rates)
**Web:** www.mahindrahomestays.com
**Rates:** From £22 per night per room, including breakfast.
Additional meals can be provided on request.

## When to go

The best months to visit India are generally October to March, India's winter. Summer time can be uncomfortably hot (with temperatures up to 45°C in Rajasthan) and the monsoon season is between May and September; the rains are particularly strong in Kerala. However, some homestay hosts encourage tourists to visit during the monsoon season as it can be especially beautiful and it is one of the best times of the year for ayurvedic treatment. Peak season in Rajasthan and Kerala is November to January, while homestays in the Himalayan region of Spiti are best visited from mid-May to mid-October in order to avoid harsh winters and heavy snows.

# IRELAND
Gregan's Castle Hotel, County Clare

How green does the Emerald Isle grow? Ireland would seem to have many eco negatives stacked up against it.... Ireland is an island – so, you have to get on a plane or boat just to set foot on this Gaelic soil. It's now one of Europe's most prosperous nations – so, there are a lot of cars on the roads, not to mention a flood of low-cost airlines that have turned it into a disposable city-break destination. It's not surprising that Ireland doesn't leap out at you when considering a European eco holiday.

While all of this is a consideration, it's not the whole picture. Ireland has developed some surprisingly progressive environmental policies over the past few years, thanks mainly to the governing Green Party. On a consumer level, plastic bags have virtually been eliminated since a tax was introduced on them in 2002. Board Bia, the national food board, has created an award for restaurants that promote sustainable food sourcing, while the Slow Food Movement has become hugely popular. So is it time to revaluate Ireland?

Gregan's Castle Hotel in County Clare on the west coast could be evidence that eco consciousness isn't simply a passing fad. Present owner Simon Haden first moved here as a young boy when his father took over the hotel in the mid-1970s. The original castle – a 15th-century tower house built for the Prince of the Burren – still stands opposite the hotel entrance. The house today at Gregan's was built in the mid-1800s as the centrepiece to a 2,000-acre Georgian family estate and has been gradually added to over the years. Simon took over the family business in 2002 and runs it with his partner Frederieke. For him, the 21-room hotel is primarily 'a place where people can relax'.

On arrival, the house and gardens offer up an overwhelming sense of stillness and tranquillity. There are no televisions or radios in any of the bedrooms or common areas. Pressing the mute button on any background noise in such a deliberate way takes a little adjustment, but forces guests to slow down and connect with the history of the house and the nature that surrounds it.

The interior has been carefully renovated to retain its history. Key antique pieces and hand-tufted rugs are softly complemented by accents of contemporary Irish art and design. Gregan's is clearly still a family affair that prides itself on continuity. Four of the staff have been working here for over 30 years – the head housekeeper Teresa used to baby-sit Simon as a child.

Like the interior, the garden is a labour of love. Head gardener Christopher Lock worked on the original landscaping when the Hadens first took over 30 years ago. It's been his personal passion ever since – designing the pond, rockery and neighbouring wood. All work is done both organically and without the help of machinery, with the exception of the rose garden, which was planted in memory of Simon's late younger brother. The perfectly

manicured croquet lawn and borders quietly offset the sharp limestone backdrop. In Christopher's view, 'when you have the gift of this view to take in, you don't want anything shouting out at you'. There are many spots to contemplate the surrounding natural beauty, including the semi-circle of Russian Rock Birch trees looking out across the valley.

The menu, served up by young Finnish chef Mickael Viljanen, is surprisingly sophisticated given Gregan's rural setting. The small, seasonal menu changes daily – focusing on the freshest local produce available and 'giving diners what they are not expecting'. Be it Burren lamb or beef, fresh Atlantic fish, Ballyvaughan lobster or locally grown organic vegetables, the Gregan's dining experience is unashamedly gourmet and artful. As well as the inventive menu, the break-taking views of the Burren also make the restaurant a popular choice with locals and passing tourists.

The lasting memory of any trip to this hotel is the jaw-dropping backdrop – the Burren, which dominates the view from every window. It's one of the most celebrated national parks in Ireland with 270 square kilometres of stark limestone pavement punctuated by deep fissures. It is home to megalithic tombs, forts and castles and many other archeological remains. A guided walk offering a unique mix of alpine, arctic and Mediterranean wildlife is unmissable.

left **Cows at the Burren Waters**

opposite **The restaurant and Prince of Burren Tower House**

Simon and his team see themselves as 'stewards' of their precious environment and take their responsibility seriously. Since 2000, the hotel's entire electricity supply has been generated by windmills on the west coast. Over the past five years, the hotel's landfill waste has been reduced by half. All of Gregan's food, office and garden waste is composted onsite and rainwater is also harvested for use, while the main water supply is from a spring on Corkscrew Hill. There is a wood-pellet heating system for the staff accommodation, with another one planned for guests. The hotel continually lobbies local and central government on planning and conservation matters that relate to the Burren. It is also one of the first luxury hotels in Ireland to pursue the EU Flower accreditation. As Haden points out, 'even though we're achieving a lot, we know there's a lot more we can do'.

# Green menu

**Take a guided walk** Learn about the flora, fauna and geology of the Burren from local guide and farmer Shane Connolly.

**Go biking** Borrow the hotel's bicycles and ride down the coast road to the Rhine – a deserted stretch of coast – where you might catch some Burren cows bathing in the sea.

**Indulge your olfactics** Take a free tour of the Burren's organic Perfumery. A herbal brew from the tea rooms is a must.

**Discover birds of prey** Visit the snowy owls, falcons and hawks at the Ailwee Cave.

**Check out the local markets** Stop off at the Ballyvaughan Farmers' Market on Saturdays or the craft fair every Sunday.

## Contacts

**Gregan's Castle Hotel** Ballyvaughan, County Clare, Ireland
**Tel:** +353 65 707 7005
**Web:** www.gregans.ie
**Rates:** From €195 per night, bed and breakfast, for two people sharing, including all taxes.

## When to go

The dominant influence on Ireland's weather is the Atlantic Ocean giving it its temperate conditions. The lowest rainfall is in early summer when the Emerald Isle is at its greenest. However, the summer holidays can become a little crowded.

# ITALY
## The Hill that Breathes

The Hill that Breathes is a holistic centre with a light heart, a big sense of humour and a small carbon footprint that lies in the heart of Italy close to the Renaissance city of Urbino.

The Hill opened in 2004, founded by Italian-British couple Gaia and John, former advertising creatives who met in London in the mid 1990s. They shared a fascination for holistic practices, both also being teachers of meditation and qigong. With a desire for a simpler life, a love of Italy, and a new family that made living in London seem less attractive, the idea of setting up a centre in Italy emerged.

Feng shui-inspired criteria set out their wish-list: plenty of woodland; a horseshoe-shaped hill surrounded by flowing water with a couple of houses so that they could expand easily; great views, but also protected so that the centre would feel like a real hideaway; and a situation close to somewhere amazing.

Surprisingly, they found it almost immediately.

While in Le Marche, Tuscany's green sister, a recommendation from Gaia's mother led them to Urbino – the Renaissance gem town, birthplace of Raphael and a UNESCO World Heritage Site. The tree-coated, horseshoe-shaped hill they arrived at contained two old farmhouses and was set against an incredible backdrop of rolling hills and flourishing woodlands leading all the way up to the broad feet of the Apennine mountains in the distance. And it even had rivers flowing all around it.

It is certainly an astonishing spot where it's evident that there's something miraculous in the air in addition to the prolific levels of pine tree-generated oxygen. Now approaching its sixth season, many guests are drawn back more than once each summer, some even returning up to four times a year, joking that they never tell their friends where they're headed in an attempt to keep the place their own secret – not something that they always manage to do.

The Hill boasts some of the best and most well-known teachers of yoga, tai chi, qigong and breathwork. Every week is dedicated to a particular discipline and there are even a couple of family yoga weeks. The legendary 'Fuck It' weeks are also a loved feature in the programme of week-long courses. Led by John and Gaia themselves, these weeks impart the special form of deep, energetic healing with a light-hearted and accessible approach for which the centre has become known.

And that's the thing about The Hill that Breathes – it's holistic in the truest sense, 'it's "whole" '. You can dive into a dynamic week of yoga sessions twice a day, with swimming in the outdoor pool and mountain biking around the hills and valleys in between. Or you could collapse into one of the many hammocks with a bottle of local wine and a novel and lie there all day until the stars come out. It really is all OK.

The house itself is now beautifully and considerately renovated using original materials and local craftsmen.

The bedrooms are stylish, spacious and very comfortable. Much of the furniture is antique and everything has been purchased locally. There are some beautiful iron pieces made by the town's ironmonger dotted about the place. Sessions take place in the stunning geodesic dome in the woods – an incredible space on the inside, the look of something from outer space on the outside.

On the hill, they are constantly working on ways not just to minimise any negative impact on the environment, but to actually benefit the environment when they can. Around 40,000 trees pose quite a job in protection alone. They are, after all, what gives the hill its name. As pine trees are the highest producers of oxygen and chi energy, the hill literally breathes. By helping to create new tree growth they also sustain the local wildlife, including deer, boar, badger, fox and red squirrel. Guests are given advice on appropriate behaviour such as keeping to tracks and picking up any rubbish.

Water is the next most important thing that needs safeguarding. It is drawn from a combination of water from the well beneath the hill, large tanks of collected rainwater and some water from the mains. Guests are encouraged to have just one shower a day and to develop a strong awareness of water usage. Solar panels provide energy to heat the tanks and power the lights.

In exchange for the eco awareness asked of the guests during the week, John and Gaia have supplied a gorgeous, salt-water swimming pool, which is free of chemicals and has stunning views across the valley.

above **Villa exterior**     right **The yoga dome**

above **The pool and view from The Hill that Breathes**

There is also a great eco system in place for processing black water (sewage) – huge tanks, independent from the mains oxygenate the black water, remove the waste matter and pollutant organisms and make it safe to reuse.

Green policies are carried into the office, where a paper-free system is in place for enquiries and bookings – the whole booking process being carried out by email. In 2007, they even stopped printing brochures for the same reason. Around 90 per cent of The Hill's staff is made up of locals and they encourage the same in their partner companies. Guides provide visits around their own communities, giving information about events and traditions, such as markets, carnival events, local village fairs and saints' days celebrations.

The scrumptious vegetarian food on offer owes much to the amazing, locally sourced ingredients (although, of course, the very talented local chef gets some of the credit too). They're not just organic, they like to use Demeter-certified biodynamic fruit and veg as much as possible; so green it's the gold standard in eco-friendly produce. There's very little by way of leftovers or waste (the food's too good), but they do compost everything they can and use recycling bins to collect plastic, glass, paper, tin and cardboard.

The holistic philosophy really is at the heart of what they do at The Hill that Breathes, following a belief that we are inseparable from our environment and that healing ourselves contributes to healing others.

Oh, and if you're looking for the secret of a long life you might just find it here. This tranquil and enchanting region boasts the highest life expectancy in Italy, which, itself, boasts an enviable rate of longevity in its people. There really must be something in the air.

# Green menu

**Take a hike** In addition to the classes, destination visits with environmental benefits are also available, including mountain walks led by an inspirational and very knowledgeable local guide.

**Pamper yourself** An array of blissful massages and treatments are on offer from a host of locals, ranging from full-body Ayurvedic massages to shiatsu.

**Visit the local market** A trip to the local weekly market in Urbino is a very enjoyable morning out, where speciality foods and arts and crafts can be purchased, at the same time as experiencing some real mingling with the locals.

**Get stuck in to the foodie philosophy** Not to be missed is a cooking lesson with the extremely passionate and eccentric local chef who not only divulges valuable tips on authentic Italian cooking and the origins and traditions surrounding the dishes he creates, but dollops it out with an entire philosophy based on Italian food.

## When to go

The Hill is open from late April to October. It tends to be dry and warm throughout, with July and August being the hottest months. A near-constant breeze sweeps amiably across the hill preventing peak summer temperatures from becoming too stifling. Local attractions and markets hold interest for all seasons with various gourmet flavours of the different months offering constant change and choice.

## Contacts

**The Hill that Breathes** La Collina Che Respira, Localita' Girfalco, Via Ca' Loreto 3, 61029 Urbino (PU), Italy
**Tel:** +39 0722 34 54 72, +44 (0) 870 609 2690 (reservations from the UK)
**Web:** www.thehillthatbreathes.com
**Rates:** From £595 (depending on the week) per person in a sharing room for three. Single and twin rooms £50 per person per week supplement.

# ITALY
## Villa Lucia, Tuscany

For lovers of 18th-century Italian villas, a new treat is in store. Situated in the historic village of Vorno, near the beautiful walled town of Lucca, Villa Lucia was, until recently, a crumbling group of rustic, stone farmhouses surrounding a grand old villa at the foot of Monte Zano.

The estate was built by the Fascetti family in the 18th century and encompasses three different accommodations set in four acres of walled gardens: Villa Lucia, Casa Cameron and Casa Joshua, totalling 21 bedrooms. Walking from one room to another, the various colour schemes sooth the eye, which has to work to pick out subtle individual detail like the row of urns that decorate the walls or the intricacies of the stairwell frescoes. You relax as soon as you arrive, with every view bathed in that ephemeral Tuscan light.

Suites, named after famous Italians, come in all shapes and sizes. Grandest of all is the Caravaggio, a three-roomed premier suite, which has a separate salon, large bathroom complete with an antique claw-footed bath and peaceful views across the garden. On the third floor, there's even a cinema with a giant plasma screen and comfy velvet sofas.

Outside there are several swimming pools nestling between ancient olive groves, a steaming, stone hot tub housed in a secret grotto, a tennis court and a novel aqua- and outdoor gym.

Lucia's main eco credential is all too obvious. The loving renovation of the 18th-century villa was no small undertaking and has taken the last five years and deep pockets to bring it back to its former glory. Owner Mike Rhode is as passionate about the green aspects of his properties (he also has homes in Marrakech and France) as he is about food and is currently experimenting with a combination of hydro-electricity (sourced from the river, which runs through the property) and turbines. Once he has ascertained the most sustainable source he hopes to convert fully.

### Green gastro

Deservedly famous for its historic sites, centuries of culture and art, Tuscany is just as renowned for its culinary excellence. The simplicity of 'casalingua' is the basis of all Tuscan cuisine.

The in-house cooking school was started by Mike in 1996 to offer gourmet travellers a chance to whet their taste buds with local flavours. However, his love of food is no accident of fate. It's in his genes. His father Willliam penned the famous cookbook *Of Cabbages and Kings* when still a young man and went on to be one of the first editors of *Gourmet* magazine. The kitchen at Lucia is at the very heart of the villa and it's impossible not to become involved as wafts of what's-for-lunch drift through the rooms.

Regional specialities using fresh local produce are the obvious green choice but they are also the key components of a 'living-life-longer' concept, very dear to Mike's heart.

'The Hayflick Limit principle (the finite number of divisions of which a cell is capable),' he explained, 'means that the more healthily we eat and drink, the longer we'll live.' And when it comes to drinking, the approach is very specific. Villa Lucia's chefs, and patron, are staunch believers in Roger Corder's *Red Wine Diet*. Rest assured, Roger isn't some red-nosed wino – he's dedicated most of his working life to researching cardiovascular functions and, as a professor of experimental therapeutics, his statements are based on scientific evidence. So feel virtuous as you sip your Barolo, or a cocktail of beneficial flavonoid polyphenols.

The cooking course began with pasta. Of course. There may be no other food in the world as ubiquitous, versatile and well loved – a basic, healthy meal made from simple

above **In summer, indoors blends seamlessly with the outdoors**
right **The main swimming pool**

above **Luxurious accommodation**    opposite (top) **Pasta masterclass**

ingredients, capable of standing alone or accommodating a variety of flavours. Local chef Glauco from the nearby village of Vinci (of Leonardo fame) generously shared his own recipes, techniques and helpful tips. We prepared Minestrone soup with foccacia (made with olive oil), aromatic limoncello sorbet, pasta and spicy Puttanesca sauce, the creamiest herb-and-roast-pepper risotto, and grilled nectarines in a devilish amaretto sabayon. All this and more doused with healthy lashings of red wine.

As the week progressed various bits of the gastro puzzle came together – a visit to the local olive press in Alle Camelia, a wine tasting in the cellars of Castello Banfi, an 11th-century vineyard, and a trip to market in Pistoia to select only the freshest raw materials. Olive groves, pasta factories, cathedrals and museums – Tuscany has choices for every taste.

To work it all off, put on your walking boots and hike up to the giant cross on the hill and admire the view overlooking Lucca and beyond. Alternatively, take a deep breath and head for the old stables and the very inviting, newly installed Vedic Spa.

## Green therapy

The new Vedic Spa, whose mantra is 'live better longer', offers anti-ageing, health and wellness programmes encompassing three basic tenets: a diet with principles taken from Roger Corder's acclaimed *Red Wine Diet*, ISHI treatments, including vino, choco and truffle therapy, and, last but not least, a strict exercise routine aimed at achieving a healthier, longer-lasting life style.

Vinotherapy, if you haven't tried it, is a novel concept using grapes harvested from the Tuscan hills combined with other active ingredients to produce a delicious anti-ageing treatment. Ditto the indulgent choco therapy (perfect for self-confessed chocoholics) and the even more unusual truffle therapy, an extravagant treatment, rigorously documented in clinical studies carried out in Italian universities.

The hammam may not be Tuscan but the black olive soap used to scrub away impurities definitely is. Each October the olives harvested around the villa make the house oil, while others are mashed into a delicious pulpy soap. Clean and healthy living with Tuscany's favourite ingredients – what more could you wish for?

# Green menu

Visit Lucca Founded in 180BC, the walled city of Lucca is justifiably referred to as Tuscany's best-kept secret. Just six kilometres from Vorno, it's famous for the Torre Guinigi and fantastic shopping along Via Fillungo. Don't go home without a bottle of its delicious olive oil, some pecorino and limoncello.

See the art of Florence Florence is only 90 minutes by train and has a wealth of art including Michelangelo's 'David' (the Uffizi museum is a must).

Climb the Leaning Tower Twenty-five minutes away is Pisa, home of the famous Florentine Galileo, which continues to attract curious travellers to climb the Leaning Tower.

Visit Siena The marbled duomo and baptistery in Siena are home to works by such great artists as Michelangelo, Ghiberti, Donatello, Duccio and Nicola and Giovanni Pisano. Volterra and San Gimignano's unforgettable towers are also within easy distance.

Have dinner at Bimbotto You would be missing out on Vorno's full flavour if you miss its best (and only) restaurant. Great pizzas, fresh pasta and local karaoke some nights if you're lucky!

Take a basket Stroll round Pistoia's fresh fruit and vegetable market on a Wednesday morning – set up in front of the famous renaissance cathedral, it's choc-a-bloc with local life.

## When to go

Vorno has a mild climate for most of the year. Rolling Tuscan hills surround the property and protect it from excessive heat in summer and freezing temperatures in winter. The best time to visit is during the quieter seasons, from April to June and from September to October, when the weather is usually good and there are fewer tourists.

## Contacts

**Villa Lucia** 165 Via di Vorno, 55060 Vorno, Tuscany, Italy
**Tel:** +39 (0) 583 971 456
**Web:** www.luxurypropertyrentals.com
www.rhodeschoolofcuisine.com
**Rates:** From €600 in a superior room per person for three nights bed, breakfast and dinner, including three treatments in the spa.

# JORDAN
## RSCN Nature Reserves, Petra and the Dead Sea

Overlooking the old city of Amman, the Wild Jordan Centre is both a great place to eat and a revolutionary force for good, devoted to promoting the protection and sustainable use of Jordan's natural heritage. Run by English Director Chris Johnson, it is part of the RSCN (Royal Society for the Conservation of Nature) set up in 1966 by a group of hunters who turned conservationist after witnessing the great decline in game. Chris is the first to admit that, 'Nature has to be relevant to peoples' lives if we are going to save it,' and his clear vision has brought about a hub of nature-based employment opportunities and a supply of over 11,000 bed nights in the Dana Nature Reserve alone. As sustainable tourism goes, it's one of the world's greatest success stories, bringing in 40,000 new eco visitors a year.

While tourism is Jordan's primary industry, there is a dilemma in that its success could destroy what it's striving to protect through overdevelopment. Chris' vision revolves around turning the country and its attractions into a boutique destination of high-value low numbers. The millennium has already witnessed a decrease in group bookings and an increase in independent travel – good for the environment and infrastructure but there's a long way to go.

### Jerash

Acres of olive and fig trees coat the deep fertile valleys in the densely populated area north of Amman where thousands of Palestinian refugees fled in 1948. A little further on lies the ancient city of Jerash. A close second to Petra in its popularity as a tourist site, its human occupation dates back more than 6,500 years but, notably, came under Roman rule in 63BC when it was conquered by General Pompey. As if its expansive ruins weren't enough, the 245-metre-long hippodrome hosts a spectacular gladiatorial battle and chariot race twice a day. Equally impressive are the colonnaded street, Hadrian's Arch and temple of Dionysus.

### Ajloun

Nearby, the Ajloun Forest Reserve is a peaceful spot on a hill covered in Mediterranean oaks, pistachio and oriental strawberry trees. The refreshing greenery offers cool comfort after the stifling temperatures of Jerash. Operated by the RSCN the choice of accommodation includes 10 tents and five wooden cabins with en-suite facilities and solar-powered heating and light. There are various gentle self-guided tours through the village orchards or along the soap-makers' trail where you can watch local women produce natural olive-oil soaps. Inhabitants from six surrounding villages are active in the reserve's community programmes, endorsing the whole concept of sustainable tourism.

Hiking along the Aljoun valley floor you may catch a glimpse of the snow-capped Sheikh Mountain in southern Syria. Closer by, the birds of prey soar above the dark

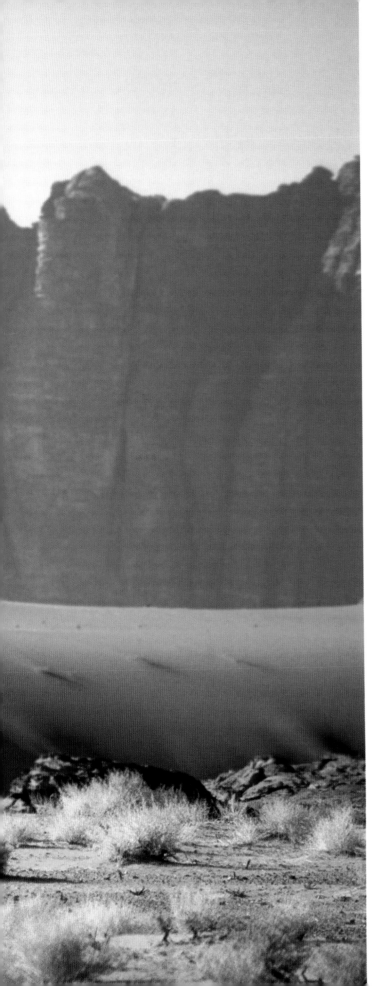

silhouettes of petrified trees and the tumbled heaps of stones that were once Roman watch towers.

## Dana

Set over 308 square kilometres, the most beautiful of all Jordan's nature reserves has to be Dana – a point validated by three choices of RSCN eco accommodation. It's worth spending at least one night in each to enjoy this landscape of rocky ravines, dunes and wooded highlands.

Accommodation comes in various guises. Dana Guest House perched high on the edge of Wadi Dana, has nine comfortably furnished rooms. It also has a great gift shop filled with soaps, herbs and silver crafted by local women. Chris Johnson told us that Dana is so successful it provides 80 per cent of the income necessary to run the whole of the park each year. Close by is Rummana campsite, with 20 large three- and four-person tents, secluded far from any roads, with the Rummana Mountain as a backdrop. It's a heavenly spot. Utterly tranquil, with a sense of suspended animation, it allows you to soak up the energy and recharge. However, most remote of all is the 26-room Feynan Wilderness Lodge at the edge of the Rift Valley, a five-hour trek from Dana (although you can then take the bus out of the other side of the wadi towards Petra). Its arabesque atmosphere is reminiscent of the ancient caravanserai that provided shelter to the camel trains that traversed the nearby trading route.

You could easily just sit and meditate at the view for three days but it would be a shame not to hike some of the trails

above **Wadi Rum, tented accommodation**

above **Roman ruins at Jerash**    opposite (top) **Feynan eco lodge**    opposite (bottom) **Dana**

that lead from the top of the Jordan Rift Valley in the north down to the desert lowlands of Wadi Arabia, taking in the vast amount of flora and fauna.

### Petra

Petra is, quite simply, spectacular. Concerned that it might turn into an anticlimax I deliberately tried to lower my expectations. I needn't have worried. The Nabatean city is so magnificent one has to keep reminding oneself that it wasn't 'built' but miraculously carved out of the solid, brick-red, rock face. Nature's weathering and smoothing of the surfaces over the centuries is just as magnificent as the carving, and the two seem to blend into a mutual kaleidoscope of warm, embracing colour.

Most recognise the photos of the so-called Treasury at Petra. Few realise the true extent of its size or scope. A solid nine hours barely scratches the surface even if you return for the mystical candlelit night visit.

Taybet Zaman, a reconstructed Jordanian mountainside village, offers the perfect place to stay, with far-reaching views across the wadi, atmospheric rooms, which offer the comfort you need at the end of a long day's walking, delicious food and an authentic hammam experience with a deep soapy massage. Local craftsmen sell their wares in the souq along the outside wall and food comes from the markets in Wadi Masa.

### The lowest point on Earth

Maybe most contentious of all, is the Dead Sea, lying at approximately 420 metres below sea level with a further depth of 400 metres. I say approximately because it's dropping every year and by 2050 is expected to be a dry valley linking neighbouring Israel. While it lasts, it's a magnificent natural phenomenon of 32 per cent salt (making all plant and animal life impossible) – that's 10 times saltier than the Mediterranean. The result is that you float like a bobbing cork while the salt draws out toxins from your pores, soaking you in a mixture of bromine, magnesium, calcium and potassium mixed with sulphur from the deposits of medicinal mud. The low altitude enriches the air with 10 per cent more oxygen than at sea level and increases the body's metabolic rate. In addition, city fumes are absent, and the high evaporation level filters out harmful UVA and UVB rays.

This is a country of cultural landscapes, a real experience where you're still likely to fall over a Roman paving stone. If you are looking for an example of Man's impact on the planet, both good and bad, it is epitomised in Jordan.

## When to go

Summers are hot with long hours of year-round sunshine. The mild winters can turn cold, with snow on the higher ground. Occasional rainfall occurs from November to March usually in the form of heavy showers.

## Contacts

**RSCN (Royal Society for the Conservation of Nature)**
**Tel:** +962 6 4633 589/7
**Web:** www.rscn.org.jo

**Jordan Tourism Board**
**Tel:** +44 (0) 207 371 6496
**Web:** www.visitjordan.com

# Green menu

Visit Wild Jordan Have an organic lunch at Wild Jordan and suss out what's what in the nature reserves. Then step back in time in Roman Philadelphia

Take time out in Ajloun Enjoy the peace and walk through the natural shrub land in the cool mountain air to a workshop where the local women make soap.

Visit Dana Trek the numerous trails and wonder at the majesty of Jordan's Rift Valley. Visit the workshop of the local villagers and buy some of their silver jewellery, herbs, jams or soaps.

Marvel at Petra Trek to the monastery – it's worth the hike or if you're really just too tired let an ass do the donkey work for you. If your visit coincides with one of the weekly Petra candlelight walks don't think twice about giving your legs the extra workout.

Ride a camel in Wadi Rum An hour from Petra, the sheer size of Wadi Rum makes it unmissable. The peaks of eroded sandstone sitting on a solid granite base soar over 700 metres into the sky making it a film-maker's dream. Camel-ride adventures across the desert are run by local Bedouin tribes.

Visit Bethany and Mount Nemo Two thousand years ago, John the Baptist baptised Jesus in a quiet spot here and it was from Mount Nemo that Moses first saw the Promised Land. It is also said to be his final resting place.

# KENYA

Lewa, the North Rangelands Trust and Kiwayu Safari Village

It may not be the African blueprint for free and fair elections, but Kenya is a true pioneer for green travel. The community conservancy model developed by the private reserve Lewa and the Northern Rangelands Trust (NRT) is a blueprint for the future of community-led eco tourism. Famous for the Masai Mara, the future of Kenyan low-impact tourism actually lies outside the national parks. As the parks become more and more choked up with packs of vehicles crowding every wildlife sighting, the private- and community-run reserves not only offer a richer experience for the guest; they are much better for both animal welfare and the local community.

While 62,000-acre Lewa is a superbly run private reserve with 60 beds, the neighbouring 80,000-acre Samburu National Park has 760 beds plus unlimited daily visitors, and this is small potatoes compared to the even more popular Masai Mara. No local communities are allowed to settle or graze within the national parks, but the community conservancy model that Lewa and the NRT are spear-heading is specifically designed to both educate and empower the local people. They have set up 14 community-run reserves to the north of their borders, creating a wildlife sanctuary of nearly 5,500 square kilometres.

The model is simple: Lewa and the NRT provide fund-raising, land management and managerial support, but the community is empowered to run the land themselves.

Established lodges run the lodge and safari operation themselves, whereas new projects partner with a specialist operator to build and run the lodge for the first five years. During this time, the community receives US$31 per person per night and has the opportunity to buy the lodge at cost price after five years.

### Sasaab and Ngwesi

Sasaab is one such lodge within the NRT. Moroccan-themed it is possibly the most spectacular and luxurious of all Kenya's safari retreats. Nine giant, multi-level tents come with luxurious veranda living-rooms, oversized beds, private plunge pools, whitewashed steps and open bathrooms, situated on a high rocky ridge overlooking the banks of the Uaso Nyiro river.

Ngwesi is another established lodge that runs its own operation. The most famous of the community-run lodges, its six bandas are beautifully constructed from local Maputo thatch and termite-resistant newtonia hardwood, previously uprooted by passing elephants. String bridges link the individual rooms and the phrase 'loo with a view' could easily have been born here.

### Lewa

There are also three different accommodation options within Lewa itself. Celebrity-friendly, 12-bed Lewa House

previous page (main) **Lola, the baby rhino at Lewa**    previous page (thumbnail) **Room at Sasaab**

(which has played host to Robbie Williams, Sting and Ronnie Wood) consists of three stone-built cottages with rustic Sanje (swamp grass) thatch roofs, built around a central lounge and dining area with beguiling views over the northern plains.

The newly built Kifaru House – meaning 'rhinoceros' in Swahili – is more grandiose. The great room, with dining table and lounge area, has a high-arched medieval ceiling with giant cedar beams and baronial fireplaces at either end. The infinity pool overlooks Mount Kenya and the separate library comes with leather-bound books and a widescreen TV. The six individual bandas that lie in its grounds have red clay walls and Sanje thatch roofs and come decked out with colonial furniture and four-poster beds. Like Lewa House, Kifaru House is only bookable on an exclusive basis. All the income that is generated by Kifaru is directly reinvested into wildlife conservation and local community development programmes.

The third option, Lewa Safari Camp (LSC) is comprised of 12 tented bungalows, which can be booked individually, with mushroom-shaped thatched roofs and balconies complete with rough-hewn sofa overlooking the savannah. Inside, the bedroom look is French-country-elegant in soft, linen colours, but the bathroom is the real African deal. Sculpted from coloured clay, Y-shaped pieces of wood create the shower divide and prop up the sink.

At the foot of the camp is a bird-watching hide and a swimming pool amid expansive, well-tended gardens.

Lewa started life in 1920 as the Craig family farm, but in 1983 the Craigs and financial backer Mrs Anna Merz set up a rhino sanctuary in response to the predicted extinction of the rhino in Kenya. As a result of poaching, the population had dropped from over 20,000 in the mid-70s to a few hundred a decade later. Lewa now has nearly 100 black and white rhino and the NRT lands are home to 50 per cent of the country's black rhino stock.

opposite **Lewa lands**    above **Bedroom at Kifaru house**    below **Pool at Sasaab**

The conservation mentality behind all these properties is to do whatever is possible for them to be as green as they can. All glass and tin cans are collected for recycling; grey water is used for watering plants and any other use they can think of; every loo is 'low-yield' and uses minimal amounts of water and guests are also encouraged to think about their water consumption and to keep it to a minimum.

Kifaru House is totally run on solar and wind power while LSC and Lewa House use solar for a portion of their power, including illuminating path lights at night. All of the Lewa properties will be converted to run on solar and wind power within the next few years.

### Kiwayu Safari Village

Kiwayu has a similarly visionary past, built 30 years ago by safari operator and eco visionary Alfredo Pelizzoli. Originally conceived as a post-safari beachside retreat, it still does exactly as promised and is one of the most charming

above **The lunch shack at Kiwayu**    below **Sunbeds at Kiwayu**

and unique hotels on the African coast. Found on the mainland coast opposite Kiwayu island, it is surrounded by mangrove lagoons and is accessible by private airstrip or a two-hour boat transfer from Lamu.

Now run by the next Pelizzoli generation, it is the epitome of barefoot luxury. The giant beach-front bandas are still built from Mekeka palm-leaf matting laid on the sand – no concrete floors here – with mangrove poles and Makuti roofing completing the natural construction. Giant clam shells stand by the door for guests to rinse sandy feet and, inside, hammocks and old Lamu beds – with stained-glass headboards and strings of shells – line the living area. The ultra-king-sized bed is made in the local village, and the driftwood bathrooms come complete with solar heating.

The main bar-restaurant is a temple to beachcombing, decorated with over 30 years of treasures that have washed up on the shore. From whale jawbones and elephant skulls to driftwood palm trunks and the decorated prows and bows of colourful dhows, the treasure chest of shells and bottle-green glass buoys make it utterly unique. There is no more spectacular way to end a safari.

# Green menu

## LEWA AND THE COMMUNITY CONSERVANCIES

Visit the game reserves Head out early on bush walk with an armed ranger or hop on a horse or a camel.

Jog with the Maasai Pull on your running shoes and go jogging with a local Maasai warrior.

Learn local skills Smoke out bees, clean gourds, hunt game and join in jumping competitions with Argosa, a young Maasai warrior at the cultural village of Ramat.

Meet the Kids Visit a local primary school and meet the effervescent Agnes, head nurse at the local clinic.

Cuddle a baby rhino Bottle-feed a hand-raised baby rhino born to a blind mum.

Run a marathon Join Tusk Trust and run in one of the world's top 10 toughest marathons (half or full) – and the only one to take place inside a game reserve.

## KIWAYU

Go beachcombing See what treasures you can find along the deserted beaches.

Enjoy sunset views Trek up into the dunes to watch the sun set over hundreds of miles of Dodori Forest and watch the game congregating at distant waterholes.

Sail a traditional dhow Cruise the coastline and cast anchor in mesmerising coves for a crab and lobster picnic lunch.

Visit Lamu Take a boat trip down to the historic World Heritage town of Lamu.

Cast your hook Fish in the mangroves or fly-fish with the local fishermen on the fringes of the lagoon.

Learn about turtles Learn about the 164 different turtle nests along the surrounding beaches at the WWF Turtle conservation project.

Meet the locals Take a tour of the local village with Shali Mohamed, join in the dancing at the local school and learn how the local women have built up their own industry making art from washed-up flip-flops.

# Contacts

## LEWA AND THE COMMUNITY CONSERVANCIES

**Lewa Properties** Osiolo, Kenia, Nairobi 00100, Kenya
**Tel:** +254 20 600 457
**Web:** www.bush-and-beyond.com
**Rates:** Include all full board, all-inclusive accommodation (two sharing) and activities. **Lewa Safari Camp:** US$440 per person per night. **Lewa House and Kifaru:** US$3,000 per night for up to six guests plus US$70 conservancy fee per person per night. Additional guests US$560 per person per night.

**Ngwesi** Laikipia, Nyahururu, Kenya
**Tel:** +254 020 4447 151
**Web:** www.lets-go-travel.net
**Rates:** From US$260 per person per night for full board and activities (two sharing), plus US$40 per person per night conservancy fees.

**Sasaab** P.O Box: 15565, Code: 00503, Nairobi, Kenya
**Tel:** +254 20 892 234
**Web:** www.tamimiea.com
**Rates:** From US$530 per person per night, for full board and activities (two sharing).

## KIWAYU

**Kiwayu Safari Village** Dodori, Lamu, Kenya
**Tel:** +254 20 600 107/891; +254 735 598 858
**Web:** www.kiwayu.com
**Rates:** From US$430 per person per night for full board, no drinks (two sharing).

**Bailey Robinson**
**Tel:** +44 (0) 1488 689 777
**Web:** BaileyRobinson.com
Bailey Robinson promotes camps and lodges that have a low environmental impact. They also give aid to various projects, including schooling, health centres and hospitals.

# When to go

There are no extremes of temperature and little humidity at the equator. Lewa averages 25–30°C. The highest rainfall is in April and May with January and February being the driest. Mid-December to mid-March are warmest with July and August coolest. Kiwayu averages 27–28°C, with February and March being the hottest. August and September can be windy and the resort closes for the monsoon between 15 April and 23 July. Lewa is closed in April and November, Ngwesi in May and Sasaab in November.

# MADAGASCAR
## Anjajavy L'hotel

Madagascar is regarded as one of the world's biodiversity hotspots, but also as a country whose natural assets are significantly at risk.

With a population fast approaching 20 million, pressure is ever increasing on the island's resources. While only 10 per cent of its natural forest cover remains, 10 per cent of its surface area has received legal protection since the end of 2008 as part of the ambitious Madagascar Action Plan implemented by the proactive Ravalomanana government. One of the goals of the MAP is that Madagascar should soon become a regional leader in the eco tourism arena.

Despite the extent of environmental degradation that has occurred through the centuries, primarily as a result of slash-and-burn agricultural methods, what remains of the forests – be they the luxuriant rainforests of the humid east, the seasonally dry forests of the summer-rainfall west, or the bizarre spiny bush in the semi-desert south ('Nature's Botanical Lunatic Asylum' as travel writer Dervla Murphy put it) – is nothing short of remarkable. Almost everything you see and touch in Madagascar is endemic, that is to say, it is found nowhere else.

Until recently, Madagascar, with its difficult geography and modest infrastructure, was predominantly a destination for fairly adventurous travellers tolerant of basic conditions. But the country has undergone massive change during the last decade and this applies also to its tourism infrastructure.

Today there are a small but growing number of lodges and hotels set in exquisite locations, geared to cater for the most demanding of guests.

## Anjajavy L'hotel

Located on the north-western coast about 120 kilometres to the north of the port Mahajanga, Anjajavy L'hotel is on an inaccessible peninsula, fronted by white sand beaches and surrounded by tropical, seasonally dry forest packed with majestic baobabs. Its location is what makes Anjajavy unique in Madagascar, able to offer its guests the twin combination of quality seaside accommodation and a fascinating wildlife experience, where lemurs roam the gardens and hotel guides escort guests along the extensive network of forest trails and introduce them to sites such as caves and eroded limestone karst formations or tsingy.

The hotel has 24 sea-facing, thatched villas, each with full en-suite facilities, which open onto a large, furnished veranda where you can relax in a hammock while watching Veso fishermen pass by in the blue waters of the Mozambique Channel. For a bit more sociability, the main building offers a lounge and an *al-fresco* restaurant and terrace bar, not to mention an enormous pool and beautiful gardens, which, most afternoons, are visited around tea time by well habituated lemurs, including the critically endangered Coquerel's sifaka.

The Anjajavy L'hotel also excels in its conservation, environmental and community efforts. Recycling is a priority – nothing is wasted – such as old newspapers, which are used for cleaning. Plastics are avoided as far as is possible. Waste plastic, tin, paper and wood are incinerated and the ash is put into landfill with the vegetable matter.

The staff are nearly all local and only five are not Malagasy – since its opening in December 2001, the hotel has brought employment to four of the most remote villages in the heart of Boina Sakalava country. Not only that but the minimum salary is almost double that of Madagascar's imposed minimum wage and the hotel provides all staff with two meals per day and uniforms. Training is good and a bonus system, equal to an additional two-thirds of salary, is also in place. Seafood, fruit and vegetables are all fresh and sourced as close to home as possible.

The hotel boutique stocks commissions from a village women's cooperative, created with support from a local Non Governmental Organisation, to which the hotel has been a major donor.

Water in Madagascar is a precious commodity and the hotel supplies its needs by taking water from a salty well and desalinating it. Guests are also encouraged to use water sparingly; towels are washed on request and in the dry season the gardens are only watered for an hour at dawn and dusk. Waste tanks are treated with natural bacterial products and there is a system that provides compost for the gardens.

The hotel prides itself in being an area of calm and quiet, providing a maximum of comfort with a minimal impact on the environment. With these goals in mind, two 'silent' generators have been installed. Low-wattage light bulbs are used to reduce electricity usage and the glass-fronted buildings need no artificial lighting during the day.

The hotel also supports the local community, contributing to the NGO, which has built four local schools (using 12V wind power), one fishing school and an adults' agricultural training centre over the last five years, as well as employing 11 teachers, one doctor, a midwife and an assistant. Twelve freshwater wells have been sunk, and use windmills to pump the water to the surface.

Privileged to enjoy its own beautiful surroundings, the Anjajavy L'hotel protects a private, 450-hectare reserve of Madagascar's most endangered and fragmented forest

left **Madagascar's majestic Baobab trees**    opposite **Thatched villa**

above **Common brown lemur**

type – its fragile, slow-growing, western, seasonally dry forests. Within this reserve, the hotel aims to protect all plants and animals endemic to the region. Significantly, it is the only protected block of this forest type between Ankarafantsika National Park and Ankarana, much further north. The hotel has a cadre of forest guards, who patrol the reserve keeping paths open and making sure that there is no poaching of wildlife. Cooperation has been established between the reserve, and the local villages who alert the hotel management if they see or hear of people poaching in the area. The hotel has also created fire-breaks to protect the forest against potential fires.

## Unique wildlife

Madagascar's wildlife is unique and, on a visit, you will have plenty of opportunity to catch more than a glimpse of it, whether on arranged trips or from the terrace looking out over the gardens, where adorable, confiding troops of Coquerel's sifaka and the common brown lemur regularly come to visit.

Birding is also excellent and flocks of emerald-green- and grey-headed lovebirds regularly comb the lawns, along with brightly coloured Madagascar red fodies, and cheeky Sakalava weavers, which suspend their kidney-shaped nests under the eaves of the hotel reception. Species easily seen include the critically endangered Madagascar fish eagle, now down to 100 pairs globally. Four pairs find protection here, mainly in the Moramba Bay area. Equally endangered and often seen in the sunset mangrove cruises, is the Madagascar white ibis. More abundant birds include the vociferous greater vasa parrot, the lovely crested and Coquerel's couas, and garrulous sicklebill vangas.

Reptiles such as the Oustalet's chameleon – which, at up to 68 centimetres, is the grand-daddy of all chameleons – the giant hognose snake and the brilliant-green day gecko, are common.

# Green menu

**Watch the local wildlife** Sit on the terrace or take various trips to glimpse Madagascar's astonishing animal kingdom.

**Take a night walk** Night walks usually reveal large numbers of noisy sportive lemurs, fat-tailed dwarf lemurs and at least two species of mouse lemur.

**Visit the locals** Visits to the school, clinic and a typical Malagasy fishing village are positively encouraged, making an interesting opportunity to talk with the children, teachers, medical staff and Boina Sakalava people who live at this remote site. Guests are encouraged to contribute pencils, books and financial aid to the school and medicines to the doctor at the clinic.

**Enjoy watersports** Five minutes walk away, there are plenty of water-based activities on offer, including windsurfing and catamaran sailing courtesy of the hotel.

**Explore by boat** A trip into remote Moramba Bay, dotted with mushroom-shaped islets, is unforgettable and will take you to deserted coves fringed with forests dominated by baobabs.

**Cruise at sundown** Enjoy cocktails and experience the calm, quiet surroundings in a boat as you cruise gently up the healthy mangrove system.

**Go mountain biking** Discover the local forest trails on mountain bikes.

**Plant a tree** Guests are welcome to plant an endangered, endemic tree as part of the forest recovery programme in the tree nursery.

## When to go

Madagascar has a hot, subtropical climate, which is colder up in the mountains. There are two distinct seasons: the lush, green, rainy season from November to March and the dry season from April to October. Both have their advantages, but avoid the cyclone season in February and March.

## Contacts

**Anjajavy L'hotel** Anjajavy Road, Anjajavy, Madagascar
**Tel:** +261 20 623 2000 (satellite)
**Web:** www.anjajavy.com
**Rates:** From €185 per adult per night (four nights or more), full board, sharing and €85 per child sharing.

**Rainbow Tours**
**Tel:** +44 (0) 20 7226 1004
**Web:** www.rainbowtours.co.uk
Rainbow Tours places its eco policy at the heart of its business, seeking to minimise its impact on the environment in everything it does, advising its clients on how to minimise their impact and working with owner-operated lodges that demonstrate a commitment to sustainable development, and benefiting their local communities. It also supports local projects and NGOs both financially and with pro bono work.

# MADEIRA AND PORTO SANTO
Atlantic garden

On the same latitude as Casablanca, the Atlantic archipelago of Madeira is much lusher than its desert-fringed neighbour. The sub-tropical climate and rich volcanic soil mean that vegetation growth here is not impeded. To the contrary, the produce yielded is so sizeable that wandering around the Funchal food market, I felt slightly like a Borrower.

Madeira hosts an unusually diverse eco system and is one of the few places in the world where acres of banana trees grow adjacent to rolling vineyards. The main island is also home to the magnificent *Laurisilva* ('laurel forest'), the largest and most dramatic of its kind in the world. *Levadas* (ancient irrigation canals) wind their way through the flora, creating natural walkways for hikes of all intensities; we pottered along an 'easy' route, opting for a jeep to take us deeper and steeper into the interior. Surrounded by nothing but deserted green peaks, troughs and the odd cow, with the endless Atlantic stretching out as far as the eye could see, I felt utterly exhilarated.

Madeirans are acutely aware that what they have is precious. In 1999, the forest was named a UNESCO World Heritage Site and five areas of the archipelago have been declared nature reserves. The largest of these, the Madeira Nature Reserve, covers a substantial 77 per cent of the main island, where development is restricted. The island's rugged and mountainous terrain also safeguards it against mass-market mayhem. That, and the lack of sandy beaches.

For those who like to flop on the soft stuff, you only have to venture a little further northeast to Porto Santo (two hours by boat) to enter beach-worshippers' heaven – a small unspoilt island with a nine-kilometre stretch of sand, akin to destinations much farther flung. But there is more to this place than its aesthetics. Locals and foreigners alike have been flocking here for centuries to submerse themselves neck-deep in the therapeutic granules of sand, which owe their healing properties to their unique mineral composition; regular stints are reputed to cure a host of ailments from psychiatric problems to rheumatism. Prior to harnessing this abundant natural asset, Hotel Porto Santo conducted ten years of scientific research to ensure it wasn't just an old wives' tale. Their results were conclusive and the hotel introduced a range of sand treatments to their spa, capitalising on its local resources combined with thalassotherapy (the sea water here is rich in iodine, chromium and strontium, which also have healing benefits).

Back on the mainland, tourism is increasingly following the eco path. Hotel Jardim Atlantico, on the west of the island, is setting the example for others to follow. To date, it has received 30 awards for its green credentials through a number of schemes such as reforestation, pollution control and energy-saving initiatives. The hotel's spa has introduced a number of enticing nature-based treatments. One of the

most popular is the 'reflexology' walk, where guests stroll along an 800-metre path comprised of 17 elements from the archipelago, such as pine cones and pebbles.

Savvy to the global agro-tourism trend, and only too happy to endorse its benefits, Madeira has launched its own initiative – The Rural Tourism Association. Visitors can stay with families or in small hotels in the most remote areas, placing an emphasis on sustainable living, with menus created solely from seasonal, homegrown produce.

The culinary offerings in Madeira add to the island's appeal. Its remote location means there is little competition from other fisherman and, therefore, plentiful hauls; black scabbard, tuna, swordfish and limpets are some of the favourites, cooked with lashings of olive oil and garlic. *Espetada* is the most famous meat dish, consisting of cubes of marinated beef cooked, resourcefully, on laurel sticks. These are all washed down nicely with Madeira's most famous export: wine or 'rainwater'.

Heading out to sea, there are many more delights to discover. A number of companies take visitors into the deep blue, with marine biologists on hand to educate. As the ocean floor plunges dramatically off the islands, whales and dolphins venture close to the shore – 320 kilometres of water surrounding the archipelago have been declared a national park for marine mammals. Within ten minutes, we were

previous page (main) **Porto Santo beach**
previous page (thumbnail) **The Hotel Jardim Atlantico**
left **Cliff hugging villages**     above **Dolphin watching**

above **Deserted green peaks**   opposite (top) **Funchal market**   opposite (bottom) **Tobogganing Madeira style**

surrounded by a shoal of the friendly flippers. Plucking up the courage, I plopped into the deep water for the ultimate 'getting-in-touch-with-nature' experience. A few moments later, we spotted a passing family of pilot whales.

Watersports, such as surfing, scuba diving and canyoning thrive on the archipelago and draw a younger crowd of adrenaline junkies. Perceptions of Madeira can be

misleading – an exclusive blue rinse paradise it is not. In fact, with around 35 per cent of the population under 25 years old, there is plenty of buzz to be sought out in Funchal. After a sip or two of Poncha, the local hooch, however, I decided to head back to my hotel for an early last night, keen to hang on to my newly detoxed self just a little longer.

# Green menu

**Enjoy the island of flowers** Visit one of the many gardens filled with blooms of all varieties, including some species endemic to Madeira, such as the spiky Bird of Paradise.

**Make your own perfume** Iconic Reid's Palace holds perfume masterclasses, where guests venture into the extensive and exotic gardens to conjure up their own olfactory creations.

**Follow the ancients** Leave your compass behind – the ancient irrigation canals (*levadas*) running throughout the Laurisilva Forest will guide walkers into the more remote parts of the island for stunning hikes.

**Take a flying jump** For the more thrill-seeking, abseiling down waterfalls is not to be missed. Canyoning here is so good that the international meeting for the sport takes place on the main island every year.

**Slide away** Extinguish carbon footprints and travel by toboggan. The specially adapted road variety takes visitors on a thrilling route down from Monte to the centre of Funchal.

**Enjoy a glass of the vine divine** A trip to Madeira would not be complete without a sip or two of the sweet nectar. Blandy's Wine Lodge in Funchal holds tours of the cellars, lectures and tasting sessions on the 300-year history of Madeira wine.
**www.symingtonfamilyestate.com**

## When to go

Temperatures on Madeira range from 18°C in the winter to around 24°C in the summer, making it a great all year round destination.

## Contacts

**Hotel Porto Santo** Campo de Baixo 9400 015, Porto Santo, Madeira
**Tel:** +351 291 980 140
**Web:** www.hotelportosanto.com

**Hotel Jardim Atlantico** Lombo da Rocha, Prazeres P-9370 605, Calhepa, Madeira
**Tel:** +351 291 820 220
**Web:** www.jardimatlantico.com

**Madeira Promotion Bureau** Rua dos Aranhas, nº 24–26, 9000-044 Funchal , Portugal
**Web:** www.madeiraislands.travel

# MALLORCA
## Mallorca farmhouses

Over the years, I have visited Mallorca many times, but it wasn't until I stayed in one of its rural farmhouses that I experienced the real essence of life here. Of course the clues were always there, during outings to the picturesque villages of Deià – the artists' community – Sóller, famous for its hillside tram and majestic Palma with its grand cathedral that utterly dominates the harbour skyline. But they were just glimpses. I hadn't realised that there was a way to enjoy eternal flavours of Mallorcan life from the second I opened my eyes until the moment that I lay my head down.

### Son Font

The omens were good. Clear skies with air that dried the bones. We overshot the turning in Calvia and ended up asking a lady for directions in Capdella; she called to the shopkeeper, who abandoned his row of customers to come and help a stranger find her way. Up and up the hill we went, passing groves of olives and fig trees laden with ripe fruit. The second we drove through the gates the awareness was instantaneous. Real Mallorca.

You get the feeling that Son Font, built in 1730, has hardly changed over the centuries; it is still surrounded by 80 hectares of well-preserved, tranquil land given to nature and equestrian activities. Views are spectacular with the rim of the Serra de Traumantana Mountains to the east and the Mediterranean horizon to the south. You can see as far

as Ibiza at dusk, when the sun dips below the headland. By day, the western terrace is the optimum spot to enjoy the blue skies, climaxing in an extravagant sunset.

The estate owes its name to the springs on the property, which provide natural mineral water of the finest quality and straight from the tap. The peace is instantly soothing, with nothing nosier than the clicking of distant cicadas after dark. I slept with the doors wide open and at dawn opened my eyes to the view from the master suite spread across the courtyard to a gnarled olive tree, as old as the hills, to the silky waters of the bay.

Son Font is the ultimate choice for those seeking traditional Mallorca – ideal for extended families who can spread over the property, sharing two magnificent salt-water swimming pools and extensive grounds. The three fincas Traumantana, Vistamar and Sa Clastra hold individual charm and benefit hugely from the warm welcome from owners Helen and Kike Alabern and their three children who live in the main house and oversee the estate. It's like staying in your own private hotel with all the personal service without the throng.

Our finca, the three-bedroom Traumantana, a converted barn, was packed with Alabern family chattels – grand piano, billiard table, antique desks and paintings and a collection of Chinese lacquered furniture picked up during an ancestor's Occidental travels. On arrival the fridge was well stocked with fresh bread, ham, cheese, wine and a mound of ripe

above **Spectacular views across the Serra de Traumantana Mountains**

nectarines and plums. The children picked figs fresh from the trees each day as we worked off our delicious lunch by exploring the paths that criss-cross the estate, free to roam wherever we pleased.

Helen and Kike are keen to do as much as they can to preserve the pristine nature of the area. Recently installed solar paneling heats all the hot water, sourced from their own well. Grey water is re-processed and stored in an

artificial lake and used for irrigation. Food waste goes into composting or to feed the animals and glass, plastic and cardboard are taken to collection points as Mallorca currently has a very limited facility for recycling.

Mornings start on the terrace with a fresh coffee and *ensaimada* fresh from the bakery. Lazy days by the pool are de rigueur but tear yourself away and you are well placed to explore the stunning scenery around Calvia and, of course,

this page and opposite **The lovely Son Font estate in Calvia**

nearby Palma. Helen will give tailor-made recommendations to fit your interests, from a restaurant serving suckling pig to hidden coves only reachable by boat.

We found our perfect island home that week – lucky, as it was hard to choose from the dozens of rural retreats that were on offer.

# Green menu

**Enjoy unspoilt beaches** The nearest beach is a mere 10 minutes away but for something spectacular drive to Es Trenc in the southeast, where unspoilt sandy beaches stretch for miles.

**Visit the Wednesday market** Mallorca has a market for every day of the week. The best is unquestionably the Wednesday market in the centre of the island in historic Sineu (worth a visit in its own right). The stalls wrap around the square, along the side streets up to the church, selling local foods, leather goods and clothes. Locals come to sell their animals and enjoy a bowl of *frit* – a dish of potatoes, vegetables and offal.

**Explore La Granja** The 10th-century mansion La Granja, situated 15 kilometres from Palma and surrounded by lush gardens with natural fountains, offers a view through the ages. Dedicated to agricultural production, it is both rustic and stately. Its history dates from Roman times, with Moorish influence, occupied by the Cistercian Order for 200 years before being sold to Don Mateo Vida. There's a handcraft show of spinning, dying, lace making and folk dancing on Wednesday and Friday afternoons. The eclectic collection of rooms range from a bizarre doctor's study to well-stocked torture room in the cellar.

**Go boating** Hire a boat from Puerto Andratx and take it round the headline to St Telmo for lunch, stopping for a swim in one of the tranquil bays.

**Visit Palma** No visit to Mallorca would be complete without a day in Palma. Wander along cobbled streets and squares, packed to the gunnels with cafes, bars, boutiques, restaurants, art galleries and museums. The majestic cathedral is a must.

## When to go

Spain has a predominantly warm Mediterranean climate, with dry summers and winters with balanced temperatures. With more than 3,000 hours of sunshine per year, it is one of the warmest parts of Europe. Spring and autumn are ideal times when the weather is comfortably warm and prices are at their most competitive. Summer is the peak time with sun-soaked day after sun-soaked day with a breeze from the coast. The Serra de Traumuntana mountain range protects the rest of the island from the northerly winds often afflicting Menorca, although the winter months do see occasional rain.

## Contacts

**Mallorca Farmhouses** 38b Church Street, Reading, Berkshire, RG4 8AU
**Tel:** +44 (0) 845 800 8080
**Web:** www.mallorca.co.uk

Set up by Jim Thomas in 1986, Mallorca Farmhouses is one of those family success stories of which dreams are made. Jim started with one property and now has over 200 on the books. The thing they have in common is their roots; whether old or new build, all the properties are homes owned by Mallorquins, who are giving travellers a chance to experience real Mallorca. Jim's company policy is to be as green as possible, using local suppliers and produce and encouraging an eco-friendly mindset in all his clients. His overall desire is to protect a centuries-old way of life and to ensure that it continues into the future.

**Son Font**
**Rates:** From £975 per property per week.

# MALTA, GOZO AND COMINO

Rural tourism

In the middle of the Mediterranean is an archipelago of three islands – Malta, Gozo and Comino. They are steeped in history, boasting the oldest standing structures on the planet (Megalithic temples Ggantija that pre-date the Pyramids by 1,000 years). They also pride themselves on a marine legacy from Phoenician times, the evident tenure of the Knights of St John and a continuation of military history with a short stint under Napoleon. Just over 185 years of rule by the British has left its mark – not just in the use of the language and elements of the culture, but also in the George Cross, which was awarded to the islands for their people's bravery during the Second World War. The landscape may remind you of various film sets – *Troy*, *Popeye*, *The Count of Monte Christo* and *Gladiator* to name but a few were shot here, with more on the cards.

The appeal of Malta stretches way beyond historians and film-makers; it is true that there are towns typical of any mass holiday destination but, thankfully, these are seeing a slow but sure transformation to meet the rigorous demands of the Malta Tourism Authority's Eco Certification Scheme – a stepping stone to the EU-recognised Eco Label Scheme. The scheme has been tailor-made for the local market and is based on ensuring improved environmental performance, conservation and promotion of local produce and culture. Measures include targets for reduced waste generation, landscaping with

local plants, fertilizing using hotel-generated mulch and using rain and secondary water to irrigate gardens.

But measures aren't all about size. It often involves the simple solutions like the use of innovative steel tanks on hotel roofs using the sun to heat water – a cheaper alternative to traditional solar power – and solar glazing on south-facing windows that helps to keep rooms cool, thereby reducing the need for air conditioning. Some venues are even inviting customers to take the stairs instead of the lift.

The capital city, Valletta, deserving a book of its own, offers wanderers electric taxis for €1 to any destination within the city walls between 7 a.m. and 9 p.m. Public transport provides a local experience and the best way to see the country and enjoy the relaxed pace of life for a few cents. Just don't be on a tight schedule.

The smaller sister island of Gozo is leading the way with its take on agri-tourismo. With stringent planning regulations in place, the development of new buildings to cater for the growth in tourism is, thankfully, not on the horizon. Although there are 13 hotels on the official 'green' list, it is the AGER Foundation, a small, independent, not-for-profit outfit that prides itself on focusing public attention on safeguarding the natural environment, that offers the real eco stays. Its unique selling proposition is the people, the tradition of hospitality, the culture and the countryside and it looks to divert the heavily weighted density of tourists

above **The old walled capital of Mdina**    opposite **Traditional organic farming**

from the traditional commercial resorts primarily on the coast, to the countryside and all it has to offer. Run by volunteers passionate about promoting sustainable rural development, predominantly on the island of Gozo, it has harvested a selection of farmers and the like to introduce traditional activities to tourists, who can opt to stay in farmhouses or visit for the day from the mainland.

Don't be put off by its less-than-glossy website, the Foundation is very professional and offers experiences as described and rural accommodation in a variety of villages at a very low cost. Its activities (for which they will collect you by horse and trap from the ferry terminal or from your farmhouse) generally cost less than €10 for children and €20 for adults.

Having tried a few of them, I can highly recommend having a go at what I called 'Shepherd's Delight', a day tending, feeding and herding sheep and goats, with the chance of shearing in the spring or making delicious

Gozitan cheese. Moreish and eaten with fresh Maltese bread, sun-dried, salted or peppered, it is a welcome reward after a day in the fields. Other trips include fishing in a traditional 'dghajsa'. The skipper introduces the various techniques of bait- and finger-fishing, with hopes of catching rainbow wrasse, blue damselfish, grouper and many other seasonal fish, which you are able to take home or barbeque on the rocks with just a squeeze of lemon picked from the fisherman's garden on idyllic Comino. And if you need a bit of salt and a few vegetables, head out one morning on a trip to pick herbs and collect salt from the natural salt planes.

below **Elegant accommodation in Mdina**    opposite (top) **Balconies in Valletta**

# Green menu

**Be at one with nature** Join the enthusiasts at AGER on guided walks, climbs and bird- and nature-watching days.
**Join the Gozo carnival** The annual carnival theme is 'grotesque' with no-holds-barred – thousands of Maltese descend on the village of Nadur in early February to scare and stare and party till dawn. Children get time off school to partake in the spectacle, which has a more cheerful and colourful aspect on Malta.
**Feast and have fun** Religious fiestas take place almost every weekend in the summer and are celebrated with flags flying from homes, band clubs and evening street parades, culminating in spectacular firework displays. The best seem to fall in August – Birgu celebrates the Feast of St Lawrence on the 10th, the feast of Santa Maria on the 15th, a national holiday best seen in Mosta. The liveliest is the feast of Saint Julian, held in the nightclub capital of St Julian's on the last day of the month. The build up and wind down cover the two weeks around the actual saint's day and the spirit and excitement amongst the villagers is utterly infectious.
**Celebrate Victory Day** The end of the Great Siege by the Ottoman Turks in 1565 falls on September 8th, also the anniversary of the end of the Second World War. Celebrations take place in the Grand Harbour in Valletta with canon fire, re-enactments and a rowing regatta. The gardens, bastions and tourist boats are packed with spectators – and it's well worth a visit.

## When to go

The nocturnal and spiritual would enjoy Malta during the high season of July and August, whereas those wishing to see or 'do' Malta are advised to visit in spring or late summer when the temperature allows you to make the most of your stay.

## Contacts

**AGER Foundation**
**Web:** www.agerfoundation.com
**Rates:** Available on request.

**Maltese Tourist Authority** Auberge D'Italie, Merchants Street, Valletta VLT 1170, Malta
**Tel:** +356 2291 5000, +356 2291 5148
**Web:** www.visitmalta.com

# MOZAMBIQUE
Guludo Beach Lodge, Vamizi Island and Lugenda, Nassa Reserve

After 25 years of civil war, 1990's Mozambique did not feature in many people's travel plans. Since then, the country has undergone a cathartic renaissance and tourism has played a defining role in its post-war culture. Nowhere is this truer than in the north of the country, which is at the cutting edge of its low-impact, eco-friendly tourism policy.

## Guludo Beach Lodge

The Quirimbas National Park and Archipelago, given international recognition at the request of the local people in 2002, is the ideal place to start. The award-winning Guludo Beach Lodge is the only lodge on a 12-kilometre-long stretch of beach that separates the African bush from the Indian Ocean and offers quintessential grass-roots eco tourism.

Its founder, Amy Carter, set up the lodge with fiancé Neal upon leaving university, and their gallant efforts won her the New Statesman 'Young Social Entrepreneur of the Year 2006'. Although at the time she did not know what social entrepreneurship was, she was, nevertheless, delighted to discover that a label existed for her pioneering vision of tourism.

Nine individual bandas peek out along the fringes of the beach, their private verandas hung with hammocks and raised beds boasting sublime sea views. The Makuti palm thatch, painted mud walls and rustic furniture are all built by a local workforce under the direction of a master craftsman. The design philosophy is that the lodge would leave no trace if it were ever to close so the camp runs on solar energy and, instead of running water, hot water is delivered to your bamboo shower twice a day and the enviro-loos boast not only a sea view, but also turn solid waste to compost.

Ninety per cent of the staff come from the local village and the daily menu is dictated by what the local fishermen catch, so high winds can mean lots of crab and squid. Not ideal for carnivores, but vegetarians can be happily accommodated.

The best part of a stay here comes when you interact with the local people. Neal very nearly became a professional footballer, so a weekly highlight is the football match between hotel guests and staff and the local village team. The kids hang from trees and most of the village roars its approval at the side of the dirt pitch.

Five per cent of your bill goes to running NEMA, the charity Amy has set up to help the surrounding villages with water projects, medical infrastructure and education. The lodge also runs its own carbon-offset scheme. The money will go directly to a local farmer who will be planting and tending the corresponding number of trees. Any leftover funds are funnelled into NEMA.

'People are coming here because they're really interested in what we're doing. One of the most rewarding things is when guests tell us they have changed the way they think about holidays. It gives you goose bumps', says Amy.

## Vamizi island

For hot running water and the height of Mozambique luxury, you need to fly out into the archipelago to the island of Vamizi. Like Guludo on the mainland, the waters around Vamizi are home to some of the most exquisite coral reefs in the Indian Ocean and both lodges offer sublime diving and snorkelling opportunities. Vamizi is said to be one of the world's top 10 dive sites.

Yet, while Guludo is down-to-earth, Vamizi is more stylishly luxurious. Ten separate beach houses, two of which can sleep four, come with large living rooms, hand-carved screens, marble bathrooms and four-poster beds draped in muslin mosquito nets. Constructed almost entirely with local materials, the lodge has been designed to melt into the environment and, inside, you can melt into the deep cane couches on the oversized verandas and marvel at this private island paradise.

Flashes of indigo are a common interior refrain, reflecting the island's colourful history; for centuries the islanders wove cloth and dyed it with local indigo, giving the name of the cloth, Maluane, to this small island chain. Vamizi is 12 kilometres long and 1.5 kilometres wide with six different beaches on the island and a small fishing village on the west coast, so it is almost big enough to get happily lost.

While it could perhaps have pushed its eco initiative further with more use of solar power and grey water, Vamizi has built a dispensary and funded a new school building on the mainland. It was voted the best new safari property in Africa by the Good Safari Awards in 2008.

## Lugenda, Niassa Reserve

Both Vamizi and Guludo are building sister Bush properties (Vamizi's on the neighbouring mainland) but you have to penetrate the north-western corner of the country for a real safari experience. At 42,000 square kilometres, the Niassa reserve is the third largest in the world.

A vast hideout during the civil war, in its aftermath the area was plundered by unscrupulous hunters. There are no rhinos left and other game species were decimated, but conservation efforts since 2001 have reaped rewards.

right **Deserted beach at Galudo**

above **Villa accommodation at Galudo**

The landscape is a vast wilderness punctuated by giant 1,000 metre-high magma inselbergs. It is thick African bush rather than savannah grasslands, so it really is a true wilderness experience.

Right in the heart of the park on the banks of the 800-metre-wide Lugenda riverbed sits Lugenda, the first eco tourism project in the entire reserve. It opened in 2007 and has eight very stylish tents, with leather-bound trunks, four-poster beds and terraces to watch the early-morning monkey show. As the sun rises, we were woken by figs crashing onto canvas as the hundreds of monkeys above us leapt through the trees.

Other concessions so far have all been for hunting, and South Africans Steve, Kim and Andrew are pioneering the eco-friendly development. They are still busy cutting new game-drive roads and have not even begun to explore all of their 625 square kilometres. Their excitement about the area's potential is infectious.

For me, the high point was looking out across the landscape having trekked up one of the vast inselbergs; as we watched elephants move through the bush, I realised we were the only people for as far as the eye could see. Now there's an experience worth fighting for.

# Green menu

## GULUDO

**Explore the coral reef** Dive and snorkel the pristine coral with myriad angelfish and learn about local coral conservation with PADI instructors who moonlight as marine biologists.

**Whalewatch** Spot humpback whales on their migratory trails between July and October.

**Play football with the locals** Pull on the number nine shirt or just join the villagers to watch the hotel staff take on the local football team.

**Pamper yourself local-style** Indulge yourself in 'beauty- on-the-beach' treatments, such as massages and hair braiding. Local women can teach you how to apply face masks used to prevent sunburn and to signify a virgin bride.

**Meet the locals** Take a tour of the village, learn how to pound cassava, the local flour, and meet characters like the tailor '19', so-called because he has 10 toes and only nine fingers.

## VAMIZI

**Go sport fishing** Cast your line for some adrenalin-fuelled 'tag and release' sport fishing; marlin, sailfish, tuna and wahoo are plentiful in the local waters. If flyfishing floats your boat, knuckle under and pit your wits against the local trevally and Spanish mackerel.

**Dhow about kayaking?** Take to the seas in a traditional dhow for a sunset cruise. If you want to get more hands-on, check out the sea-kayaking around the bays.

**Spot turtles and whales** Not only can you spot the humpback whale migration (July to October), but turtles are plentiful around these waters between July and April. Stay dry on board or snorkel and dive with the fish.

**Go birdwatching** Full-blown twitchers and amateur birders alike will love the guided trails through the marshy reserve, home to 112 bird species.

## LUGENDA

**Explore new territory** This area is so unexplored the rangers are still cutting new game routes. Check out this real safari wilderness and help familiarise the big cats to the sights and sounds of the jeeps.

**Climb the inselbergs** As the morning sun rises on your back trek up giant inselbergs to help determine which way the elephants are heading and see who's been spending the night high up under the stars.

**Canoeing and fishing** Paddle upstream in the rough-hewn canoe to visit the local fishing camp for lessons in traditional fishing techniques.

---

## Contacts

**Guludo** Quirimbas National Park, Mozambique
**Tel:** +44 (0) 13 2376 6655
**Web:** www.guludo.com
**Rates:** From US$225 per person per night, including all meals, no drinks.

**Vamizi** Vamizi Island, Mozambique
**Tel:** +27 11 884 8869
**Web:** www.maluane.com
**Rates:** From US$560 per person per night, including meals, local beer, house wine and soft drinks.

**Lugenda** Niassa Wildlife Reservation, Mozambique
**Tel:** +27 11 467 1277
**Web:** www.raniresorts.com
**Rates:** From US$344 per person per night, including meals and drinks.

## When to go

Guludo and Vamizi are open year-round, peak seasons being August and December. Lugenda is closed during the rainy season from December to April, but rains on the coast are usually short intermittent showers with temperatures in the high 30°Cs. Dry-season temperatures hover around 28°C with an annual sea temperature between 26–30°C.

# NAMIBIA
Wilderness Safaris and Wolwedans

Say the word Namibia to anyone who has travelled to this former German colony and you will be amazed by the size of the smile that transforms their face and the enthusiasm with which they ask, 'have you been there too?' Namibia is a destination that invariably excites and delights its visitors. It infects them with a desire to return again and again.

Lying between South Africa and Angola, Namibia is a big country in all respects but population – only 2.1 million people in a country four times the size of the UK. It boasts breathtaking, southern landscapes that present enormous pristine vistas. Tall, stark mountains push up into clear, deep, azure-blue skies, lines of red dunes stretch across the oldest desert in the world, and wild, cold seas confront the magnificent Skeleton Coast. The country's tropical north with encircling grasslands is home to an abundance of wildlife, some species found nowhere else in the world. Alongside live the San Bushmen together with the Herero and the Himba, one of the last nomadic, hunter-gatherer peoples left on the planet. Nature is king in Namibia and Man is only a visitor in much of this wonderful country.

Tourism in Namibia is being developed intelligently. Government-run wildlife reserves such as Etosha, where you can see every type of African game (except hippo and buffalo) and privately owned reserves like the Hanssen family's famous Africat at Okonjima, with its leopard and cheetah rehabilitation programmes, are being developed as some of the most environmentally responsible destinations in the world.

## Wilderness Safaris

Wilderness Safaris have been particularly successful in developing lodges in partnership with many Namibian communities. On my first trip to Namibia I visited Damaraland camp, one of the oldest and most successful of such joint ventures. On the edge of the Huab valley, in the Torra conservancy, the camp offers really comfortable, en-suite, tented accommodation and truly delicious local food. I was impressed by the enthusiasm with which the staff from the local community welcomed us, their pride in their camp and their genuine commitment to the preservation of the wonderful semi-desert flora and fauna. Guests and staff singing together around an open fire in the evening, under a clear, bright, starry sky was an experience I will never forget. The early morning mists, which extend inland from the Skeleton Coast made for a chilly start to game viewing, but we were rewarded with sightings of both elephant and rhino, which find good forage in the valleys of ephemeral rivers like the Huab. Animals roam long distances so sightings are never guaranteed, but guides will show you the amazing adaptation of their food plants to the harsh local environment.

above **A lone oryx at Wolwedans**   opposite **Astonishing colours of a desert landscape**

In addition to their joint community ventures like Damaraland, Wilderness Safari's many other successful camps and lodges throughout Southern Africa have helped to fund their award-winning education programme, Children in the Wilderness. To date, more than 7,000 children from urban areas have been introduced to their own wildlife heritage through weeks spent at Wilderness properties. Game drives, boating and walking safaris build the children's confidence and self esteem and an understanding of the environment comes naturally.

## Wolwedans, Namib Rand Nature Reserve

Namibian tourism's inspiring eco credentials are also clearly demonstrated in Wolwedans. The privately owned 180,000-hectare Namib Rand nature reserve, in the centre-south of the country, was established by native-born Namibians, Albi and Stephan Bruckner, from their

family's former sheep farm and surrounding territory. The conservation of Wolwedans' fragile semi-desert eco system owes a great deal to their vision of sustainable tourism and intense desire both to share it with like-minded tourists and to provide employment for local people. Converting farmland to conservancy requires hard work as well as dreams and, since the removal of miles of unwanted farm fencing and unused buildings, game now migrates freely and the natural landscape has been restored across this award-winning reserve.

Visitors can fly in to a private landing strip, but we drove the 487 kilometres (five hours) south from Windhoek into the heart of the Namib Naukluft area. Twenty kilometres off the C27 gravel road you reach the main farmhouse reception area, where an instant, warm welcome confirms your status as a new member of the Wolwedans family. You meet a local guide, assigned specifically to you, whose

expertise and knowledge will unravel the secrets of the area during your stay.

The Dune Lodge is perched on a red dune plateau in an area so untouched that you feel that no one could possibly have breathed in the air before it reaches your nostrils. The guest chalets are solid, wooden structures with canvas walls that roll up to allow uninterrupted views of the desert or the night sky. Perched on stilts, each offers full bathroom facilities, an indoor and outdoor sitting area with chairs or loungers and a huge bed with a sumptuous duvet, which positively hugs you to sleep. Solar panels provide water heating for each room so showers are hot. Wooden walkways connect with the central area, complete with 'sundowner' deck and open fire, ideal for enjoying a civilised drink and good conversation. There is also a well-stocked, library, plus two dining rooms, a sundeck and a pool.

The food, sourced locally, is outstandingly good and there is an impressive wine cellar built into the cool sand of the dunes. Staff are like extended family and chef presents his menu in person each night, in English and one or more of the local languages, including those with 'clicks'. Everything at Wolwedans is exquisitely prepared and executed. Nothing is superfluous; it is the epitome of elegant, but sustainable, tourism.

Our guide, Samuel, took us on scenic game drives in a comfortable, specially adapted vehicle. The desert is surprisingly full of game. There are plenty of zebra, ostrich, oryx and springbok, but you should not ignore the raptors – battaleur eagle, pale chanting goshawk – and smaller creatures like the sociable weaver birds, which build huge nests like hayricks in the occasional trees found in the landscape. Chameleons, lizards and the mischievous ground squirrels scuttle along the ground.

However, it is the landscape that is the star at Wolwedans: you will explore deep, remote valleys, rich with vegetation and the sound of baboons or you may stand on a dune ridge looking out over vast plains of semi-desert with no other human in sight. It is a rocky wonderland where you truly feel at one with nature at its most unspoiled.

There is no 'them and us'. Everyone shares experiences, conversation and a sense of wonder at the privilege of being at one with nature in this untouched environment. Achieving this quality of apparently effortless hospitality and relaxed gentility must say a great deal about Stephan Bruckner's vision and leadership. Wolwedans is a place to recharge all your senses and you will want to return to this most civilised of places in its truly wild environment.

below **A room with a view**

# Green menu

### DAMARALAND CAMP

**Track elephants** The most exciting thing is tracking the desert-adapted elephant in the river valleys. In the mornings, mist that has rolled in from the skeleton coast provides moisture for drought-tolerant plant species. A walking safari with a local guide will give you an enthusiasm for botany to rival a Namibian David Bellamy.

### WOLWEDANS

**Walk the Toktokkie Trail** Take a walking camping safari within the reserve. Named after the local beetles, a two-day walking safari, with one night camped under the stars, will really give you a sense of the scale of the landscape and the range of micro-vegetation systems in the rocky ravines (kloofs) and on the open, gravel plains.
**www.trailhopper.com**

**Watch the stars** Roll up your chalet walls and star gaze from the warmth of your bed, curled up with a hot chocolate. You'll never have a better opportunity to see constellations like the Southern Cross or Draco, than in the clear desert skies. Bring a star map and your best binoculars.

**Check out the desert chefs** Stephan Bruckner's latest venture is the Namibian Institute of Culinary Education (NICE). Located in Windhoek, NICE is a great place to eat. The school not only provides training for prospective chefs and workers in Namibia's growing tourist industry but gives young people the prospect of quality jobs of which they can be proud. If you go back home through Windhoek, check it out.
**www.nice.com.na**

## Contacts

**Namibia Tourism Board**
Web: www.namibiatourism.com.na

**Wilderness Safaris** Cnr Schinz and Merensky Street, Ausspannplatz, Windhoek, Namibia
**Tel:** +264 61 274 500
**Web:** www.wilderness-safaris.com
**Rates:** From US$300 per person per night sharing, fully inclusive.

**WOLWEDANS**
**Wolwedans Dune Camp** Windhoek, Namibia
**Tel:** +264 61 230 616
**Web:** www.wolwedans.com
**Rates:** From US$280 per night. All fees include park fees but exclude guide fees; minimum two-night stay for all accommodation.

## When to go

There is no bad time to visit Namibia, but the country is at its hottest from December to February and the north is at its wettest. My favourite times are spring and autumn, when daytime temperatures are lower, although evenings can be chilly.

# NEW ZEALAND

## Release Eco Retreat

New Zealand is a country of vast open spaces where you can drive uninterrupted for miles, witnessing a stunning range of diversity from glorious, empty beaches and steamy, sulphur-laden geothermals to rugged mountains and extraordinary animal and plant life. Fantastic activities, such as ice-climbing on South Island's Franz Josef Glacier or horse riding in the foothills of the Kaikoura Ranges abound, while walking in the Waipoua Forest on the far tip of North Island, among some of the largest trees in the world, is little short of a spiritual experience.

It is no surprise, then, that New Zealand's unsullied natural environment is one of its main draws for foreign visitors and one that it is keen to protect, as illustrated by the government's '100 per cent Pure New Zealand' campaign, launched in 1999. One third of the country is protected for conservation, with new national parks opening every year to encourage controlled and responsible tourism throughout the whole country.

In fact, concern for the environment is no new thing for New Zealand. The Maori concept of 'Kaitiakitanga' sees human beings as the guardians of the world, assisting the gods and the ancestral spirits in preserving and protecting the environment, which also includes cultural elements such as art and language. Kaitiakitanga is a holistic philosophy that aims to deliver the planet to future generations with its 'mana' intact.

### Release Eco Retreat

Fulfilling the pure ethos is Release, a stunning new eco retreat in the Central Otago area of New Zealand's South Island, the brainchild of 'the two Nicks', Frame and Hay, who met in 2002 while diving with whale sharks in Honduras. Fast friends and three years later, after a stint in Colorado, they came back to New Zealand in 2005 to start creating their vision for a series of 'ultimate lifestyle retreats'.

In their search for a location, they lit upon the Wanaka area of South Island and managed to secure a plot of land on an elevated site away from the well-known tourist honey pots of the Central Otago area. It enjoys a surprising degree of anonymity and, with an 80-metre frontage, the spot they chose enjoys the most beautiful views out over the lake and the mountains. In addition, and very importantly in a setting this far south, it enjoys plenty of sun and supports its own warm, little microclimate.

The Nicks chose their architect, Marc Scaife, and together they fine-tuned the contemporary design that is now the first Release retreat. Their fingerprints are literally all over the project – Nick Hay being the master craftsman and Nick Frame the 'lowly plumber, gas-fitter and drain-layer'.

The main structure is an impressive steel-and-timber frame with cedar cladding. The front deck is elevated three metres from the ground looking out to Black Peak and the Mount Aspiring National Park. The vision was to create a

sustainable retreat that would last a lifetime. Details such as a passive solar design means that there is little need for heating and there are countless water- and energy-efficient features such as storm-water catchment, wool insulation, grey-water irrigation and argon-filled windows.

The house can accommodate up to six adults in three separate suites. It has a stunning, central living area, kitchen, deck and hot tub and comes with a full concierge service that will arrange a vast range of adventures as well as food and wine.

All the design features ensure that this is a total New Zealand experience, from the custom-built furniture, cool

above **Living room with stunning, all-round views**
opposite **The continental climate of Central Otago's Rippon Vineyard produces wines with a subtly different character**

home wares, eye-catching art work and organic skin-care products right down to the carpets and tea-towels.

The Nicks describe themselves as 'just two blokes having a go and trying to do the right thing'. Their aspirations for business are not huge but they want to make a difference. They treat their guests with a hands-on approach, openly sharing their Wanaka secrets, from riding in the Sticky Forest to revealing where the trout hide. Next step, plans for Release 2 are afoot. I can't wait.

right **The walk up Mount Roy will make your legs ache, but the view is worth every step**

# Green menu

**Visit the southern lakes** The Southern Lakes are one of the most diverse and beautiful regions in New Zealand from dramatic landscapes of Fiordland in the south, to the rugged mountains, Queenstown and Lake Wanaka in the north.

**Hike, bike, climb, sail or walk** Part of the Te Wahipounamu World Heritage Area, Lake Wanaka lies at the gateway to Mount Aspiring National Park, a pristine environment of striking mountains and deep alpine lakes, where hikers, mountaineers, rock climbers and day walkers enjoy the area's spectacular natural beauty on foot, bike and boat.

**Walk the Rob Roy Glacier** Climb an easy track through forest to alpine meadows, dominated by the awe-inspiring Rob Roy Hanging Glacier, just one hour's drive from Lake Wanaka and a three-hour walk through the foothills of the Southern Alps. See jaw-dropping waterfalls and watch and listen as sections of the constantly moving glacier break away and shatter as they tumble 300 metres down the mountainside.

**Go fly fishing** The Lake Wanaka region offers an impressive variety of angling opportunities, boasting three major lakes, a host of small, still waters and a number of quality streams and rivers, from small, snow-fed streams to the mighty Clutha river – New Zealand's second longest, which flows 340 kilometres before it reaches the Pacific Ocean. Many of the high country rivers contain some of the clearest water in the world where rainbow and brown trout are easy to spot but not always easy to catch.

**Climb to the top** Lake Wanaka is the rock-climbing capital of New Zealand and renowned by climbers from all over the world. There are literally hundreds of routes with the main area being the spectacular Matukituki Valley on the edge of Mount Aspiring National Park. Hire a private guide to explore this amazing area and enjoy a gourmet picnic lunch off the beaten track, surrounded by soaring rock faces and the calls of the kea (alpine parrot).
**www.wanakarock.co.nz**

**Cruise and walk** Cruise by boat to the magical Mou Wahu Island in the middle of Lake Wanaka, then take a guided bushwalk to the serene Arethusa Pools for lake and alpine views. Experienced guides share their knowledge of local history as well as the beautiful native plant and birdlife, including the endangered buff weka that inhabits the island.
**www.ecowanaka.co.nz, www.dualimage.co.nz**

**Sup a sip of wine** Central Otago is renowned for its excellent wines and the shores of Lake Wanaka are the location of the world-famous Rippon Vineyard, arguably one of the most beautiful settings for a vineyard anywhere in the world. Fully organic, Rippon does not use herbicides, fungicides, pesticides or soluble nitrogenous fertilisers on the property and all its organic waste is recycled. Enjoy a wine tasting looking out over the vines to the lake and mountains beyond.
**www.rippon.co.nz**

**Ski the slopes** Lake Wanaka is home to four international ski areas, Cardrona, Treble Cone, Snow Farm and Snow Park, with something for everybody from powder to terrain parks, cross-country to downhill.
**www.cardrona.com, www.treblecone.com, www.snowfarmnz.com, www.snowparknz.com**

# When to go

New Zealand lies in the 'roaring 40s' latitude, with prevailing winds from west to east; ranging from a gentle breeze in summer to a buffeting gale in winter. The Southern Alps act as a barrier for the moisture-laden winds from the Tasman Sea, creating a wet climate to the west of the mountains and a dry climate to the east. Its maritime climate means the weather can change with amazing rapidity and consequence. October to March is usually the best time to go.

# Contacts

**Release Private Retreat** 9 Mount Gold Place, Penrith Park, Wanaka, New Zealand
**Tel:** +64 21 762 695
**Web:** www.releasenz.com
**Rates:** From US$596 per night for the whole house, including a welcome pack for your first breakfast and a few local treats.

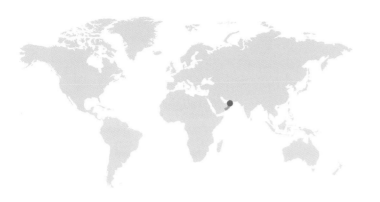

# OMAN

Bedouin camping and Zighy Bay Hideaway

In tourism terms, Oman is something of a newcomer to the international market and, unlike neighbouring Dubai, is taking it all at a dignified pace, preferring to protect her heritage before rushing headlong into development. This is good news for eco tourism as 90 per cent of hotels remain owned by nationals and the power of the tourist pound goes directly into local communities.

'Oman is only 38-years-old', said Ali our 28-year-old driver and guide, as we passed Muscat's polished cars and white, low-line horizon of shops and houses. 'Prior to that, it was a collection of individual states.' Today's Oman is ruled by a much-loved sultan who selects his own ministers but allows a democratic process for selecting mayors and local councils.

Much of the country's history lies inland, which can only be accessed by car or on foot as there is no railway network and most roads are under a decade old. There is a network of local buses (with very posh bus stop shelters) across the country but most people travel in shiny, white cars.

Ali showed great pride pointing out the school building in every village – understandable when you consider that in 1970 there were only three government, male-only, primary schools in the whole country. In just under 40 years, that has risen to over a thousand, educating girls as well as boys. It seems that 21st-century Oman has developed into a progressive country while managing to honour its Islamic traditions.

## So what of green?

Food throughout the country is sourced locally with fish – caught along the 1,700 kilometres of coast – dates, goat's milk and meat providing the nutritious mainstay diet.

In terms of power, although it's unlikely to replace gas while it remains so economical, the Omani government is actively researching sources of renewable energy, including solar and wave power.

Oman's buildings are generally traditional, two-storey, whitewashed villas constructed in a time-honoured style, surrounded by walled courtyards and palm groves. And the sultan who wishes to protect his people's way of life is adopting a sensitive approach to new building.

However, to capture the full joy of Omani eco, camping Bedouin-style is the ultimate experience…

## Touring the country Bedouin-style

The southern slopes of the Hajar Mountains, which drop from heights of over 3,000 metres straight into the warm Gulf, are famous for their oasis villages and flourishing date groves. They are in stark contrast to the spectacular sand dunes of the sparsely populated Wahiba desert. Slightly larger than Italy, with fewer than three million inhabitants, we saw more goats than people.

The scenic, rugged coast south of Muscat is laced with deep sapphire waters entwined with coves hiding white,

sandy beaches stretching the length of Oman. It's a hot, arid and unforgiving shoreline but exceedingly beautiful. The coppery glint of the Al Hajar morphs into a lunar landscape of truncated mounds followed by shiny, white boulders of gypsum. Just after the fishing village of Quriyat, you'll see the first of many natural phenomena that make the area a geologist's dream – a vast limestone crater, known as the Bimah sinkhole and filled with blue-green water and curious little fish that come and tickle cooling toes.

A little further on, we glimpsed shy, flat-footed gazelles darting below the watchful eyes of several black eagles and a flock of Egyptian vultures. Some 300 kilometres south of Muscat, the seafaring town of Sur, renowned for its dhow-building, is worth a stop. At its zenith, it operated a fleet of over a hundred great ocean-faring dhows that sailed between India and Zanzibar. You can still spot dozens nodding gently in the ocean bringing in the dawn catch.

West of Sur lies the vast Wahiba desert of undulating sand, rising up to 200 metres. An off-road, roller-coaster ride across the waves of the ever-changing pattern of dunes towards the Desert Nights Camp had us all screaming with excitement. Later, I sat in my cotton-cloth tent listening to the children running down the side of the adjacent dune in the pitch black. It is so quiet in this valley of sand that voices are magnified – I could hear every syllable over 300 metres away. Unused as we are to absolute stillness, its eerie abnormality exaggerated my internal senses.

*above and right* **The Wahiba Desert**

left **Wadi Oasis**    above **Zighy Bay villa pool at sunset**

Each square tent, approximately five square metres with one central pole, had two cast-iron beds covered by a thin but comfortable foam mattress, a pillow and a counterpane. A tapestry of kelims, carpets and sarongs covered the sandy ground. It's an empty space – just 15 tents with a number pinned to each flap on one side of the wire-enclosed compound. We squatted cross-legged round hexagonal tables to eat rice, chicken and goat kebabs and regaled the company with the day's activities. At the centre, a raised deck with cushions and carpets beckoned for stargazing and once the generator was switched off, there wasn't a hint of light pollution for miles. The only sound was the rise and fall of our own breath and the slip-slip of Ali's shoes on the sand.

All slept soundly until sunrise, when the early-morning rays turned the inside of the tent rose pink, then showered in water drawn from the well and drip-dried in the sun. Just outside the enclosure were various tracks made in the night; antelope, birds of prey and snakes had all left their telltale prints.

We met up with a Bedouin tribe exercising their camels and followed them some way taking in the flora and fauna of the desert. You can choose to ride their camels; drive up and down the vertiginous dunes to terrifying effect or be

still and take in the vast space and pure peace of the dunes. Goodbyes were said Bedouin-style – by shaking hands and touching noses like an Eskimo.

In stark contrast to the arid desert are the small villages embedded into the mountain around Wadi Bani Khalid's emerald waters. We dived off rocks into the cool oasis lake to the sound of longhaired goats bleating contentedly as they quenched their thirst. A more pastoral scene is impossible to imagine. From here it was north again, passing through Ibra – famous for its Wednesday morning 'women only' market – and the stunning abandoned village of Birkat al Mawz. We stopped in the ancient capital Nizwa to admire the elaborate filigree work on the silver kanjar daggers being sold in the recently renovated souq and enjoyed the banter and bartering of locals in the fruit and vegetable market.

A stretch of winding road took us to the jewel of the Al Hajar mountains. Our ears popped as we climbed over 3,000 metres to the summit of Jebel Al Akhdar, the highest region in the Arabian Peninsular. The temperature fell with each vertical kilometre, passing dappled paths leading through terraced farms fed by ice-cold water running through the *falaj*. Wild juniper, peach, orange, apricot and grapevines clung to the slopes against all odds. Up above,

above **Much of Oman's heritage lies along its 1,700 kilometres of shoreline**

a panoramic view of cascading shadows across a giant canyon; down below, fascinating marine fossils embedded in black rocks under gnarled shrubbery.

The other side of Jebel Akhdar, slightly more accessible from Muscat, is in many ways even more dramatic. We wound our way through Wadi Mistal up towards the steeped terraces of the cliff-top Wakan village. The path to the top seemed endless, climbing hundreds of steps through sweet-smelling limes, date palms and pomegranates but the view was surely worth the puff.

Back in the valley another new experience awaited. Yes, we'd admired the desert from all angles but nothing could have prepared us for trekking along the bed of the vast white-pebbled Wadi Abhyad, stopping to admire the sulphur sedimentation and the hundreds of bubbling rock pools of fish. High drama indeed and another altogether different taste of Oman.

### Zighy Bay, Six Senses Hideaway

Further north along the coast lies the Musandam Peninsula. No surprise that this is where Six Senses have chosen to locate their stunning eco Hideaway. Zighy Bay is set in seclusion between the crystal-clear Gulf of Oman and the Hajar Mountains, an area often referred to as the 'Norway of the Middle East' due to its fjord-like landscape. It's of great geological interest due to its exposure of fossils, hidden in the mountains, which are made up of old coral and sediments that were once the sea bed.

Renowned for its marine environment, the coast offers excellent diving and snorkelling. As well as colourful fish and corals, the Gulf of Oman is also home to green turtles, humpback dolphins, hammerhead sharks and the largest fish in the sea, the plankton-feeding whale shark.

The 79 pool villas at Zighy Bay are a blend of the surrounding traditional Omani village style, combined with luxury, modern amenities. They offer a spacious environment with rustic chic décor, and the Gulf's first eco boutique hotel, which blends well with its surroundings, was built according to old Omani traditional style. The staff is proud of their environmental management system and hope to contribute to the sustainable development of the local community. A good template for things to come.

# Green menu

**Go fishing** With over 1,700 kilometres of shoreline, much of Oman's heritage and culture is attached to its sea. You can catch a 'big' fish just minutes from the mainland. Cast your line for a giant grouper, tuna or trevally from the ocean floor 200 metres below. The government runs a 'common sense' designated fishing season to ensure that stocks are not depleted. Free divers without oxygen harvest abalone (a mussel type of shellfish worth £100 kilo) only in November. At Six Senses, a catch-and-release system is in place for all fish that is caught.

**Step into another world** Elaborate forts, castles and watch towers punctuate the land. Step inside (you'll probably have the place to yourself) and imagine life in a desert oasis.

**Follow the route of millennia** Watch the tadpoles swim along the beautifully engineered *falaj* surface canals that have watered Oman's crops for millennia, threading through villages, along precipitous cliff faces bringing life to parched lands.

**Settle into market life** Enjoy a cup of local *kahwa* (coffee) with some fresh dates. Buy some bukhoor incense from the market to burn in a clay dish.

**Swim outdoors** Swimming in an oasis is not something you can do every day.

**Go sightseeing** From Zighy Bay, head for Fujairah, pausing at Bidiyah to admire the oldest mosque in the United Arab Emirates. Then move on to the Friday Market in Masafi, and on into the canyons, uphill along winding roads, to reach an altitude of 1,100 metres to visit ancient stone houses that show the utilitarian way of life lived many centuries ago.

**Cycle Khab al Shamsi** Wadi Khab Al Shamsi near Zighy Bay offers the keen mountain biker some of the best technical trails in the region. Cycle the hard dirt track that winds its way up Rus Al Jebel. The trail passes many ancient stone settlements and dramatic cliffs as it steadily climbs higher.

## When to go

Oman is best visited between September and May. The months between June and August are particularly hot. Rainfall varies according to the region but stays low throughout the year.

## Contacts

For more information on Oman and rates contact:
**Oman Tourist Office**
**Tel:** +44 (0) 20 8877 4524
**Web:** www.omantourism.gov.om

# THE PHILIPPINES

El Nido, Palawan

When you enter your tropical paradise luxury beach chalet, you are usually shown the mini bar and an array of enticing freebies lining the designer bathroom, but here we were shown a row of brown paper bags laid out over the bed. 'This one, the 'Eco-Nido bag', you can take home; it's for all the rubbish you have brought with you,' says Mary, who, like most of the staff, is local. 'This one is to carry with you during your stay to collect things from the beaches' – she's not talking pretty shells (strictly *verboten*) – 'plastic bags look like tasty jelly fish to turtles, but it's their last supper,' she explains. The El Nido Resort collects nearly a ton of non-biodegradable stuff this way each year. Another bag, the 'buri bag', made from recyclable polyethylene, is for use during our activities around the resort (in case, I suppose, you suddenly feel self-conscious about the eco credentials of your own beach bag). Next on the tour, it's the bathroom, not for more bags, but an explanation on recycled water and the desalination and sewage treatment plants. Stealing a second, I notice that the freebies are in delicate ceramics with ill-fitting corks – no chance of taking those home.

Lecture over, I lie back in bed and gawp at the view in front of me. Nature as outstanding as this, will inspire you to sacrifice anything in order to preserve it – it's quite possibly the most beautiful place on earth. El Nido is one of a string of 45 tiny tropical islands afloat in the South China Sea; each with a sheer limestone cliff with jagged crenellations jutting into the sky and a dazzling, milk-coloured beach gently lapped by pristine water surrounded by equatorial rainforest. The El Nido Resort is a small cluster of stilted water- and beach-cottages at the foot of a massive curtain of rock covered in vegetation and teeming with life; macaque monkeys and hornbills mingle with monstrous hanging roots. I scan the elevated limestone caves and flowering shelves for edible swift's nests, after which the resort takes its name ('nido' means 'nest' in Spanish). Be reassured, they're not on the menu. By the water there are a pair of mating monitor lizards, totally undisturbed by the presence of a five-star resort on their beach.

It's a beautiful resort but what makes it so different are all the ways you can engage with nature by getting in it, on it and under it. You can learn how to rock climb up a cliff or how to abseil down one; you can hike up through the jungle to the top of the island for an amazing view, or kayak round the corner to a series of spectacular hidden lagoons with the clearest water and the most prehistoric vegetation; you can even paddle round there at dusk and have a meal for two set up on a little platform floating in the middle of the mangroves. And snorkelling with the local school of giant jackfish followed by a sunset dinner on your own isolated spit of sand, seemingly suspended somewhere in the blue, is another appealing option. After dinner, when you see that shooting star, you will hope that the boat forgets to pick you up at the end of the week.

Snorkelling and scuba diving are the main attractions for many. The Philippines form part of the Coral Triangle (with neighbouring Indonesia, Papua New Guinea and Malaysia) where there are more marine species, more types of fish and more varieties of coral than anywhere else on the planet. Full of anticipation, I break the glassy surface of the crystal-clear water with the tip of my fin and drop over the side of our flimsy bamboo 'banca'. As an experienced diver, I wonder what new treasures of the marine world I will meet; it could be a black-tipped reef shark, a pair of mating mandarin fish, a juvenile zebra batfish, a manta ray, a ghost pipefish or a blue-ringed octopus, all found in and around the beautiful coral gardens of this gloriously warm, tropical water.

What I see is not what I expect; scarred rock and crumbled corals, abandoned by sea life save for a large Napoleon wrasse guarding an isolated mound of stubborn soft coral. Deeper down, a troop of yellow-fin snappers smother an isolated coral cabbage patch, next to piles of rubble, as far as the eye can see. A hawksbill turtle, one of the three endangered turtles in the area, rises to the surface to breathe, just as I do, keen to get away from the depressing devastation of the dynamite and cyanide fishing that obviously has been taking place here.

left and above **Stilted water villas**

Back at base, I learn about the real eco work of El Nido and it's got nothing to do with bags. The management has been buying up islands in the Bacuit Bay to prevent illegal fishing. It works with the local community to monitor snorkelling and dive sites and install mooring buoys (to prevent anchor damage on the coral). Most importantly, it has installed 24-hour guards on each of the islands. Without further interference, the coral will eventually recover. Each guest pays a fee to support the marine conservation project in the area, which in 1998 was formally established as a marine reserve by the government.

If you want to contribute further, don't buy tropical fish for your aquarium. It is reckoned that 80 per cent of the Western trade in coral fish alone comes from Palawan and nearly all of these have been caught with cynanide. Tragically, this results in much habitat damage and up to two-thirds of the fish will die in transport, meaning that more and more fish must be caught.

The good news is that with our tourist dollars (or pounds, euros or yen) we can convince the desperately poor, local people that there is more money to be made out of showing us tropical fish, turtles and sharks than in bagging them up for export or eating them.

above **Water villa suite**    right **View across Bacuit Bay**

# Green menu

**Take to the water** Swim with the resident school of giant jackfish (some a metre long); take the plunge in one of over 20 dive sites, where there is plenty of astonishing marine life to see; or go hobie-cat sailing.
**Gaze at the views** You can't miss the view across the whole Bacuit bay.

**Explore the area** Kayak in secret lagoons, take a mangrove tour, discover stunning geological formations in Cudugnon limestone cave, and an ancient burial site or isolated islands.
**Go hiking and rock-climbing** Take a healthy hike up to the Pangulasian lookout point (with nature guide or self guided), or go rock climbing on Lagen wall.
**Get twitching** Take your binoculars and, with a guide, look out for over a hundred species of birds.
**Indulge in a massage** These don't come any better and there are even couples' massage rooms.

## Contacts

**El Nido Resort** Palawan, Philippines
**Tel:** +632 894 5644
**Web:** www.elnidoresorts.com
**Rates:** From US$305 per person per night for a waterside or beach-front cottage.

## When to go

There are two seasons: dry (December to May) and wet (June to November). April and May are the driest, least windy but hottest months, August is the wettest and January is the coolest month. Temperatures range from 22–33°C. Water temperatures range from 24–29°C.

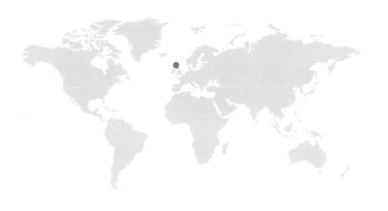

# SCOTLAND
## The Knoydart Peninsula

The remote and beautiful Knoydart Peninsula in the north-west Highlands of Scotland has been aptly described as the 'last wilderness in Britain'. A wild and rugged landscape with a turbulent history, the mountains of Knoydart rise from the depths of two majestic sea lochs, Loch Nevis (in Gaelic, the 'Loch of Heaven') and Loch Hourn (the 'Loch of Hell').

Rather than being stuck in Purgatory, travellers to this magical region of Scotland are rewarded with some incredible views, a real sense of remoteness and wonderful Highland hospitality.

Although part of the mainland, Knoydart has a distinct, island feel. The peninsula is only accessible on foot by a challenging 19-mile walk on a rough hill track over three mountain passes or, more comfortably, by a 45-minute boat journey across Loch Nevis from the tiny fishing community of Mallaig.

In times gone by, Knoydart was known in Highland folklore as the 'Rough Bounds', infamous for its rebellious clansmen and a haven for cattle raiders and criminals.

The peninsula is home to several pairs of rare golden eagles and, on the boat journey over to Knoydart, dolphins and porpoises are commonly sighted in the sheltered waters between the mainland and the Isle of Skye. Locals occasionally report Orca, or killer whales, making their way to the upper reaches of Loch Nevis in the winter in search of the seal colonies.

We decided to join a week-long, guided, walking holiday with Wilderness Scotland, who specialise in sustainable activity holidays on foot or by bike, kayak, canoe and sail boat and who do much to support conservation.

Our journey began with a four-hour train ride on the spectacular West Highland railway, passing the magnificent scenery made famous in the recent *Harry Potter* movies. From the station it was a short walk to the quayside, where we boarded our private boat.

The wind was picking up as we edged our way out into Loch Nevis, the mountain-tops hidden behind the clouds. Thirty minutes later, the first glimpse of the rocky shoreline of Knoydart appeared through the mists. A few moments more and we landed in a small bay where we were met from a tiny pier by our hosts who whisked us off to their beautiful timber lodge overlooking the bay.

We awoke the following morning to glorious sunshine and a home-cooked breakfast and fresh coffee on the veranda, with the mighty Cuillin mountains on Skye clearly visible across the Sound of Sleat. I wandered down to the sandy shores in front of our lodge. A splash out in the bay caught my attention and a tiny head could be seen swimming towards the rocks – my first sighting of an otter.

During the course of the week, we explored Knoydart and the surrounding islands. On our way to the Isle of Rum, a national nature reserve to the west of the Knoydart

Peninsula, we sighted Minke whales in the distance and dolphins playing in the wake of the boat.

Rum is the most mountainous of the 'Small Isles', a collection of remote Hebridean islands to the south and west of Skye. One of the most striking features is the baronial castle that sits at the head of Kinloch bay. This castle was home to an eccentric Edwardian landowner who, reputedly, used to keep crocodiles in the moat and raced his classic cars around the island.

We headed instead for the high pass above the castle for an incredible view and followed an ancient hunting trail, once used by local clansmen to access the deer on the higher slopes. Rum has one of the highest densities of red deer on the planet and has often been mooted as a potential location for reintroducing wolves to Scotland. As we climbed higher, the vegetation became thinner and, at the summit, we were rewarded with a fabulous view in all directions. Before us, the island chain of the Outer Hebrides spread along the horizon and to the south we glimpsed the summit of Ben Nevis, the UK's highest peak.

left **Inverie, the 'capital' of Knoydart**
above **Cloud inversion on the summit ridge of Ladhar Bheinn**

Far beneath us a yacht sailed gracefully across the azure waters between the islands of Eigg and Canna, its sails glinting in the sunlight.

Back at Knoydart, glowing from the day's adventure, we ate dinner – a mountain of fresh langoustines, caught that day by a local fisherman and landed at our lodge shortly before we sat down to eat. Wonderful, locally sourced food was a theme throughout the week, with crab caught in the bay and a crofter from the next glen supplying superb Highland lamb. The lodge's organic garden is a continual source of wonderful herbs and vegetables.

Although visitors will be struck by the sense of peace and tranquility on Knoydart, this was not always so. In the mid 1980s, following a series of disastrous land owners, it was only hours away from being sold to the Ministry of Defence to be used as a bombing range. This prompted a national outcry and a number of important nature conservation organisations and generous individuals supported a subsequent bid by the community to buy the peninsula for the local people.

Ultimately successful, this bid by the Knoydart locals heralded a new era for the region. Although much of the economy is based upon the traditional activities of fishing, crofting (small-scale farming) and forestry, the mainstay is eco tourism and visitors to Knoydart play a vital part in the preservation of its natural and human heritage.

Visitors contribute to a range of important nature conservation initiatives, including support of the John Muir Trust, Scotland's leading wilderness conservation organisation, which works in partnership with the local community. Wilderness Scotland makes a contribution to these initiatives for every guest who travels to Knoydart with them.

The joys of Knoydart are only four hours from Glasgow by train and boat. This remote and beautiful peninsula offers a wonderful experience at any time of year.

below **The ruins at Carnoch on the shores of Loch Nevis**     opposite **Heading ashore at Doune on the Knoydart Peninsula**

# Green menu

**Take a wee dram** A highlight of any visit is a night in the remotest pub in Britain, a lively hostelry frequented by locals, sailors and visitors. The peninsula's residents include a selection of superb musicians and a 'ceilidh' featuring live traditional music is a common occurrence.
**Eat slowly** Eating fresh, local food cuts down on carbon emissions and is simply delicious.
**Guard Scotland's wild places** Become a supporter of the John Muir Trust, which manages the remote northern side of the Knoydart Peninsula and is undertaking an ambitious reforestation programme.
**www.jmt.org**
**Leave your car** Travel from anywhere in Britain by train via Glasgow and the West Highland line (with overnight sleeper services to Fort William from London Euston a popular option).

## When to go

While the Knoydart Peninsula can be visited year-round, the best time for favourable weather is April to October. Its west coast location does mean that rain is possible at any time of the year, but long periods of dry settled weather are not that uncommon. May and June are usually a good time to visit, with long summer days and abundant plant and animal life.

## Contacts

**Wilderness Scotland**
Wilderness Scotland offers a range of guided and self-guided holidays on the Knoydart Peninsula.
**Tel:** +44 (0) 131 625 6635
**Web:** www.wildernessscotland.com
**Rates:** From £385 for a 4-night, self-guided break in a charming local guesthouse.

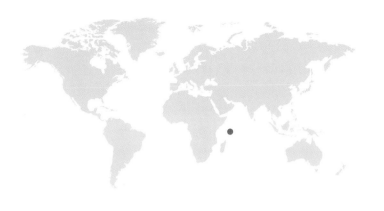

# THE SEYCHELLES
## Frégate Island eco paradise

The Seychelles is a destination faithful to its epithet 'another world'. The islands broke away at the dawn of time, splitting from the southern super-continent Gondwana, eventually settling in splendid isolation, sprinkled over 400,000 square kilometres of the Indian Ocean, just four degrees south of the equator and northeast of Madagascar. More recently known as 'Repiblik Sesel' in Seselwa, or native Creole, the Seychelles gained independence from Britain in 1976 and became Communist. Turning their back on the rapid developments of the capitalist world meant that they remained largely unchanged. However, after the decline in coconut farming (incidentally not indigenous to the area) today's most important industries are tourism and fishing.

On the island capital, Mahé, consumerism is creeping in; slick new residences are sprouting up and a handful of up-market hotels are under development. Despair not. To counterbalance recent growth, two areas have been designated UNESCO World Heritage Sites and, in addition to numerous nature reserves, there are strictly controlled regulations to protect the unique flora and fauna.

### One island – one resort

An hour by boat from the island capital of Mahé, Frégate Island rises 125 metres out of the Indian Ocean. The Seychelles swishiest eco paradise encompasses three square kilometres of tropical vegetation with just 16 palatial villas.

Its roots, however, lie firmly in an impassioned eco ethos rather than extravagance.

Long before it became fashionable to be thinking about the planet's welfare, Frégate's billionaire owner had a vision to protect the fragile infrastructure of the island. He built himself a relatively modest house and set about restoring the endemic wonder of his home. Today he shares it with a maximum of 40 guests, whose key luxuries are peace, privacy and an island to themselves. Yes, there are private butlers and infinity pools, four posters and sunken Jacuzzis but the indulgent trappings never detract from the wonder of the island's conspicuous and diverse nature.

Wandering down a path sheltered by giant Banyan trees, I came across a giant Aldabra tortoise, which looked up once, snorted and continued unperturbed. I was the first to set foot or leave a print on a small sandy beach banked with ylang-ylang and giant, pink-granite boulders. I turned over the wooden sign, which read 'Beach Occupied'. Free to observe and contemplate, I swam, watched the hermit crabs busy themselves and dozed in the shade. A picnic lunch of fresh lobster, freshly squeezed lemonade along with a garland of frangipani arrived just as I was feeling peckish. Up above, a Frégate bird swirled and dived. The pirate of the air, unable to swim or land on water, uses a combination of speed and skilful manoeuvres to steal the 'loot' of other seabirds. While exploring the Seychelles in

above **Spa**    opposite (top) **Dine with a view in the main restaurant**    opposite (bottom) **Spa pool**

1744, Lazare Picault was so impressed by its aerial acrobatics that he named this island Frégate. If you're adverse to creepy crawlies, this isn't the place for you. Millipedes by the millions munch their way through the island's carpet of freshly fallen leaves, which are deliberately left unswept so as not to disturb the natural habitat. Geckos, lizards, spiders and snakes scurry and slither along the jungle floor and the sound of constantly rustling leaves is the island's main soundscape.

### As free as a bird

In 1995, Frégate was home to the last 20 magpie robins in the world. Following a decade of painstaking conservation efforts to restore its natural breeding and nesting habitats, the island is now refuge to over 140 of these blue-black songbirds – still over 90 per cent of the global population of what is classified as the world's seventh-rarest bird.

But they're not vaguely tempted to rest on their laurels and are pushing forward with a strategy of reintroducing the magpie robin to as many of its original habitats as possible, in order to best protect the species and help preserve its genetic diversity. Small family groups introduced to the nearby islands of Curieuse, Aride and Denis are being monitored with great interest.

Resident ecologist Steve Hill explained that Frégate is widely recognised as the spearhead of eco tourism in the Seychelles and is one of the most important sanctuaries for rare endemic and indigenous animals. In addition to magpie robins, the island has important colonies of Seychelles white-eyes and Seychelles blue pigeons. It is home to a flourishing population of the critically endangered Seychelles terrapin and the world's second biggest population of Aldabra giant tortoises, and it is also an important nesting island for green and hawk-bill turtles.

Reforestation is taken very seriously and well over 80,000 endemic trees have been planted over the past decade as part of a programme to restore natural habitats, with two trees being planted for every new arrival.

The Seychelles' climate delivers fruit and vegetables 365 days of the year. The plantation grows a huge assortment of vegetables, fruits and over 160 varieties of herbs, leaves and spices – picked twice a day to form the basis of the island cuisine. Amazingly, 99 per cent of food consumed comes from on or around the island. A giant hydroponics (water system) green house uses three key mediums (coconut husks, fine gravel and pebbles) to stabilise the plants, enjoyed by over 600 mouths a day. There are 17 varieties of banana, abundant papaya, avocados that grow up to three kilogrammes in weight, swathes of purple, Thai and continental basil; and the biggest yield of chillies in the Seychelles. Make sure you lunch in the banana grove one day. After picking a basket

above **Barefoot** *al-fresco* **dining**    below **Villa bedroom**

full of fig, guava, passion fruit, palm heart and star fruit your chef will prepare kingfish on a salad 'blissed' in balsamic vinegar that tastes of heaven.

### Going carbon negative

Frégate has introduced a fleet of 14 solar-powered guest buggies as part of an ongoing drive towards achieving carbon-negative status. The new buggies will lead to a reduction in $CO_2$ emissions of almost 42 tonnes per year – the equivalent of seven years worth of emissions from the average European household. Visionary chairman

Marc Aeberhard has also commissioned extensive ongoing research into the application of emerging energy technologies to reduce dependence on fossil fuels. All staff quarters have solar-assisted hot-water systems and successful experimentation in the use of pure coconut oil and recycled food oil is underway, with one island tractor already running on a mixture of diesel and used frying oil. Marc explains that the ethos at Frégate is, 'not so much why nature is intruding into our sphere but how we can minimalise our intrusion into Mother Nature's garden'. Paradise indeed.

# Green menu

Take a nature walk No trip to Frégate would be complete without a stroll along its ancient paths carved by giant Aldabra tortoises... Green jungle tours with the resident ecologist show a kaleidoscope of plants and the island's thousands of inhabitants.

Indulge yourself Visit the spa – entering through a granite canyon, flanked by freshwater pools and cascading waterfalls will definitely put you in the right mood. The spa embraces all elements of the island's nature in the holistic treatments combining ancient techniques from India, Australia and Polynesia with botanical treatments prepared from Seychellois ingredients.

Sail the waves Frégate's Yacht Club, Marina and PADI Dive Centre opposite the plantation offer sailing and boat trips to the numerous sites around the island. The marina overlooks a turquoise lagoon, protected by a small reef, which restricts the waves and makes the beach particularly safe for swimmers and snorkellers.

Take a dive Close to the shore, Lion Rock is one of Frégate's most popular dive sites. You may find young reef sharks hiding; nurse sharks, lobster, lionfish, puffers and eagle rays are often seen. Stingray Point, west of Anse Victorin, has individual coral formations home to Moray eels, octopus and Scorpion fish and occasional green sea turtles. You may see various stingrays, including two resident shovelnose rays.

Spread your wings Discover the inner islands of the Seychelles. Praslin Island, home to the Vallée de Mai, which General Charles Gordon claimed was the original Garden of Eden in 1881. The tranquil island of La Digue can be explored by bicycle or by traditional ox-drawn cart. The famous beach, Anse Source d'Argent is simply stunning and a stop at the Veuve Reserve to see the rare Paradise flycatcher is well worthwhile.

## Contacts

**Frégate Island Private** Postal Box 330, Victoria, Mahé, Seychelles
**Tel:** +248 670 100
**Web:** www.fregate.com
**Rates:** From €1,300 per person per night sharing, full board (excluding alcohol, taxes and service charge).

**Bailey Robinson**
**Tel:** +44 (0) 1488 689 777
**Web:** www.baileyrobinson.com

The Seychelles islands are at the forefront of leading conservation models. Bailey Robinson strongly promotes the more eco-friendly islands, including Frégate, Denis, North and Cousine, which was nominated for the Tourism for Tomorrow Conservation Award. All profits go to the conservation of its wildlife, and providing local community education and involvement.

## When to go

For diving and fishing ,the north west Monsoon period from October to May is characterised by a lack of wind, calm seas favourable for fishing, snorkelling and diving, with visibility at its best. The humidity is high during the rainy season, which experiences heavy, short, sharp showers ... after which the sun reappears.

For land activity, the south east monsoon period from May to October is characterised by steady South East Trade Winds with rough sea conditions and strong currents. Rainfall is minimal and humidity is at its lowest. Perfect for trail walking.

# SLOVAKIA
## Aquacity

The temperature is -160°C and I am wearing shorts and a vest. Madness. A thin crust of ice forms on my arms and I concentrate on breathing in and out, trudging round and round a tiny, cell-like room in a circle of similarly-clad hopefuls, anticipating a cure. But curiously, I'm not cold, just invigorated, if a little apprehensive.

Welcome to the cryotherapy centre at AquaCity Resort, surely one of the most unlikely places in one of the least-discovered corners in Eastern Europe; in fact, the last place on Earth you might think of turning up at, in the hope of fixing those nagging sporting injuries.

Yet, nestled between the medieval country town of Poprad and the jagged peaks of the High Tatras Mountains is one of the world's greenest, most cutting-edge eco resorts.

AquaCity is the brainchild of local entrepreneur Jan Telensky, an ambitious man with a Midas touch and spectacular vision.

Telensky was born in communist Czechoslovakia and, in 1968, after fighting the Soviet invasion, fled the country for Britain, aged 21, with a forged passport and £2 in his pocket. Penniless, he slept in the graveyard at Dunstable before landing a job.

By the age of 29, he was a millionaire; his business ideas just seemed to click. When communism fell in 1989, he returned to his home country of Slovakia and married a local girl from Poprad.

Telensky was out walking with his wife one day when he tripped over a rusty pipe. He later found that the pipe tapped water from a vast, underground, geothermically heated reservoir, and the inspiration for AquaCity was born.

The resort opened in 2002, an eco-friendly project with a difference in an era when spas were becoming ever more lavish and exclusive. AquaCity, on the other hand, is affordable and accessible to all.

As well as an Olympic-sized pool, there's a huge outdoor water park with warm and cool pools, waterslides and flumes. Vital World includes an ice cave, a Roman-style tepidarium, a giant Jacuzzi, saunas and a 'summer meadow', drenched with UV light to lift the spirits on a dark day. The cryotherapy centre, where patients undergo extreme cold for short periods, comes complete with doctor, gym and a cryo-chamber that takes about six, which is used to treat athletes with muscular injuries from all over Europe.

It's all thanks to this underground lake, 70 kilometres long, 30 kilometres wide and up to 500 metres deep, fed by pure water from the High Tatras Mountains. The water in the pools is 1,400 metres below the earth's surface and is 15,000 years old, filtered by layer upon layer of rock and rich in magnesium, natrium, calcium, carbon dioxide and hydro-carbonates.

Heat from deep inside the Earth raises the temperature to 49°C. The water is pumped to the surface by natural pressure and then cooled to 36°C for use in the warmest pool. The temperature difference heats AquaCity's two hotels, provides all the hot water for the bathrooms and even supplies the under-floor heating for the car park, keeping it free of snow in winter. This adds up to an annual saving of some €2.5 million.

The city of Poprad is a stakeholder in AquaCity, owning 15 per cent of the project. Local schools use the pools and local businesses use the conference facilities. The excess power provides energy for the city too.

AquaCity has made quite a difference to this sleepy town, for which the main employer was previously a depressing washing machine factory. As well as this amazing leisure facility on the doorstep, the resort provides employment and has created a market for local produce, the use of which keeps the food miles down in the restaurants.

It's not just the free power that makes AquaCity green. The water is filtered using a UV system, similar to that used for drinking water, and the pools are crystal clear with no acrid sting of chlorine – a real bonus for people with sensitive skin. It's filtered six times a day and, in effect, is changed completely twice every day. What chlorine is used amounts to about 10 per cent of that used in a conventional pool – and the pools have smooth, stainless-steel linings, not old-fashioned, bacteria-gathering tiles.

This is not to say the facilities are austere. On the contrary, they're quite decadent. The new Blue Diamond Pool, mineral-rich and, of course, geothermically heated, has bubble benches, jets, a swim-up bar and shimmery holographic tiles around the outside. The glass panels include solar cells for heating and wind turbines contribute yet more to the power, meaning that AquaCity is 80 per cent of the way towards Telensky's goal of becoming 100 per cent carbon-neutral.

Recognition has been quick to arrive. Four million visitors have come and benefited since the project opened and AquaCity has become the first destination in the world to achieve 'Live Earth' certification, a global accreditation that offers an internationally recognised certification of sustainability; encompassing environmental, social, cultural and economic factors. In 2007, Telensky was voted the 'World's Leading Green Travel Personality' at the World Travel Awards.

As for the group of us in the cryotherapy chamber... After two minutes of that extreme cold, the doors open and we burst out, blood rushing back to our extremities. We leap onto exercise bikes as instructed by the medical team and pedal like crazy, endorphins going wild, our bodies warming up. After a few sessions over my three-day stay, I feel amazing – and it hasn't cost the earth.

above **Cryotherapy: the coldest chamber on Earth**

# Green menu

**Buy local goods** Stroll into Poprad, with its pastel-coloured houses dating back to the Middle Ages. As well as local handicrafts, gorgeous, fluffy sheepskin rugs are an absolute bargain.

**Walk, bike and ski** Hire a bicycle or take the local narrow-gauge train into the mountains for walking or in winter, skiing. The scenery is incredible and it's completely unspoilt.

**Visit Spišská Sobota** Take a short walk to Spišská Sobota, an amazing, 12th-century village on the doorstep of AquaCity; a visit is like stepping back in time. The village is on UNESCO's World Cultural and Natural Heritage List and is full of traditional bars and restaurants where you can dine at amazingly low prices.

## Contacts

For flights, hotel reservations, spa treatments and excursions, contact:

**Czech Travel**
**Tel:** +44 (0) 845 2703800
**Web:** www.czechtravelonline.com, www.aquacityresort.com
**Rates:** From around £90 per night per room depending on the season, half board including entrance to the waterpark and spa.

## When to go

Summer for families because of the outdoor pools and slides; any time for the spa. Winter is especially beautiful, with snow covering the mountains.

# SLOVENIA
The green oasis of Europe

Slovenia, although so recently rent by war, is a naturally very beautiful country, where you can spend the morning hiking in dramatic Alpine scenery scattered with pretty Austrian-style chalets and the afternoon eating fresh fish by the sea in a little harbour that wouldn't look out of place in Venice.

Initially, this tiny new country, formed in 1991 as one of the remnant states of former Yugoslavia after 45 years of Communist rule, focused its tourism along the 46 kilometres of Mediterranean coastline, but it is beginning to recognise the potential of its beautiful rural inland areas. The Tourist Association has been quick to respond to the negative environmental impact of mass tourism and is actively encouraging a new approach to sustainable tourism that respects the natural environment and conserves the 'socio-cultural authenticity of host populations'.

All well and good, but their progress is, necessarily, slow. Currently 'green' credentials amount to unspoilt remote rural areas where native hoteliers set up their businesses and have used local materials when restoring old buildings. This, of course, helps to regenerate the local community but may be more of an accident that a thought-out eco policy. In terms of the eco credentials required for European awards, two Slovenian hotels have hit the grade but, unfortunately, they cannot boast beauty in architecture or setting. There are also 20 'eco farms' – part of the Slovenia 'agri-tourismo', which has been so successful in Italy – but,

again, the accommodation and food is not of a high quality at the moment.

Nonetheless, Slovenia's large areas of unspoilt nature are a big draw – not for nothing is it often referred to as the 'Green oasis of Europe'. It is one of the countries in the EU with the greatest level of biodiversity; a paradise for nature-lovers who want to get out and enjoy the spectacular scenery, which ranges from tranquil lakes to fast-flowing rivers fed by beautiful waterfalls, from peaceful alpine forests to rolling hills with olive groves and vineyards. It also has the totally magical Triglav National Park, one of Europe's best-kept secrets.

This has all been around for millions of years but, until recently, there has been nowhere sympathetic to stay. Early entrepreneurs assumed we would appreciate exploring the country's natural splendour from concrete blocks complete with thumping discos and tacky casinos. Fortunately a new breed of Slovenian hotelier has arrived, normal local people from other walks of life, offering us an upmarket, authentic experience of their country but on a very small scale. Far from the crowds, in beautiful locations, they offer home-cooked, organic food in cool, stylish accommodation built in sympathy with the natural surroundings.

### The Sončna Hiša

The Sun House or 'The Sončna Hiša' offers a little beam of luxury shining on the edge of the Pannonian flatlands

straddling the Hungarian border. Ales Kegelj, a web designer, has created his petite boutique Bed & Breakfast in the modest back garden of his parents' village home. There are just five bedrooms including the 'Natura', which has a 'silver birch' theme echoing the surrounding trees and the 'Lime Grass' room, which echoes the grasses found in the nearby river.

## The Pristava Lepena chalets

Another ray of sunshine falls on a mountain-side clearing in the Triglav National Park. The Pristava Lepena is a small cluster of chalets lovingly constructed in the traditional style from local wood and reclaimed stone. It is a rural retreat in a spectacular setting for active nature lovers. The area is home to many endemic plant and animal species in one of the largest national parks in Europe. The local owner, Milan Dolenc, a retired civil engineer, was brought up with horses and guides experienced riders into the national park on beautiful white Lipizzaners. The riding is rugged; wading knee-deep across rivers, climbing up into the mountains, galloping across meadows filled with wild flowers.

One of the big attractions here is the Soča river, which is such a striking colour that it is known as the 'Emerald River'; part of the Narnia film, *Prince Caspian*, was recently shot here. People like to fish in it, ramble along it, abseil into it or, increasingly, to raft and kayak down it. Just lazing by it with a good book, is also highly recommended.

previous page (main) **The Lime Grass room at The Sončna Hiša**
previous page (thumbnail) **Nebesa Mountain Resort**
left **Fishing in the Soča river**    below **Lipica horses**

above **Pule Estate**    below **Sečovlje Salts Flats**

the level of comfort or dimmed the stylish interiors, but refers only to the meditative pleasures you may like to undertake here while you contemplate the immensity and beauty of nature from your perch 900 metres above the valley floor.

### The Pule Estate

Hidden away amongst the rolling hills south of Ljubljana, is where the owner of the Pule Estate, Mr. Anderlič, has created a luxurious escapists' treat out of an eclectic collection of his ancestors' abandoned farm buildings. These have been painstakingly restored from old photographs by local craftsmen, with authentic materials and no expense spared. There are five Lipizzaner ponies housed in beautiful stables, better appointed than the dwellings that his great grandparents were no doubt accustomed to. The restaurant shares the stable building (just a glass wall between you and the hay) and serves some of the best food in Slovenia. The surrounding area, mostly ancient beach and oak woodland with gentle hills and meandering streams, can be enjoyed on foot (picnic baskets with plaid blanket supplied), on a bike or on horseback.

If our green future is all about avoiding the building frenzy and infrastructure required for mass tourism then we should encourage these Slovenian hoteliers who are tempting us to pursue life's more simple pleasures and enjoy a holiday in the country in their exclusive rural hotels. After all, who wants to go to a hotel to escape, when there are scores of other people doing the same thing?

Further down the Soča, perched at the top of an imposing hillside, 'between red and fallow deer breeding herds', is the Nebesa Mountain 'Resort'. This is a row of just four wood-and-glass huts, which stand to attention in front of a panoramic curtain that takes your breath away. 'Nebesa' meaning heaven was the name given by the local shepherds, which was later adopted by a long-abandoned ski resort. The owners, Katja and Bojan Roš, a journalist and a local doctor, have managed to transform the remains of the ski lodge without losing the spirit of these ancient pastures with their shepherd cottages and hay lofts. The owners state that, 'in the mountains, taking pleasure must be tempered with a measure of asceticism'. Fortunately, this philosophy has not affected

# Green menu

Visit the Skocjan Caves A UNESCO World Heritage Site since 1986, these caves are a magical underground wonderland. www.park-skocjanske-jame.si

Explore the Vintgar Gorge One of the most popular natural features in Slovenia. Follow the trail along the Radovna river gorge, where there are galleries and bridges constructed in the rock to view the spectacular cascades and rapids, which end at the Šum waterfall, the highest in Slovenia. www.bled.si

Walk the Sečovlje Salts Flats These flats produce salt in the traditional way based on a 700-year-old method. Over the centuries, a unique habitat has formed for halophytic plants and animals and migrating birds. There are sign-posted walking and bicycle trails. Stop off to visit the Saltworks Museum to find out more about this part of Slovenia's history and culture. www.kpss.si

Go bird-watching Fontanigge is home to 272 bird species. In 1993, the Salina was listed as an internationally important marsh under the auspices of the Ramsar convention due to its extraordinary assortment of various seawater, brackish, fresh-water and land eco systems.

Cycle along the wine route Bicycle along one of the well sign-posted wine routes in the Vipava valley, next to the Italian border. Stop for lunch in a traditional 'Gostilna', family home serving traditional homemade dishes typical of the area. www.slovenia.si/tourism/cuisine

Visit the Lipizzaner stud farm The original stud farm at Lipica supplied military horses to the Spanish Riding School in Vienna. Watch a fantastic dressage show with music and a guided tour. Carriage rides and rides out are also available. www.lipica.org, www.theridingcompany.com

## Contacts

**The Pule Estate** Posestvo Pule, Drečji vrh 16, 8231 Trebelno, Slovenia
**Tel:** +386 5 137 7201
**Web:** www.theridingcompany.com
**Rates:** From €145 bed and breakfast per person per night, sharing.

**Nebesa Mountain Resort** Livek 39, 5222 Kobarid, Slovenia
**Tel:** +386 5 384 4620
**Web:** www.nebesa.si
**Rates:** From €119 bed and breakfast per person per night, sharing.

**The Sun House** Son̆cna Hiša, Banovci 3c, 9241 Veržej, Slovenia
**Tel:** +386 2 588 8238
**Web:** www.soncna-hisa.si
**Rates:** From €95 bed and breakfast per person per night, sharing.

**The Pristava Lepena** Lepena 2, 5232 Soca, Slovenia
**Tel:** +386 5 388 9900
**Web:** www.theridingcompany.com
**Rates:** Fom €76 half board per person per night, sharing.

The Riding Company, whose motto is to 'leave nothing but hoof prints' is an admirably eco-conscious agency that works mainly with small family-run businesses in rural and mountainous areas who are dedicated to preserving their environment and traditional way of life. They make a donation to Climate Care on behalf of every guest to offset the $CO_2$ emissions of their flight, and support their colleagues abroad in their environmental work, including the Eco-Ranger project and Daktari Bush School in South Africa, the Bulgarian-Swiss Biodiversity Conservation Programme and The Brooke, a leading overseas equine-welfare charity.

## When to go

September is good for hiking and climbing, as the summer crowds have gone. December to March is best for skiing, while spring is best in the lowlands and valleys when everything is in blossom. July and August are hot and crowded, especially along the coast, which has a Mediterranean climate. Summer is mostly dry with average highs of 29°C. Winters can be cold, with temperatures around 0°C in the central areas.

# SOUTH AFRICA
## Grootbos and Phinda

*'Do not go gentle into a land filled with turbines but rage, rage against the dying of the countryside.'*

Under Milk Wood, Dylan Thomas

It's not just green that you get at Grootbos, it's also blue. The huge windows of the starkly modern Forest Lodge look out over one of the most beautiful bays in South Africa at the point where two great oceans meet at the very tip of the African continent. It is here that the enlightened owner of Grootbos has chosen to establish what David Bellamy has called 'the best example of conservation of biodiversity I have ever seen'. Named as a UNESCO Heritage Site, the region has 9,000 species of Fynbos plants, most of which do not grow anywhere else on the planet, making it one of the hottest of the world's biodiversity hotspots. Just strolling from your luxury stone-and-thatch chalet to the reception, you will pass an astonishing variety of proteas, ericas and exotic grasses sheltering amongst the ancient Milkwood trees.

The Grootbos Foundation was set up in 2004 to restore and protect this natural environment, one of the world's six 'floral kingdoms', which is under threat from agriculture and urbanisation. It helps the local people by retraining them as gardeners and makes Fynbos pay its way through the on-site nursery, which supplies an expanding wild-flower market, including the Eden Project in Cornwall. It also runs the Siyakula Township Project where children are taught how to grow vegetables to feed themselves.

To contribute to these and other projects, all you have to do is to have a great time. Lounge in the stylish cocktail bar or hang over the edge of the infinity pool knowing that your money is being spent exactly how you'd want. Pleasures here are simple; take a steed from the stable and trot up into the hills to savour the view, then lie back on your private veranda during the heat of the day and take in the scent of the aromatic wild herbs. As the dusk melts into darkness, stretch out on the warm earth and take in the enormous night sky.

The nature isn't obvious here; it's not big or dramatic like the Drakensberg or the Kruger and there is no sign of the 'Big Five' game animals. For the novice it is better brought to life with specialist knowledge from the local guides. These biologists and conservationists will accompany you on walks, horseback rides or drives, teaching you to appreciate the complexity of the unique Fynbos ecology. They will also organise boat trips to see some wonders of the marine world, the 'Big Five' of the deep – dolphins, penguins, seals, sharks and whales – for which the area is famous.

There are two five-star lodges to choose from; the relaxed Garden Lodge for families and the more formal Forest Lodge for sophisticated grown-ups. Both lodges are built out of natural materials, mostly by local craftsmen.

This is a perfect place for a short break, for taking time out from hectic lives to be reminded of the beauty and

above **Grootbos Forest Lodge suite and pool**

simplicity of nature, and to dream. Perfect, too, for those with green fingers as well as a green conscience.

## Phinda

If you want to go wild, then nestled below the verdant sub-tropical carpet of the Lebombo Mountains of Northern KwaZulu-Natal, andBEYOND's Phinda private game reserve is one of South Africa's great success stories of game reintroduction. Lion, cheetah, black and white rhino, buffalo, elephant, leopard and giraffe are among ubiquitous game in an ambitious restocking operation dubbed '*phinda izilwane*', return of the wild animals.

Looking across the plains, it's hard to believe that as recently as 1990, the land was derelict, spoiled and penniless after years of harmful farming and poor land

management. Today, it is regarded as one of South Africa's most remarkable eco destinations following a successful conservation programme, integrating a pioneering partnership between private enterprise, conservation ideals and a rewarding relationship with the neighbouring communities of Makhasa and Mnqobokazi, who now own the land. Phinda (meaning 'the return' in Zulu) has gone back to its people – and to its animals.

In 1989, a mining company wanted to bulldoze dunes along the eastern peninsula to remove titanium and other metals. This caused uproar among conservationists, who managed to convince the government that it should have an environmental assessment prepared. The South African Government carefully weighed the potential economic benefits of allowing the mining against the disruption and further degradation of an area that was already greatly in need of restoration. A sigh of relief came in late 1993 when the panel conducting the environmental assessment advised the government against the mining proposal. A new tourism industry took root with the St Lucia Park at its core, and the Phinda nature reserve (just north of Lake St Lucia) created more jobs than the proposed mining operations would have done.

Disputed land claims, squatting in protected areas, uncontrolled fishing practices and the spread of exotic plants all present big challenges to achieving sustainable development. However, when the Greater St Lucia Wetland gained World Heritage Site status in 2000 because of its outstanding natural value and rich biodiversity, it became fully protected from external threats.

opposite **King of the Jungle**    above **Phinda Forest suite**

Bordering the Wetlands, Phinda covers an enormous 23,000 hectares of prime conservation land. Electric and barbed-wire fences are fast disappearing, linking seven distinct habitats, home to an abundance of wildlife, including Africa's 'Big Five', a plethora of rare mammals and over 380 bird species.

While Phinda's variety of topography is remarkable, what really makes this reserve unique is its proximity to the Indian Ocean, a mere 40 minutes away. Where else in the world can you swim with a whale shark before breakfast, watch warthogs frolic over lunch, followed by a finale of elephants supping at dusk? The change in scenery merely increases the bush's potency. But Phinda isn't just about safari; it's also a dynamic working model in land management and creative wildlife conservation – andBEYOND's flagship operation. Our guide, Richard, explained that life at Phinda is like the three-legged *poitjie* – or cooking pot – combining care for the land, with its wildlife and its people.

Guests can look forward to exciting game-drives in open safari vehicles led by experienced rangers and Zulu trackers, as well as thrilling optional activities on the river. Just after dawn, we heard the low rumble of a 40-year-old elephant in musk, as he tramped through the forest making light work of palm trees, picking them like daisies. As he chewed on a six-metre Marula branch that he'd plucked like a grape from a vine, we learnt that pachyderms have a catholic diet – for every tree knocked down or destroyed, eight more will be sown via the elephant's dung. I could see why 90 per cent of children vote for the elephant as their favourite animal. A dazzle of zebra crossed our path – one without a tail and then, quite unexpectedly, a small movement in the bushes (only spotted by our tracker) led us to a huddle of cheetahs, barely a week old – five furry bundles about to make their way in the world.

Accommodation at Phinda comes in six eco-friendly, low-footprint guises. There are two out-of-this-world, private, sole-use lodges – Bond-like Getty residences, in

addition to four diverse lodges: Forest, Vlei, Rock and Mountain. Forest Lodge consists of 16 stilted suites set deep in the heart of a rare, dry sand forest, with a rim-flow swimming pool and expansive viewing deck offering a panorama of the game-filled plains. Nearby Vlei (meaning 'wetland') is an intimate cluster of six glass-and-thatch suites with private plunge pools, often frequented by passing antelope. At the other end of the reserve lies Mountain Lodge's 20 suites, each with a plunge pool and private viewing deck taking in long views of the Lebombo Mountains and bushveld. Adjacent Rock Lodge has six intimate stone-and-adobe-walled suites suspended from the side of a rocky cliff, each with a secluded plunge pool and deck offering an unrivalled outlook of spectacular Leopard Rock. Your hardest choice will be where to stay.

above and right **Phinda Rock suites and pool**

# Green menu

## GROOTBOS

**Whale-watch** Watch from the shore as Southern right whales come within metres of land to mate and calve from June to September each year. Sea-based trips are also available.
www.whalewatchsouthafrica.com

**Save a penguin** Visit the African or jackass penguin on Dyer Island and support the 'Faces of Need, Dyer Island Conservation Trust' project. Penguin numbers are dwindling as their habitat is threatened.

**Take a boat to Geyser Island** Visit the 60,000 Cape fur seals who live on this nearby island. Watch them bask, play and swim.

**Shark-spot** Gansbaai is the great white shark capital of the world. They visit the channel between these two islands, not called 'shark alley' for nothing. For the brave or the mad, there is also cage shark-diving.
www.whitesharktrust.org; www.sharkwatchsouthafrica

**Yell for the local team** Watch football at Masakhane township's new Fifa-standard pitch, built with the support of Grootbos' 'Spaces for Sport' project. Before the end of 2007, they had 17 football clubs but not one level pitch. More soccer fields are in the pipeline.

**Hop on a horse** Grootbos has 20 resident horses, all of which are available to guests and some of which are suitable for beginners.

## PHINDA

**Go fishing** Boaters and shore anglers have the opportunity to catch a number of different game fish; barracuda, yellow fin tuna and kingfish to name a few. Sodwana has produced record billfish and sailfish. Deep-sea fishermen should note that Phinda supports catch and release.

**Learn leopard ways** Observe Phinda's leopards with a specialist ranger and tracker team, staying out all night if necessary.

**Capture a rhino** Play an important role in conservation by participating in Phinda's rhino-darting partnership programme. A veterinarian darts the rhino and, once it is safely anaesthetised, guests perform their assigned tasks.

**Learn to track** Learn the art of tracking wildlife on foot accompanied by a specialist ranger and tracker team.

**Explore local culture** Learn about Zulu culture when you explore the Mduku and Mnqobokazi communities surrounding Phinda with the Isikolethu ('Our Culture') Community Experience. A visit to the Sangoma (medicine man) and Mdluli Ancestoral Home delivers a fascinating cultural insight.

**Take a turtle night drive** From November to January, enjoy a thrilling night drive along the beach in search of the elusive leatherback and loggerhead turtles that come ashore to breed. A surfside supper is served, creating a truly memorable wildlife experience.

**Discover the birdlife** With 600 species recorded, the Zululand Birding Route is southern Africa's birding diversity hotspot. A network of 14 self-drive routes offers a range of great birding localities that will thrill the most seasoned birder.

# Contacts

**Grootbos Private Nature Reserve** P.O. Box 148, Gansbaai 7220, South Africa
**Tel:** +27 28 384 8000
**Web:** www.grootbos.com
**Rates:** From US$352 per person per night, including all meals, guided walks and drives through the reserve, bird watching, horse-riding, and guided land-based whale watching.

**Phinda**
**Tel:** +27 11 809 4300
**Web:** www.andbeyond.com
**Rates:** From US$373 per person per night, sharing, including all meals, drinks, laundry, game drives and scheduled activities.

# When to go

For Grootbos visit from June to September when the whales come. For winter game viewing at Phinda go in May, while November is best for spotting turtles.

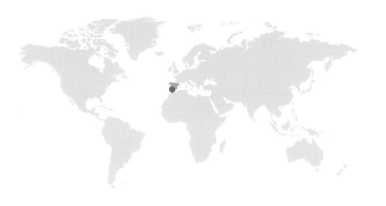

# SPAIN

## The Hoopoe Yurt Hotel

The Yurt Hotel concept is simple. First take a 10-acre olive grove and cork oak forest plot set in an idyllic location with spectacular views of the rugged Grazalema mountains of Andalucia, in southern Spain. Then give each set of guests their own yurt with a private bathroom (and homemade olive-oil soaps), as well as an acre of private meadow with hammocks and comfortable, shaded seating areas. Add in first-rate cooking using local ingredients and the fact that you are treated as a guest not a customer (there are only five yurts), and you have a holiday that allows you to genuinely unwind and get back to nature, without forgoing any of the usual luxuries you might wish for.

Yurts originated in Mongolia as travelling felt tents that could be folded up and moved from place to place. However, this is a far cry from traditional camping. The yurts are lovely to look at, with their ribbed roofs and diamond-shaped wall supports and inside, extremely spacious double rooms with comfortable beds and treated wooden floors are individually decorated with traditional Mongolian furniture and exotic textiles. And it's not just the guests who stay in the yurts – owners Henrietta and Ed Hunt have built a yurt home for themselves and their two small children to live in all year-round, consisting of a central 30-foot yurt with four smaller ones attached.

This truly is an idyllic place to unwind, relax and soak up the sights and sounds of nature right on your doorstep.

Fall asleep in a hammock under the shade of a cork oak tree, lulled by the sound of goats' bells and crickets. Or use the hotel as a base to explore nearby Ronda and some of the famous white villages of Andalucia. When you get back you can cool off with a dip in the chlorine-free swimming pool, with fabulous views of the surrounding mountains, while you look forward to the evening's gourmet meal.

So you don't need to be an eco nut to have a memorable and enjoyable holiday at the Yurt Hotel. However, if you are interested in environmental issues then the Hoopoe Yurt is about as green as it is possible for a hotel to be. Henry and Ed do not see themselves as eco evangelists but, during the five years that they have owned the plot, they have set out to be as ecological as they can, so long as it is practical and financially viable. All of the stones used for walling and terracing have been collected from the land; the yurt platforms are made out of Spanish pine and many of the steps are reclaimed railway sleepers; and since finding a yurt-maker in the south of Spain, all the yurts are sourced from him. Henry reckons it would be possible for them to pack up and leave within a month leaving no trace of the hotel apart from the swimming pool.

When the Hunts bought the plot it was covered with scrub and brambles. Over the years they have cleared most of it by hand, freeing up the olives and cork oaks, and creating fire breaks round all of their borders. This has allowed many

above **Private meadow**    opposite **Views of he Grazalema mountains**

species of wild flower to return to the meadows they have created and the variety of bird and insect life has increased in parallel – one keen bird watcher counted almost 50 different species during a one-week stay.

The Hoopoe Yurt Hotel generates minimal carbon emissions. All electrical power is generated from solar panels. The hot-water pipes are all exposed black pipes that heat up in the sun so the gas boilers can be left on the lowest setting – one small gas bottle will last each bathroom for a whole season. Ed has stripped an old, industrial fridge of its working parts to store all drinks, vegetables and fruit. The doors are left open at night when the air is cool, so

when drinks are taken out and placed in the powered fridge to cool they are already half-way there.

Being in the south of Spain water is a precious commodity. Showers and sinks are low-flow since they are gravity-fed from the spring. Grey water is collected and either piped directly to the plants or stored for watering. The dry-compost loos do not use any water and Henry and Ed have deliberately chosen to plant Mediterranean drought-resistant plants, which are watered by drippers rather than by a hosepipe.

Guests hand all recyclable waste to Henry and Ed. Organic waste is composted and recyclable material is taken

above **Cortes de la Frontera**   opposite **A yurt interior**

to the local village recycling units. Even waste from the loos is composted and recycled onto the garden.

Henry and Ed recognise the importance of sourcing local food, goods and services when it comes to minimising their overall environmental impact. They buy as much as possible from the local village and artisans; failing that, they get what they need from Ronda, which is only 30 kilometres away. The only equipment that they have had

to ship in are the compost loos. Food is a big part of the Yurt Hotel experience; all of it comes from the south of Spain and almost all of it is either grown in the kitchen garden or bought from the village market. Four nights a week they provide *al fresco*, three-course meals under the pergola, and the fact that guests almost invariably choose to stay in for all four nights is a testament to Henry's fantastic culinary skills.

# Green menu

Visit a white village Cortes de la Frontera, a typical Andalucian 'white village', is a 20-minute walk or a brief cycle ride away. Bicycles are provided for guests.

Explore underground Nearby, on the road to Ronda, are the Cueva de la Pileta, home to ancient cave paintings and underground galleries with giant stalactites and stalagmites, and the Cueva del Gato, where icy-cold water pours out of the mountain into a rock pool – very refreshing in the heat of the summer.

See Ronda The Hoopoe Yurt Hotel is half an hour from Ronda, one of the oldest towns in Spain. The town is perched above the dramatic 100-metre Tajo Gorge. Walk across the New Bridge with spectacular views to the charming old town, which has lots of buildings of historical interest from Ronda's Moorish past, or eat out at one of several excellent restaurants overhanging the gorge. The world-famous bullring is definitely worth a visit.

Spend a day birdwatching If you are interested in birds, spend the day with local bird expert Peter Jones who will take you into the mountains for a spot of twitching. Alternatively, combine your stay with a visit to the National Park of Donaña on the shores of the Guadalquivir river. Its beaches, dunes, wetlands and pine forests are home to a rich variety of birds and other wildlife, including the almost extinct Iberian lynx and Spanish imperial eagle.

Take part in local events Henry and Ed make a point of telling their guests about local events and *ferias*, and encouraging them to attend. They also encourage them to eat in the local restaurants on the nights when they are not cooking.

Enjoy a massage There is a local masseuse who walks down to the Hoopoe Yurt Hotel to provide massages for the guests. There are also local yoga classes that guests can attend.

## When to go

Spring is the best time to visit, when the countryside's colours are at their most dramatic and the daytime heat is comfortable, though you will probably need to wear another layer in the evenings. From mid-June everything becomes hotter and drier, cooling down from around September. By October, temperatures are still pleasant, in the 20°Cs, though there is more likelihood of rain. The Hoopoe Yurt Hotel is open from May to mid-October.

## Contacts

**The Hoopoe Yurt Hotel** Apartado de Correos 23, Cortes de la Frontera, 29380 Málaga, Spain
**Tel:** +34 951 168 040 (radio phone with no answer phone), +34 660 668 241 (mobile)
**Web:** www.yurthotel.com
**Rates:** From €130 per night per double yurt, including breakfast for two.

# SRI LANKA
## Jetwing's Eternal Earth Project

Sri Lanka is green in so many ways. The whole tear-shaped island (the same size as mainland Britain) is covered in a verdant canopy of tropical vegetation – everywhere you look you'll find terraces of lime paddy fields dotted with ripe papaya and mango trees; whole mountainsides covered with bottle-green tea bushes; plantations of emerald banana trees; and row upon row of smoky-jade, shaded leeks surrounded by lush meadows of grazing cows.

### Earth Lung and Jetwing

Despite tragedy and national disasters, Sri Lankans are both a resilient and visionary people who use their energy planning for the future. Earth Lung is just such a vision, as explained by the Minister of Tourism at the UN WTO Ministerial Summit on Climate Change and Tourism, 'The question is', he says, 'What can we do to ensure that we make a real and solid difference? In tourism, little Sri Lanka has come up with a lead initiative, with a resolve to make our island nation a carbon-neutral tourism destination by 2018, making it the most sought-after destination in Asia.'

This vision has been embraced wholeheartedly by hotelier Hiran Cooray, Deputy Chairman of the hotel and holiday company Jetwing, who has taken pro-active steps by establishing the Jetwing Eternal Earth Project, aimed at educating school children about earth-saving practices, such as responsible waste disposal, the reduction of carbon emissions and prevention of harmful land clearing and soil erosion, as well as the importance and sustenance of bio-diversity and so on. As part of the project, Jetwing also gives the kids seeds. Once these have grown into saplings, the children can sell them back to the company, who will plant them in protected, forest plantation areas. The community involvement in the project is also harnessing a relationship with the tourism industry and nurturing an awareness among local communities of its value.

All Jetwing's hotels follow good environmental practices, including the use of energy-saving light bulbs, discontinuing the use of plastic bags, conducting training classes for the village schools, composting, using grey water for the watering of the gardens and using biodegradable cleaning products and natural insect repellents instead of aerosol cans. Wherever possible, purchases come from area suppliers.

In addition, social initiatives are to the fore and a development project to combat rural unemployment has been designed to develop the youth for suitable employment within the group or elsewhere. The naturally positive attitudes, talents, enthusiasm to learn and good discipline are often overshadowed by poor English, the biggest hindrance to finding a job, especially within the private sector. The first stage of this programme to fill the 'skills gap' started at Vil Uyana, with English lessons that continued for six months. On successful completion, 60 youths passed

previous page (main) **Stilt fishermen in Gallee**   previous page (thumbnail) **Kurulubedda – stilted river hideout**

out at a ceremony under the patronage of the Secretary to the Ministry of Tourism.

### Vil Uyana – a tropical escape

For many, Sri Lanka's coastline is its main asset but a trip inland through hills and tea plantations to the cultural triangle of Dambulla's painted caves, Polunnaruwa's famous rock temples and statues and the spectacular rock fortress of Sigiriya, is where the island's true heart lies.

Conveniently, the area is also home to Jetwing's Vil Uyana, a new and exciting concept of eco hospitality. The brainchild of environmental architect Sunela Jayawardene, who is inspired by rural and local traditions, it comprises 25 dwellings set in 23 acres of wetlands, lakes and reedbeds and is a haven

opposite **Vil Uyana eco villas with Sigiriya in the distance**     above **The 'tea plantation bungalow' at Warwick Gardens**

for wildlife. 'My inspiration,' she says, 'for the land-use and buildings comes from the pre-colonial vernacular architecture of this island. I have seen structures such as these in forgotten villages, deep in the heart of Sri Lanka.'

## Warwick Gardens – A Tea Planter's Bungalow

Further south, Nuwara Eliya is the 'Little England' of Sri Lanka, set against beautiful backdrops of mountains, valleys, waterfalls and tea plantations. Supposedly one of the coolest places on the island, its climate is like an English summer. Everywhere there is evidence of British influence, including country cottages and Queen-Anne-style mansions. A six-hour drive (at an average 16 kilometres per hour) from Colombo, Warwick Gardens is a century-old, tea planter's bungalow that typifies a new age in eco tourism. Situated at an altitude of 1,770 metres near Ambewela, the 30-acre estate has been lovingly restored. The stonework is crisp once more, the five suites are freshly painted and the gardens are being reclaimed step by step.

Warwick is run like a house party. A breakfast of fresh local fruits is served outside on the western terrace encircled by nodding agapanthas, to the sound of the rushing stream down below. Deep-seated loungers on the south terrace are a perfect place to loll and enjoy the view of the tiered gardens. Vegetable and herb gardens provide fresh greens to accompany the spicy curry and dal dishes along with string hoppers, a national dish made from a vermicelli-type rice-mixture.

The peace is deceptive. Down in the valley over 100 students study and you will be charmed to see Sri Lankan school girls dressed from head to toe in white, with their hair in plaits, commuting up and down the path,

### Kurulubedda – stilted river hide-out

Further south still, near the Dutch fortified sea town of Galle, Jetwing's Kurulubedda (meaning 'bird forest') lies hidden deep in the mangroves. A short chug on a rickety boat down the Mahamodara river, are two hidden stilted dwellings. Greeted on the pier by a sarong-clad butler carrying bunches of purple lotus pods (the national flower), you're only a few steps from your jungle hide out, which comprises a comfortable first-floor bedroom and a large terrace over a cool plunge pool. Thick vegetation camouflages the dining pavilion next to a small paddy field and marshes teaming with birdlife. There's an *al-fresco* lounge area surrounded by greenery and a small lawn bedecked with loungers for relaxation and lazy daydreaming. It's perfect for a day or two.

below and right **Warwick Gardens 'bungalow' and suite**

# Green menu

### VIL UYANA

Climb up to Sigiriya Rock Fortress You can't leave without having climbed past the murals of beautiful nymphs to the renowned Sigiriya Rock Fortress just 5 kilometres away.

Visit Sri Lanka's cultural cities Visit Polonnaruwa and Anuradhapura, Sri Lanka's cultural cities and get an insight into Buddhism from the head monk of the temple.

Explore Uda Walawe National Park Sri Lanka is the best place in Asia to see the Asian elephant. Uda Walawe National Park virtually guarantees sightings. During September and October, the 'Gathering', an annual migration to the receding shores of the Minneriya National Park has up to 300 elephants present on the exposed lake bed, by now a verdant meadow of lush grass.

### WARWICK GARDENS

Go for tea Surrounded by tea bushes as far as the eye can see, a walk up the hill to the tea factory is a must. Every hour, 260 kilogrammes of leaves drop down a shoot into a huge roller to be crushed. From there they go through various contraptions, originating from the turn of the 19th century, into the 'ball breaker' where they pour out of three shoots, now resembling tea leaves as we know them.

Enjoy a massage Have an early-morning Indian head massage or close wet-shave with the local barber and his mineral stone shine.

Ride the estate Ride a Thoroughbred racehorse through the tea plantations and around Lake Gregory in Nuwara Eliya.

Visit Ambewela Farm Thirty minutes from Warwick, this farm covers hundreds of acres. Dairy is the mainstay, alongside 100 snowy-white Salan goats, pens of rabbits, roaming chickens and calves, which are milked at 12.30 p.m. each day to the strains of Beethoven.

### KURULUBEDDA

Go birding on the river Take a boat ride along the Mahamodara river and enjoy the birdlife. White-breasted kingfishers, drongos, Brahmini kites, parakeets and the dramatic Asian paradise flycatcher dart along the banks while purple-faced leaf monkeys, peculiar to Sri Lanka, stare at you from the huge bamboos that frame the river.

Visit the walled city of Galle Sri Lanka's sapphires and moon stones are renowned as being the best quality in the world and it is said that King Solomon bought his gems, spices and peacocks from the old fortified town of Galle. Little has changed since the 17th century and it remains a great place to shop for local gemstones and spices before watching the sun go down over the western wall.

Enjoy local life A cinnamon spice plantation is only a boat ride away, so too a temple and a village laundry. Enjoy a cup of hand-rolled bio-tea with home-styled patties followed by dinner under the star-studded sky.

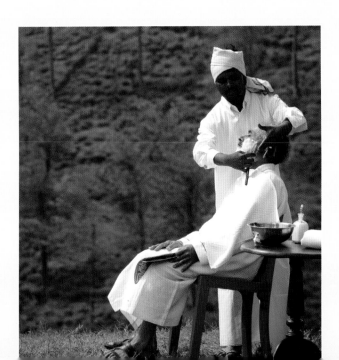

## When to go

Sri Lanka has two monsoons, which occur from May to July and December to January when rainfall peaks. It benefits from a tropical climate with temperate upland areas and coastal zones cooled by sea breezes.

## Contacts

**Jetwing** Jetwing House, 46/26, Navam Mawatha, Colombo 2, Sri Lanka
**Tel:** +94 11 234 5700
**Web:** www.jetwingtravels.com, www.jetwing.com
**Rates:** Available on request.

# SWEDEN
## Icehotel and Ängavallen Farm

Sweden's Icehotel on the banks of the Tome river comes and goes with the seasons. Each year, the process begins when the farmers, equipped with tractors and special saws, harvest huge blocks of ice from the river. By fusing the water with air to form a mixture known as '*snis*', water snow cannons transform the river, creating a substance that is hard as cement and will both insulate the hotel and protect it from the sun. But the waters are only on loan. In May the whole structure melts back into the river – respectfully returned to its source only to be re-incarnated the following winter. There's something poetic about its cycle; man so often eclipses nature, here its annual sequence is a celebration of nature's supremacy.

While the Torne river is both the source of inspiration and the building material of the Icehotel, human activities still affect the local climate, which has resulted in a commitment to be become $CO_2$ negative by the year 2015. To achieve this goal, a surplus of renewable energy (Icehotel currently buys electricity that is '*Källmärkt*', meaning 100 per cent renewable) will be produced in partnership with Gävle Energi. Green goals encompass all operations in Jukkasjärvi, including all activities and ground transportation, and all Icebars and events around the world.

In this part of the world, knowledge about snow and ice has always been a necessity. The Samis have over 300 words for snow (we could only think of ten: ice, snow, sleet, slush, hail, brash, icicles, icebergs, glacier and igloo). The hotel's initial impact is slightly disconcerting. A 'normal' timber reception hall leads down to long ice corridors passing wooden chalets – there's nothing very special about it. Then two reindeer-coated doors with antler handles open and the transformation from the mundane to the fantastic is instantaneous. An ice palace with an ice-crystal chandelier, ice beds, glassy furniture and ice sculpture. By day it's an ice museum open to the general public for a small fee, but from 6 p.m. it's a residents-only domain. Each of the dramatically different suites is designed by artists from around the world, ranging from fabulous to pure fetish – we chose a suite resembling an avalanche of giant snowballs designed by Australians Daniel Rosenbaum and Dylan Pillemer.

You'll eat well during your stay. 'Wild is wonderful', says Icehotel's chef Jens Seitovaara, 'I find my inspiration in nature's own mix of colours and flavours'. He likes to compose his menus like a symphony, always searching for the ultimate harmonies and contrasts. Air-dried moose filet, ptarmigan, reindeer and Arctic char form the staple diet in these climes.

People frequently ask whether it's really possible to sleep in temperatures of -5°C; last year, in its short four-month life, 15,000 people did just that – but for those preferring traditional accommodation, cosy cabins are an alternative. The Icehotel has been such a success that it has opened

above **Dog-sledding**    opposite **Designer ice bedroom**

numerous Icebars in various cities around the world. Colourful vodka-based cocktails served in ice-carved glasses cause no end of high spirits in the original Absolut Icebar, which provides a bit of Dutch courage before heading off to your fur-lined ice bed for the night. Most of us found sleeping in a giant igloo surprisingly comfortable, although we were very grateful to thaw out in the sauna and steaming showers first thing the next morning.

The whole trip is characterised by an exciting smorgasbord of outdoor adventure – dog sledding with Arctic huskies, reindeer racing, ice fishing, snowshoeing, abseiling, ice sculpting, moose tracking, thrilling snow safaris and cross-country skiing.

On cold, clear nights from December to March, the Aurora Borealis, or Northern Lights, streak across the northern skyline like a winter greeting from the sun. Usually a bluey-green colour, they create traces like the blood of a wounded dragon. It's not wizardry. They appear when charged electrons from outer space encounter the atmosphere surrounding the Earth and their moving energy is converted into light. It's a wonder of the world that will stay with you forever.

## Ängavallen Farm

At the other end of the country in Skåne (an area known as Sweden's Pantry), lies one of Europe's first organic farms, actually started way back in 1971 when owner-manager Rolf Axel Nordström created his own response to what he saw as cruel, industrialised animal husbandry. His philosophy couldn't be simpler, 'I wanted to fulfil a childhood dream and treat the animals raised to provide food for humans with the same degree of dignity, love and respect as our family cat and dogs'.

His motto 'from field to fork' covers all phases of food production, including a feed of pure vegetable matter, which is free of chemical fertiliser and poisons. Animals are born, bred and die on the farm reducing any stress from transportation thus eliminating any trace of toxic cortisone (the fear enzyme) in his meat. The result is exceptionally tasty and tender produce from animals you know have led complete and happy lives. Interestingly, meat from animals that only consume grass and hay contains more Omega 3 fatty acids. In the case of pigs this means living a 'normal' two-and-a-half times longer than industrially bred stock,

above **Ängavallen Farm in Skane**

and there's something good about watching them wander freely in large pastures remaining with their mothers as long as they like. This does make the end produce rather more expensive, but in today's times of enlightened awareness many people are happy and able to pay.

Ängavallen can sleep up to 40 people in charming, converted farm buildings, with cosy, loft sleeping areas that are great for kids. Environmentally compatible rooms surrounding the newly built herb garden are named after herbs or traditional farm occupations like 'Milker', 'Fodder Master' or 'Blacksmith'.

It's not just Ängavallen that's green. Nearby Malmö is the world's fourth greenest city with a clear vision for sustainable urban development along the Western Harbour and promotion of fair trade. Funky architecture like the 190-metre 'Turning Torso' mingles with green roof tops, reservoirs and bat boxes – and by 2012, the city will also be able to boast that every one of its school restaurants is 100 per cent organic.

# Green menu

### ICE HOTEL

Make an ice sculpture The material – the crystal-clear ice – is plentiful around Jukkasjärvi. Artists introduce you to the magical world of ice sculpting using special ice implements. Feel the flow of your own creativity and make something cool.

Take a ski and snowshoe tour Kit yourself out in special ski gear and ski into the woods to a little shelter for warm drinks and homemade cake. Then time to redress and follow the marked trails to find your way back.

Enjoy a starlit dinner in the wilderness Visit the Esrange Space Centre, the base for scientific research of the Aurora Borealis. You will be given a guided tour of the facilities and an introduction to the Northern Lights while the Icehotel chef prepares a wilderness dinner for you to enjoy as you gaze at the flashing sky.

### ÄNGAVALLEN

Stuff a sausage Have a go at stuffing your own sausage *à la* 'Generation Game' mixing garlic, spice, port and whisky according to your own taste. They'll be smoked for three days and sent home to you.

Picnic idyllic Visit one of the nearby white, sandy beaches, taking a picnic basket from Ängavallen for lunch.

Lunch organic Walk around Malmö's rejuvenated Western Harbour and have lunch at the organic Salt & Brygga where even the leather sofas are organic. Or enjoy a cup of coffee at Barista Fairtrade Coffee and take a packet of used coffee grounds home as free fertiliser – a saving of 100 kilogrammes of waste a year that makes a lot of customers very happy.

**Ängavallen Gård** 235 91 Vellinge, Sweden
**Tel:** +46 (0) 4042 3250
**Web:** www.angavallen.se
**Rates:** From €63 per person per night or 650 SEK (charges in SEK), with up to four guests per room, and including Ängavallen's ecological breakfast buffet.

## When to go

### Icehotel

March is the best month to visit; the temperatures are warmer, the days longer and there is a very good chance of seeing the Aurora Borealis (Northern Lights) on clear, cold nights.

### Ängavallen

Ängavallen is open all year but perhaps most fun in summer when it's warm enough to swim in the sea or go for long bike rides in the countryside or to Malmö or Copenhagen.

## Contacts

**Icehotel** 981 91 Jukkasjärvi, Sweden
**Tel:** +46 (0) 9806 6800
**Web:** www.icehotel.com
**Rates:** From €128 per person per night (all charges are made in SEK).

# SWITZERLAND

## The majestic Alps

In a way, Switzerland has long been the model of a green, eco-friendly holiday destination. Visitors have been coming for more than two centuries to marvel at the snow-capped Alps, the aromatic forests, the lakes, rivers and waterfalls, and the awe-inspiring glaciers. The Swiss, for their part, have been careful to preserve their landscapes, and provide convenient access to them – not just for the sake of foreigners, but for their own physical and spiritual wellbeing as well.

Perhaps the latest manifestation of this was the launch in summer 2008 of an integrated 20,000-kilometre network of non-motorised transport routes, SwitzerlandMobility. You may choose to cycle against a backdrop of the glacier-strewn peaks of the Bernese Oberland; hike through the secluded valleys, thick with sweet chestnut trees and scattered with *campaniles*, of Italian-speaking Ticino; mountain-bike along the high, ancient, whale-backed ridges of the French-speaking Jura; skate through the orchards along the shores of Lake Constance; or canoe past the colonies of storks along the river Aare – whichever, the most memorable way to see Switzerland is under your own steam.

Planning a journey is easy. The network connects with Switzerland's exemplary public transport system at 18,000 stops. Famously punctual, and with the timetables of trains, postal buses, lake steamers and even cable cars co-ordinated, this 20,000-kilometre network extends to even the remotest valleys, and is the densest in the world.

Escaping the car is easy here. Several mountain resorts are totally traffic-free, from internationally celebrated Zermatt, Saas-Fee, Wengen and Mürren to smaller family favourites such as Braunwald and Bettmeralp. But you do not have to limit yourself to remote mountain communities to feel close to nature here. In Zürich, for example, the financial capital, you only have to see locals swimming at laid-back lidos along the lake and the river Limmat, just five minutes' walk from the banks and luxury shops, to realise that a clean, unpolluted environment and a very high quality of life are very important to people here.

Water is a leitmotiv that runs through this country. In Leukerbad, the largest spa resort in the Alps, 3.9 million litres of hot, mineral-rich water gush out of the rock every day and people have been coming since Roman times to wallow in the healing waters, against a spectacular mountain backdrop. Now visitors can enjoy some of the finest spa facilities in Europe, and be pampered in any of more than 250 treatments.

Adding to Switzerland's popularity for wellness holidays are the invigorating alpine air and the pure nature of local produce, frequently used in treatments. The same lush, alpine-meadow flowers whose goodness makes its way into two of the country's most natural products – cheese and milk chocolate – can be used to make invigorating hay-flower wraps or stimulating baths. In Engelberg ('Angel mountain',

named after a medieval monk heard celestial hosts singing up here), you can bathe in warm, pure whey, fresh from the cheese maker, in an open-air tub on the alp. The liquid is rich in minerals and B vitamins and said to be refreshing and calming for the skin.

Switzerland offers countless more experiences close to nature. At some 240 farms, for example, you can sleep on sweet-smelling straw in the barn, before tucking into a farmer's breakfast of natural local products. Elsewhere you can sleep in a cornfield or a tepee, in an igloo, a barrel or up a tree. Up in the Alps, there are hundreds of secluded mountain huts where walkers can stay inexpensively and dine lavishly before watching fiery sunsets give way to night skies filled with millions of stars. One of the most unusual and eco-friendly places to stay is the Whitepod Eco Camp at Les Cerniers high above the Rhône valley, about 90 minutes from Geneva. It offers guests accommodation in hemispherical pods built of Swiss pine insulated with cork.

left **Mountain hut accommodation**　　above **St Moritz**

above **Badrutt's Palace hotel**  above (right) **The great Aletsch glacier – a UNESCO World Natural Heritage site**

Each has its own bathroom (with loo and shower); water comes from a local well, electricity from a solar panel, and heating from a wood-burning stove. As well as spectacular mountain views, the camp offers snowshoeing through the snow-covered forest and activities ranging from dog-sled rides to skiing on nearby slopes.

Holidays do not have to be basic to be eco-conscious. The luxurious Badrutt's Palace Hotel in the glamorous resort of St. Moritz, for example, has invested in a pioneering system of extracting heat from the local lake – saving nearly half a million litres of oil a year, cutting emissions of $CO_2$ by 1,200 tonnes. A fascinating excursion is the resort's Clean Energy Tour, which takes in visits to local hydroelectric and wind-generating plants, as well as a ride on the scenic Corviglia funicular, powered by the photovoltaic cells that line its tracks, producing some 18,000 kWh of electricity a year.

Impressive enough, but more memorable still are the mountain experiences that are to be had here. Hiking high on slopes suspended between glaciers and glittering lakes; or in winter, exploring tranquil, forested valleys blanketed in snow, on snowshoes, cross-country skis, or snuggled in the comfort of a horse-drawn sleigh – sublime, natural experiences that Switzerland has been offering in style for many generations.

One of the best places to do this is the Swiss National Park. Founded in 1914, it is the oldest national park in the Alps (and also one of the most carefully protected in Europe). Visitors are only allowed in on foot – bikes, skis and horses are forbidden – and must stay on the 80 kilometres of marked paths. As a result, the landscape is pristine, and the chances of seeing wildlife excellent: the park is home to around 100 species of birds and 30 species of mammal, including red deer, chamois and ibex. An excellent new, high-tech Visitor Centre opened in 2008, offering facilities such as hand-held computer guides that you carry around the park. You can stay also within the park at the Chamanna Cluozza log cabin, built in 1910 or in the charming Hotel Il Fuorn.

# Green menu

Take an unforgettable train ride The Albula–Bernina line of the Rhaetian Railway, which runs from Thusis via St. Moritz to Poschiavo, was awarded UNESCO World Heritage status in 2008. It passes over giddying viaducts above deep gorges, through countless tunnels, and past glaciers as it climbs over the Bernina Pass at 2,253 metres – which makes it the highest Alpine rail crossing in Europe. Wonder at man and nature Impressive World Heritage sites include the Aletsch Glacier, the largest in Europe; and the panoramic, terraced vineyards of the Lavaux high above Lake Geneva. Created by monks in the 11th century, they reveal a people's extraordinary care for their landscape over many generations.
www.rhb.ch
Loll about in Leukerbad Indulge in a thermal bath.
www.leukerbad.ch
Soak in a whey bath Little Miss Muffet eat your heart out in Engelberg as you soak in a bath that Cleopatra would envy.
www.engelberg.ch
Clean up your act Take the Clean Energy Tour® in St. Moritz and see for yourself the power of wind, sun, water and biogas.
www.stmoritz.ch/clean-energy-tour

## When to go

For snowy holidays, travel between Christmas and Easter – although the season may be slightly longer at the highest resorts. The other time that the high Alps are at their most beautiful is from May, after the snows have melted, to September. The weather can often be fine in October – and the autumn colours are sublime.

## Contacts

**Badrutt's Palace Hotel** Via Serlas 27, CH-7500 St Moritz, Switzerland
**Tel:** +41 (0) 81 837 1000
**Web:** www.badruttspalace.com
**Rates:** From €224 for a standard double room, including breakfast and all taxes.

**'Sleep-on-straw' Mountain Huts and Other Unusual Accommodation**
**Tel:** +44 (0) 0800 100 200 30 (free phone),
+44 (0) 20 7420 4900
**Web:** www.MySwitzerland.com

**White Pod Eco Camp** Les Cerniers, Batt. Postal 681, 1871 Les Giettes, Switzerland
**Tel:** +41 (0) 24 471 3838
**Web:** www.whitepod.com
**Rates:** From €260 per pod (sleeping 2–4 guests) per night, including breakfast. In summer, individual guests can stay at the resort refuge, from €42 per person per night, half board.

**Chamanna Cluozza Log Cabin**
**Tel:** +41 (0) 81 856 1235 (June to mid-October),
+41 (0) 81 856 1689 (mid-October to May)
**Web:** www.nationalpark.ch/english/B_2_1.php
**Rates:** From €44 per person, bed and breakfast; closed from mid-October to May.

**Hotel Parc Naziunal Il Fuorn** CH-7530 Zernez, Switzerland
**Tel:** +41 (0) 81 856 1226
**Web:** www.ilfuorn.ch
**Rates:** From €90 per night for a double.

**Switzerland Mobility**
**Tel:** +41 (0) 31 307 4740
**Web:** www.SwitzerlandMobility.ch

**Swiss Trails**
Swiss Trails has an extensive range of routes and tours.
**Tel:** +41 (0) 44 450 2434
**Web:** www.swisstrails.ch

**Swiss Travel System**
Check out a range of excellent travel passes and discounts.
**Web:** www.swisstravelsystem.ch

# THAILAND
Six Senses, Tonsai Bay and Lisu Lodge

Thailand certainly deserves its reputation as the land of smiles. An infectiously laid-back attitude pervades up and down the country, from the relentless hedonism of Bangkok to the tranquil Central Plains; the chilly mountains of the north, with their tribes and traditions, to a tropical, southern peninsular drenched in sun, white sand and some of the world's most exclusive resorts. And it's this Buddhist *joie de vivre* that's driving environmental efforts, as communities steeped in tradition embrace modern 'green' practices. The former king fronted campaigns to boost his country's eco credentials and this long-term project is one that sees the government, the people, and the country's booming tourism industry working towards a common goal. Thanks to innovative hoteliers, some of Thailand's most exclusive resorts are now offering luxury with a conscience.

## Six Senses

Sonu and Eva Shivdasani, owners of the Six Senses chain of luxury resorts, are two of the pioneers in the field and for their efforts have received several environmental tourism plaudits, including the coveted Tourism for Tomorrow Award, which recognises best practices in sustainable tourism development all over the world. As Sonu puts it, 'our guests do not want to enjoy themselves at the expense of others'.

There are several properties in Thailand, including Phuket, nearby Phang Nga Bay and Koh Samui. Six Senses Phuket rises from the tangled tropical parkland to offer dazzling views across the Andaman Sea. Its unique charm on this rather developed island is testament to Sonu and Eva's vision and their power for recycling – the couple insisted on reusing the shell of an existing hotel to create the resort. This ethos of 'making new' is carried through on everything from the use of bio diesel to the toiletries. They have also gone to the trouble of employing an in-house environment coordinator to ensure that the eco-chic balance of the hotel and its private island Bon is maintained. A short boat ride from the hotel, Bon offers blissful isolation, all-natural spa treatments and a choice of non-motorised watersports, not to mention Thailand's best-kept reef.

Yao Noi in Phang Nga Bay offers a kind of tranquillity you forget exists. The resort comprises pool villas and one extra-special 'hill top hideaway'. Each villa has its own butler who will pick you up in an electric buggy and drive you to the private beach, the beautifully landscaped restaurants or, of course, that fabulous spa, while the cliff-top resort on Koh Samui offers the gourmet national cuisine created by a former chef to the Thai royal family.

In every resort, the aim is to lessen greenhouse gas emissions through energy efficiency; reduce water consumption by managing freshwater resources; preserve the eco system

and raise social and cultural issues by involvement with local communities. 'We always aim to give guests space, privacy and a oneness with nature', Sonu explains.

### Tonsai Bay eco resort

Also on Koh Samui is the similarly sumptuous and environmentally inspired Tongsai Bay. Here you'll find a glorious secluded beach that surpasses the Six Senses' smaller sandy offering. The multi-eco-award-winning resort encourages *al-fresco* living – not hard when the great outdoors looks like this. All Tongsai Bay's beautifully furnished suites and villas have stylish decking areas, complete with beds so you can sleep under the stars … just as the resort's founder, the late Akorn Hoontrakul, did when he first spotted Tongsai Bay from the sea in 1985. Hoontrakul claimed it was 'love at first sight' and, after buying the land, he slept on the beach for three months in order to plan the construction of his dream resort to be in harmony with its natural environment. His legacy lives on, as all the hotel's staff members are offered an environmental orientation course so an eco ethos becomes second nature.

### Lisu Lodge, northern Thailand

From eco indulgence to a hill-top adventure, the Lisu Lodge combines basic comfort with absolute authenticity. It offers guests a chance to live among the Lisu tribe people who manage the lodge and, by doing so, help provide the funds to sustain the community's traditional way of life. In doing so, it has also received a number of awards for its eco contribution and efforts.

previous page (main) **Lisu Lodge**
left **Six Senses Samui swimming pool at night**
above **Tongsai Bay Restaurant**

Opt to be picked up from Chiang Mai by one of the tribe's people, and you'll be bundled into the back of an open truck and driven up, up, up into the ear-popping heights of northern Thailand. The lodge offers between two- and six-day adventures that cater for those looking for a bit of fun and a chance to chill-out in the wilderness, or for hardcore trekking, rafting and camping options.

As the truck pulls into the grounds of Lisu Lodge, you're met by Tey, who like the other women living in the local village and working at the lodge, wears the traditional Lisu costume of brightly coloured robes and an elaborate beaded hat accessorised with a mobile phone tucked away in a pouch on her dress. Tey escorts guests to a wooden house on stilts with five rooms. The resort comprises three such houses, all basic but immaculately clean. Pushing open the bamboo window shutters reveals lychee trees and dense groves of

banana and pawpaw, all set against a hazy, mountain background. A welcome drink of fresh lemon grass juice is served and you're left to relax and admire the surroundings before dinner and a traditional dance performance.

The unobtrusive placement of the lodge allows the villagers to earn the cash that they need without jeopardising their dignity and becoming some sort of voyeuristic 'human zoo'. Local Lisu people work in the gardens, the kitchen, the lodge shop or as housekeepers. Others act as knowledgeable guides to the local area. Daily outings end with a village tour, stopping for a cup of green tea with the shaman and his wife. Yes, the Lisu locals are getting a percentage of the lodge's profits for letting tourists into their homes, but it is their genuine kindness and evident pride in a project that has enthralled international guests for over 14 years that makes this a truly worthy and wonderful holiday experience.

below **Six Senses pool villa suite**    opposite **Yao Noi**

# Green menu

### SIX SENSES

Read your *Little Green Book* All rooms come complete with a *Little Green Book* outlining the resort's exotic plants and wildlife as well as detailing how you can donate to various local social or environmental projects or offset your carbon footprint for the trip.

Enjoy the natural spa All resorts have a fabulous spa, where you can try all-natural Thai herb treatments among others using organic or eco-friendly products.

Take a Local Tour All resorts have tours on offer that introduce you to the local people and surroundings – from local islands and fishing and crab-catching to mangrove forestation.

### TONGSAI BAY

Watersports Make a splash with non-motorised watersports, such as snorkelling, sailing, sea kayaking and windsurfing.

Choose, learn and cook Potter around the verdant organic garden that grows herbs and vegetables for use in the kitchens of the resort, then pick your own ingredients for a cookery class run by a former cook to the Thai royal family, Chef Chom.

### LISU LODGE

Go rafting Travel downriver to a traditional Thai country village, followed by a short transfer to the Elephant Camp for a scenic picnic lunch.

Ride an elephant Enjoy an hour of elephant riding through the beautiful mountainous jungle to the river.

Go trekking Trek for five days from the area near Pha Mieng, through the jungle to the remote village of Hmong Pha Mieng. Meet the inhabitants of this small hilltribe village.

Learn about village ways Visit the cultural centre and 'museum' created by the villagers or walk from Ton Lung temple to visit the herbal garden with a village guide.

Take a ride Take a guided bike tour around the Lisu Lodge area or climb into an ox-cart and ride through farmlands and orchards to the Thai village of Baan Pang Mai Daeng.

## When to go

Thailand is generally hot, particularly between March and May. The monsoon season runs from July to October, when the climate is hot and humid with torrential rains. The best months are in the cool season between November and February when there is less rain and the daily average temperature is 26–27°C.

## Contacts

### Six Senses
**Tel:** +44 (0) 20 8780 3519
**Web:** www.sixsenses.com
**Rates:** Phuket from £98 per room per night staying in a Studio Room with garden view. Yao Noi from £392 per room per night staying in a Pool Villa. Koh Samui from £271 per room per night staying in a Villa.

**Tongsai Bay** 84 Moo 5, Bo Phut, Koh Samui, Surat Thani 84320
**Tel:** +66 (0) 2381 8774
**Web:** www.tongsaibay.co.th
**Rates:** From £171 per room per night in a beachfront suite.

**Lisu Lodge** Asian Oasis, 7th floor, Nai Lert Tower, 2/4 Wireless Road, Bangkok 10330, Thailand
**Tel:** +66 (0) 5327 8338
**Web:** www.asian-oasis.com
**Rates:** A one-day adventure starts from £33 per person; a five-day adventure starts from £260 per person.

### Bailey Robinson
Every hotel in Bailey Robinson's Thai portfolio has been vetted for its green credentials to ensure that eco responsibility is a priority. Holidaymakers are actively encouraged to visit local communities with indigenous guides and to find ways of contributing to improve their lives or contribute to nature initiatives such as turtle and gibbon rehabilitation programmes.

# USA
## California

LA might be called the 'city of angels' but in reality it's the city of stars and movies dominate practically all everyday conversations. Where Rio has a statue of Christ the Redeemer as its skyline icon, LA has the huge HOLLYWOOD sign to remind residents of what makes this city tick. It's only when you visit Universal City, which incidentally is working on various energy-saving policies, that you understand the vast acreage that is dedicated to this industry. From Universal Hill you can also see across the city to the Warner Brothers empire – a great reminder of how close the competition is (and in America there's no such thing as second place).

A visit to Universal makes everything in LA fall into place. Such is the energy, magnetism, pizzazz and excitement of the place even I (with zero theatrical talent or desire to entertain) experienced an internal urge to tread the boards. For someone who thinks karaoke is the greatest form of torture – it must have quite a spell. You just want to be part of its magic.

While LA is never going to be a pedestrian destination, green is creeping into its psyche. The quaint Venice Beach Eco Cottages are currently the city's greenest option for accommodation. Just four blocks from the beach, these solar-powered, urban, clapboard retreats, run by a husband (actor)-and-wife (environmental economist) team, offer a comfortable, eco-friendly place to lay your head.

### Santa Barbara and along the coast

Ninety miles north, the charming town of Santa Barbara, known as the American Riviera, is the birthplace of the modern environmental movement. The nation's first Earth Day celebration was held here back in 1970. Today, many residents use alternative-fuel vehicles and there's a general sense of wellbeing that you don't get in LA. You can choose between numerous walking tours, car-free itineraries, bike paths, deep-sea diving, birding, ocean kayaking and whale-watching between the coast and the unspoilt Channel Islands.

The 'livin' *la vida locavore*' tour reflects the fast-growing demand from health-conscious and environmentally aware people who follow a simple concept of eating locally grown and harvested foods. The average distance that food travels in the US before reaching a dining table is a staggering 1,500 miles. Santa Barbara has a perfect growing climate for most fruit and vegetables, and an abundance of organic farms, eco wineries and restaurants that pride themselves on farm-to-table cuisine.

The next 100 miles of coast is probably America's most famous. The Big Sur, as it is called, sees the Pacific's rolling white horses crash into the rocky bluffs, where the mountains fall straight into the ocean. Cormorants populate rocky pinnacles turned white from guano and giant elephant seals collapse in blubbery heaps to sun themselves on sandy beaches. Perched along this coastline is the eco-conscious

Post Ranch Inn, described by one guest as an 'aphrodisiac' – it's the best place to enjoy the coastline views.

A little further along, the impressive harbour-based Monterey Bay Aquarium is taking action for the oceans by promoting sustainable seafood, creating marine protected areas and protecting California's threatened sea otters. Among various thrilling, interactive shows and goliath tanks, there's a clear conservation message. The National Seafood Watch programme lists how to make the right choices for healthy oceans, explaining what your best menu choices are according to where you live and what you should avoid at all costs.

## Sacramento and Lake Tahoe

Heading inland, California's capital city is definitely worth a stop over. Old Sacramento remains reminiscent of a gold rush town with its traditional buildings, many of which house museums such as the extensive California State Railway Museum, which showcases railroading's human

left **Cavallo Point in San Francisco Bay**     above **Trams and Alcatraz**

above **Post Ranch Inn**    opposite **Solage Calistoga in the Napa Valley**

face. After a visit here you can ride a steam locomotive or even spend a night aboard the riverboat Delta King.

Lake Tahoe is, in a word, spectacular – a vast stretch of water surrounded by mountains covered in wild flowers from spring to autumn and a winter wonderland from November to April. The north side of the lake is indisputably more scenic and a walk through the hillside meadows at Squaw Valley is a treat every step of the way. Blanketed in mule ears, lupines, buckwheat and mountain elderberry, it enraptured Walt Disney so much when he visited in 1960 that he designed the *Big Thunder Mountain Railroad Ride* at Disneyland after the ridge line of red granite rocks.

It is also home to one of America's greenest and friendliest hotels. Jeff and Patty Baird's Cedar House Sport Hotel, just minutes from Truckee and Lake Tahoe, was inspired by its setting, high in the Sierra Nevada Mountains. Water, heat- and energy-efficient, the cedar structures (sourced from a reforestation project) are a charming example of what can be achieved with careful consideration. Water drains from the green roof down pretty hanging chains to the landscape below. In the bar you'll find delicious local wines and complimentary snacks. Jeff and Patty have partnered up with local mountain guide companies, creating outdoor adventure packages that include hiking, biking, kayaking, snowshoeing and dog-sledding to name but a few.

### I lost my heart to San Francisco

In terms of setting, San Francisco is probably the world's most beautiful city. Like Rome, set on seven hills, it enjoys kaleidoscopic views of the skyline, sea and hills. Bustling with packed open trams, markets and busy pavements, it's a cosmopolitan magnate, overflowing with cultural variety. A short stroll from China Town and Union Square, the Orchard Garden Hotel is the city's greenest option, with eco-friendly guestrooms that even have recycling bins in the bedroom.

The brand-new and incredibly eco California Academy of Sciences is an aquarium, natural history museum, planetarium and research centre all rolled into one, under a huge teletubby biodome roof. You can fly to Mars, go beak to beak with a penguin and climb into the canopy of the living rainforest feet away from an albino alligator – all with a zero footprint. And if you've still got time, cross the road to the de Young Museum or stroll around the Japanese Tea Gardens before heading to Fisherman's Wharf to watch the sunset.

Just across Golden Gate Bridge in Marin County, in a tranquil bay next to the seaside village of Sausalito, the original officers' quarters at historic Fort Baker have been lovingly restored to their former glory as Cavallo Point – the Lodge at the Golden Gate. The huge amount of space lends a casual campus feel to the property where front porches creak to the sound of rocking chairs facing out over the panoramic view of the city and bridge. There's a Michelin-starred chef and a funky Healing Arts Centre and Spa offering anything from blissful cranio-sacral massage to hypnotherapy or organic cooking classes in an attempt to re-connect with your inner child. Its effort to support sustainability and stewardship of the national park it sits in are a priority. If you're lucky, you might see a humming bird from your window.

### Solage Calistoga

Last on our green list, but by no means least, is a stunning new property in the lush Napa Valley. Solage Calistoga, a designer, eco property at the northern end of the valley, has the good fortune to lie above a geothermal spring, which provides guests with healing mineral waters in which to bathe, and a speciality mud-bath fabulous for skin and joints. The openess of the property takes full advantage of the magical scenery and forget-me-not coloured skies. In between trips to the hundreds of wineries you can borrow a bike to visit nearby Calistoga or dine on a feast of local food in Solbar under the stars.

# Green menu

**Visit California's Galapagos** After a foray in the local markets in Santa Barbara, take The Adventure Company trip to the Channel Islands – California's Galapagos. Sea lions tussle in clear waters between giant kelp that stretches out like a sea monster's tentacles, as flocks of brown pelicans cruise over the ocean looking for an easy catch.

**Go eco with the fish** No question but to visit the Aquarium at Monterey Bay – promoting inspiring, entertaining and visionary green policies that are infiltrating eateries from coast to coast.

**Glide over the tree tops** The Heavenly Flyer Ziprider on the south side of Lake Tahoe will carry you to 9,156 feet in the air and will then whoosh you down the mountain at approximately 50 miles per hour for about 80 seconds of pure adrenaline rush.

**Raft the Truckee River** Spend a leisurely two hours at Lake Tahoe floating down five miles of the pretty Tahoe tributary with an occasional grade one rapid to wake you up.

**Go on two wheels or three** Absolute must-dos in San Francisco include cycling across the Golden Gate Bridge with Blazing Saddles and taking a guided GPS tour in a three-wheeled, self-drive Go-Car.

**Tempt your taste buds** Visit myriad wineries in Napa. Hike through the vines or bike into Calistoga. And don't miss the speciality Calistoga Mud bath.

**Drive green** Fuel-efficient, Toyota Prius, gas-electric hybrid cars are now available at airport locations in California. **www.hertz.com**

## When to go

California enjoys a year-round Mediterranean climate. Summers are hot (especially further south) while winters are milder with wetter weather and snow in the mountains.

## Contacts

For all consumer enquiries and rates contact:
**California Tourism**
**Tel:** +44 (0) 20 7257 6180
**Web:** www.visitcalifornia.co.uk

# USA
## Pennsylvania – Route 6

Having crossed the Atlantic many times over the years, it wasn't until I visited Pennsylvania that I found the real McCoy. A sentiment, I soon discovered, shared with compatriots. Good living, good food, old-fashioned hospitality and wholehearted trustiness all added up to a flavour of that illusive thing in the 21st century: the American dream. So where was it exactly?

Most have heard of the trans-American Route 66 but far fewer know about the wonders of Pennsylvania's Route 6, rated by *National Geographic* as one of America's most scenic drives. It's more accessible in terms of span (comfortably covered in a week) and an idyllic tour, covering some of America's best-kept countryside. Stretching 400 miles across the state's northern tier, it passes quirky historic villages, deep streams hidden in narrow gorges, endless mountains and a continual blanket of forest.

### Perfect Pocono

There's no better place to start than in the eastern historic town of Milford, home to America's first Chief Forester and visionary conservationist Gifford Pinchot (1865–1946). He was the son of a business man who had made a fortune out of lumber and land speculation but regretted the damage it had caused. Above all else, Pinchot wanted to save trees and his legacy was to ensure that Pennsylvania, meaning 'Penn's Woods', became the country's first protected state.

Pinchot believed that a passion for nature is sown in childhood, and one place that seems to embody fun for all ages is the Pocono Mountains region – home to rolling mountain terrain, beautiful waterfalls, thriving woodlands and 170 miles of winding rivers.

Pinchot wasn't the only forward thinker. In Harrisburg a new wind-energy initiative has put Pennsylvania at the forefront of a renewable energy movement that is looking to become a world-class leader in this field. As the current governor explained, 'We know this economic development investment strategy works because we've seen it work before.' The future in Pennsylvania is now looking green in more ways than one.

### Penn wilds

As you progress along its winding path, one thing, one colour dominates all. Green. That is, unless you visit in the autumn when the hillsides explode with vibrant reds and golds.

Pennsylvania has over 17 million acres of forests (covering 60 per cent of the territory), seemingly endless and endlessly soothing. By the time you reach Wellsboro, your eyes will have adjusted to the blanket of trees that stretch from one horizon to the next, punctuated with romantic-looking, old, federal-style houses and clapboard barns.

One such abode, immersed in woodland just off the road, is Bear Mountain Lodge, the snug timber chalet of local Jim

previous page (main) **Longwood Gardens**   previous page (thumbnail) **Sweetwater Lodge**

Meade. Breakfast is served in town at the authentic porcelain 1939 Wellsboro diner, which dishes out ample platefuls of home cooking. After that, armed with a backpack of goodies, head off to hike, bike, ride or raft along 50 miles of Pine Creek Gorge, the 1,000-foot canyon of the east. Or trek the four-mile Turkey Trail to Pine Creek Gorge, where you'll hear the rich language of the wild turkey.

From May to September a band of volunteers offer free public star tours for novice stargazers in Cherry Springs State Park. Its dark skies are a haven for astronomers. Take a blanket and thermos and 'kick back' to the stars.

## Allegheny National Forest

The hills continue to swallow the road as you continue west into historic Smethport. The Victorian, federal-style mansions of West Main Street are like something out of *Gone with the Wind*, offering a glimpse at an opulent past.

It's also elk country and home to the largest, free-roaming herd in the east. Over 500 roam the county and, during the mating season between September and October, these shy creatures can be observed in their natural splendour from a series of safe, public, viewing sites.

Most visitors come to this region for the stunning scenery. Plenty come to hike, boat or just sit and admire the 20-mile Kinzua reservoir, cloaked in forest. Marked trails through untouched woodlands of black cherry, hemlock, maple, ash, and beech are interspersed with common sightings of deer, fox, bear, beaver, ruffed grouse, blue heron and the great bald eagle. Environmental tours with a ranger are also available.

Close by, Kane is the eponymous town of the general who built the famous Kinzua viaduct, which, until a tornado struck in 2003, was the world's longest and highest railway bridge. You can stay in his last home, Kane Manor, now a

opposite **Scenic Pennsylvania in Autumn**   above **Allegheny National Forest and reservoir**

quirky bed and breakfast with a light residue of yesteryear grandeur. Or, for something plusher, opt for the lodge at Glendorn, an ancestral 1,280-acre estate near Bradford.

Route 6 comes to a gentle end on its western frontier at Lake Erie. The forests melt into a bucolic landscape of grazing cattle, meadows and hay barns. The undulation of waves over the sandy beaches at Presque Isle deludes the senses that the majestic waterfront, with over 200 miles of coastline, is a sea, rather than one of North America's great wonders – the Great Lakes. But, fear not, the journey doesn't end there.

## Pittsburgh

While Pennsylvania's highest elevation is only 3,200 feet, the sheer number and density of its hills and ravines give it one of the most dramatic changes in elevation per linear mile of any state. Southwest Pennsylvania's unique topographic blend of steep, winding hills and flat river areas makes it one of the best places for hiking and biking.

Pittsburgh sits at a unique confluence of rivers. Three rivers meet at its heart – Allegheny, Mononghahela and Ohio – and act as a vast watershed of more than a dozen river systems extending into New York and West Virginia. With the second-largest number of registered pleasure boats in the country, the rivers are ideal for sculling, kayaking and canoeing, rowing and white-water rafting.

The Youghiogheny River Trail, along with the Montour Trail and the Three Rivers Heritage Trail System, are all part of the Great Allegheny Passage, a 150-mile, rails-to-trails project that creates a continuous non-motorised corridor from Pittsburgh to Washington D.C.

I expected an industrial non-entity. What I found was an architectural and cultural haven. Pittsburgh is home to a stream of household names: Warhol, Heinz, the Pittsburgh

above **Blue Kinzua reservoir**    opposite **Amish buggies in beautiful Lancaster County**

Pirates… No surprise then that it has been voted as America's most liveable city; metropolitan vivacity mixed with a laid-back feel of the countryside. Its creative planning elicits instant excitement – and it's proud of its eco efforts, having led the way with its green convention centre, powered by a wave of solar panels – an attractive and environmentally intelligent feature on Pittsburgh's riverfront.

For a first-stop orientation take the Duquesne Incline cable railway to Mount Washington for a panoramic view of the skyscrapers and river-life, followed by a guided Segway scooter tour. Visit one of the museums – science, art, history, botany, and architecture are covered consummately, some in green buildings like the innovative Children's Museum, next to the National Aviary. However much time you spend in this city, you'll want to return.

Travelling east you'll pass Lancaster County, the land of the Amish community, a humble, plain-dressed people who still travel by horse and buggy and farm the land using teams of horses and mules. Their simple way of life and respected traditions take the place of commercial temptations. Markets full of homemade goods give a timeless sense of a different world – surrounded by pristine farms and a back-to-roots way of life with a strong sense of community.

### The final leg – Brandywine Valley

Historic Brandywine Valley, just west of Philadelphia, is the perfect place to end a trip to Pennsylvania. And Sweetwater Lodge is a bed and breakfast with a difference. A tranquil retreat set in 50 acres, with seven guest cottages, a pool and spa (owned and hosted by Grace Kelly's nephew), it provides a comfortable base to visit 1,050 acres of gardens, woodlands and meadows at nearby Longwood Gardens. In 1906 when a historic arboretum was slated to be cut for lumber, the industrialist and philanthropist Pierre du Pont decided to save the trees and created a spectacular horticultural showcase of ever-changing beds, a conservatory, children's garden and dazzling fountains – an appropriate finale to an sustainably green tour.

# Green menu

Go grey Grey Towers in Milford, the ancestral home and parkland of visionary Gifford Pinchot provides the perfect scene-setter for green Pennsylvania.
www.greytowers.org

Take a hayride Thunder Valley Stables in McKean near Erie, offers horse-drawn hayrides hauled by magnificent percheron geldings through the pumpkin fields to a creek full of pre-historic fossils.
www.thundervalleystables.net

Watch wildlife Visit Asbury Woods, a rescued wetland in urban Erie, which includes interactive animal attractions that are especially good for kids.
www.asburywoods.org

Eat fresh The best and freshest seafood in town is at the Westin's Original Fish Market Restaurant.
www.starwoodhotels.com

Visit the Tom Ridge Environmental Center Housed in an energy-efficient, green building, the centre offers exhibitions about how the 3,200-acre Erie peninsular was formed during the Ice Age and what the impact of modern day life has been on its eco systems.
www.dcnr.state.pa.us/trecpi/

Take a bite The Burgh Bits and Bites organic food tour around the buzzing Strip district embraces the best of Pittsburgh's local characters and flavours.
www.burghfoodtour.com

Take to the water In the heart of Downtown Pittsburgh, Kayak Pittsburgh rents solo and tandem kayaks, canoes, and hydrobikes for peaceful urban exploration.
www.kayakpittsburgh.org

Go mountain biking Pittsburgh offers premier single track and mountain biking in an urban setting. Pittsburgh Off-Road Cyclists has extensive information on local mountain bike trails and an active community in their forums.
www.porcmtbclub.org

Enjoy living tradition Visit Central Market in Lancaster, one of the oldest farmers' markets in the country, where traditional living carries on and Amish goods are on sale. Check out Hannah's Quilts and then visit the Lancaster Quilt and Textile Museum, housed in the old bank that did not survive the 1930s Depression.

# When to go

Pennsylvania's weather is similar to the rest of the northeastern United States. Spring and autumn are mild, ranging from 13–24°C. Winter lows can dip to 0°C in January and February. During peak summer months, temperatures soar well into the 30s. If visiting Philadelphia, most concert series and museum exhibits occur between October and June.

# Contacts

For further information on Route 6, key attractions and some the state's best bed and breakfasts contact:
**Visit Pennsylvania**
**Tel:** +44 (0) 844 880 6852
**Web:** www.visitpa.com, www.paroute6.com

# CREDITS AND ACKNOWLEDGEMENTS

**With my heartfelt thanks to:**

- Antonia Cunningham went to Cambridge University before turning her hand to publishing, where she found her way into travel editing and writing. She has written several guide books, specialising in Copenhagen and Denmark and a number of children's non-fiction books.
- Petra Shepherd has been with the Travel Channel, Europe's largest pan-European TV channel, since its launch in 1994. She works on flagship magazine programme Travel Today, which features a four-minute green story each month.
- Photographer Daniella Cesarei has the enviable task of documenting a diverse range of people, places (and fabulous hotels) as she travels the world with her trusty Cannon.
- Lotte Jeffs is a travel editor and journalist whose work takes her from pop stars' dressing rooms to awesome, exotic and unexpected locations around the world. Of all the hotels she's reviewed, Lotte was blown away by Thailand's eco chic resorts.
- Neil Birnie is the co-founder and director of Wilderness Scotland, the leading eco tourism business in Scotland. A former environmental lawyer, Neil is a passionate advocate for eco tourism's role in nature conservation and sustainable development.
- Having spent fourteen years flourishing in the television industry, Sham Sandhu is currently indulging in his three passions: travel, yoga and massage, contributing regularly to various media whenever the opportunity arises.
- Sue Bryant is an award-winning travel writer and photographer with a particular interest in environmental impact. She contributes to the *Daily Telegraph*, *The Times*, *The Daily Express,* BBC Radio Four and numerous magazines, websites and guides.
- Tom Barber was a staff writer at *GQ* and freelanced for the *Evening Standard* and *Tatler* before launching award-winning travel company Original Travel in 2003. Tom has since visited even more far-flung corners of the globe – all for research purposes, naturally.
- Matilda Bathurst is a rising star, currently studying English Literature at Cambridge University. She recently spent months travelling in India, interviewing and writing articles for the New Indian Express.

- James Bedding is a journalist, travel writer and translator specialising in adventure activities and environmentally-aware travel. Half-British, half-Swiss he has held a variety of jobs, including working as a handyman for a community of nuns on a mountain above Lake Lucerne.
- After reading English at Oxford, Kat Thurston Tiefenthal spent years touring, setting world records as part of the British paragliding team, submitting travel articles to top up funding. Now living in Austria, she runs theridingcompany.com specialising in riding holidays in beautiful places.
- David Wickers was Chief Travel Correspondent on *The Sunday Times* for 17 years, and three times recipient of Travel Writer of the Year awards. Currently Travel Editor of *Good Housekeeping*, he is also a founding Director of Bridge & Wickers, a tour operator specialising in tailor-made, luxury holidays to Australia and New Zealand.
- Louise Roddon is a regular contributor to the travel pages of *The Times* and *The Telegraph*. Her work also appears in *The Daily Mail, The Express, Sunday Times Travel Magazine,* and *Thomas Cook magazine*. She is the published author of four books.
- Monique Chambers is evangelical about Malta and Gozo; and all that the islands have to offer. She writes about tourism and leisure for various on- and off-line publications and is currently working on a series of destination travel guides for the discerning globetrotter.
- Hilary Reed is a former geography teacher who is now a partner in a small independent travel agency. The need to share her passion for wild places and their amazing eco systems has motivated both her careers.
- Victoria Trott is a Wales-based freelance writer and photographer who contributes to the *Daily Mail, Living France, French Magazine* and *Spain Magazine*. She is co-author of *Frommer's Provence & the Cote d'Azur with your Family* and has revised the latest Michelin Green Guides to Provence and Brittany.
- Derek Schuurman is the co-author of *Globetrotter Guide to Madagascar* and *Madagascar Wildlife: A Visitors Guide*, and works for the award-winning specialist tour operator Rainbow Tours in London. He has visited Madagascar many times since 1992.

- Felix Milns writes about eco-friendly travel for a wide variety of newspapers and magazines, including the *Financial Times*, *Telegraph*, *Times*, *Guardian*, *Tatler*, *Centurion* and *Departures*. He is currently campaigning green skiing through *InTheSnow*, the ski magazine he edits.
- Mary-Clare Gribbon is passionate about Greece, having travelled around the islands extensively. She spent six months working as an environmental volunteer for an NGO in Nepal and has backpacked around India, South-East Asia and Morocco. Mary-Clare is also a foodie and has written for *Food & Travel Magazine* and *Exposé*.
- Liane Katz is the *Guardian's* online Travel editor and the editor of the *Guardian Green Travel Guide*, published in 2009.
- Angela Bailey is a freelance editor and proof reader.

**All pictures supplied by the author, contributors, hotels, resorts and tourist boards with special thanks to the following:**

www.istockphoto.com/tombonatti: page 10 (globe); www.istockphoto.com/racnus: 12 (panda); www.istockphoto.com/deejpilot: (plane); www.istockphoto.com/miflippo: 16 (rucksack); www.istockphoto.com/veni: 17 (hiker); Antonia Cunningam: 85, 88 and 89; Wonderful Denmark (www.visitcopenhagen.com) Cees van Roeden: P84 and 86 (bottom); Tourism New Zealand: 194, 196 and 197 (bottom); Richard Laburn: 236 and 240; Ben Nilsson/Big Ben Productions: 256, 257, 258 and 259; Daniella Cesarei: 268; Kodiak Greenwood: 275 and 278.

Every attempt has been made to include all relevant contributors to this publication. The publisher apologises for any information that is missing or incorrect.

# Heaven on Earth Kids
The world's best family holidays

SARAH SIESE

# Heaven on Earth
A calendar of divine hotels around the world

SARAH SIESE

*What they said:*

'Every discerning traveller should have a copy on their coffee table'
Sir Richard Branson

'*Heaven on Earth* is an inspired and long over-due collection of the world's best hotels'
*Elegant Traveller Magazine*

'A must-read offering an inside track for those who truly want to get the very best from their time away'
Kate Thornton, Presenter, *Holiday* BBC1

'Swallow it whole, and take with water'
Ruby Wax